# HALLYU

# How Korea Captivated the World

# HALLYU

Chang Dae-whan Ph.D

매일경제신문사

It was approximately four years ago, on June 20, 2019, when I published the book, *The Korea We Don't Know: A 70-Year Miracle of Korea*. I had a clear motivation for writing the book: At that time, Korea was impressing the world as a miracle and wonder in itself. However, there was a widespread phenomenon among Koreans, wherein we only focused on the negative aspects of Korea rather than acknowledging the positive ones. As the publisher of various news media outlets, I felt a sense of duty to address this issue. I even experienced a sense of defeat, wondering, "What is the reason for all this cynicism and self-blame?", even though the news media that I oversee—Maeil Business Newspaper, Maeil Broadcasting Network(MBN), and Maekyung.com, etc.—have consistently presented the facts as they are.

I am aware of the situation. It may have come about through the conflicts and grievances that inevitably arise between classes and generations, as well as labor and management during the compressed growth process. Politics is meant to resolve such problems, yet politics in Korea has become increasingly divided into extremes, perpetuating and deepening the conflict.

The media's mission is to address identified problems. Therefore, my efforts began with 'numbers.' It is undeniable that even when presented with the same facts, opinions can vary depending on one's perspective, and evaluations of history may also differ based on one's understanding. Statistics are invaluable in such situations. While it is true that numbers can also be subject to distortion, they tend to be more objective than other sources of information.

I thoroughly examined the achievements of Koreans over the 70 years since the establishment of the Republic of Korea government, with a keen focus on various statistics. I also delved into how Korea is perceived on the global stage. I subsequently conducted a neutral assessment of Korea's strengths and weaknesses and laid out the necessary steps to sustain a miracle that has already lasted 70 years. The culmination of this effort resulted in the book, *The Korea We Don't Know: A 70-Year Miracle of Korea.*

I would like to seize this opportunity to express my gratitude to my readers for their interest and encouragement. Many of you may be wondering how I managed to compile such detailed statistics while fulfilling my role as a newspaper publisher. To those queries, I would respond that my emphasis on data-driven management and my personal interest in collecting statistics enabled me to bring this book to fruition. Nevertheless, there was a tinge of self-consciousness about it.

I also received feedback from readers who expressed disappointment because, as time passed, the statistics presented in the book became outdated and did not reflect the current situation. I recognized the necessity for these updates. Initially, I had intended to merely revise the numbers, but I soon realized that the book required more extensive revisions, including addressing areas of disappointment. Consequently, it evolved into an entirely new and different edition.

Above all, an unexpected and significant variable emerged: a global pandemic.

At the end of 2019—less than six months after the publication of the book—the world witnessed the emergence of the COVID-19 virus, which originated in Wuhan, China. By early 2020, it had escalated into a global pandemic, giving rise to a multitude of problems, including a sharp economic downturn, an unemployment crisis, trade disputes, a debt crisis, and a regression in globalization as well as democracy.

In response, I examined the ripple effects of the pandemic, which encompassed the loss of normalcy in daily life, the positive and negative aspects of the Korean government's quarantine measures, the onset of a third phase of negative economic growth and the employment crisis that followed, as well as the rapidly changing workplace environment and asset market. I also explored the opportunities and threats associated with this crisis. I even emphasized how the values of democracy and economic freedom have gained increased significance and elaborated on why and how Korea must progress toward becoming a future-oriented, innovative nation with a per capita income of $100,000 as we navigate the new era of systemic competition in the 21st century. That's how I took a somewhat ambitious step and published another revised edition in March 2021.

Now, a little over two years have passed, and it's time to update the data once again. However, it occurred to me that it might be more effective to consolidate key statistics into an index instead of continually updating them. This approach would allow for a greater emphasis on areas that had previously been overlooked. It was this realization that led me to adopt a storytelling approach. Numbers, on their own, have limitations in bringing the written word to life. Behind these numbers lie countless fascinating stories. This is precisely why I chose "HALLYU" as the title of the new book and decided to prioritize narratives over numbers.

I frequently have the opportunity to travel abroad, primarily to participate in forums and conferences held overseas, where I engage in discussions with foreign scholars. The 'World Knowledge Forum,' hosted by Maekyung Media Group, has now been running for 24 years. It serves as a knowledge festival and a platform for the exchange of ideas, where Korean and foreign opinion leaders share their perspectives on crucial global issues. For this forum alone, more than 200 foreign scholars visit Korea and hold meetings with me.

There is a common theme that emerges from these interactions: the wonder of Korea. It's not just flattery; Korea is indeed a marvel in its own right. As I mentioned in the preface of *The Korea We Don't Know: A 70-Year Miracle of Korea*, world-renowned historian Paul Kennedy shared the following with me during his visit to Korea in the fall of 2016;

"The Republic of Korea is really a puzzling case. It seems to me that the country should have been wiped from the map a long time ago, but it wasn't. It is a miracle that Korea continued for 5,000 years while surrounded by such powers as China, Japan, and Russia and has even thrived."

He is absolutely right. Korea stands as a remarkable miracle in world history. In 2022, I had the privilege of visiting Austria to commemorate the 130th anniversary of diplomatic relations between Korea and Austria. During this visit, I met with Wolfgang Sobotka, the Speaker of the National Council, in Austria's capital, Vienna. During the meeting, it became evident to me that he genuinely sought cooperation with Korean companies, and it is likely that this was why he wanted to meet with me. The initial topic he raised was Austria's historical ties with Korea, particularly the story of Francesca Donner—an Austrian who married Korea's first President, Syngman Rhee, and thereby became the country's inaugural First Lady. This connection, established at a time when many Koreans couldn't differentiate Austria from Australia, underscores the significance of the relationship Austria has with Korea, he stressed.

Within the basement of our newspaper building, there is an operational rotary printing press, which is used not only to print Maeil Business Newspaper but several other publications as well. One of these publications is the UK's Financial Times (FT). Due to this partnership, Maeil Business Newspaper and Financial Times have maintained a longstanding collaboration, involving the exchange of personnel and articles. I also have a personal connection with CEO John Reading, who previously served as a Korea correspondent and assumed the role of CEO at the newspaper in 2006. I also had the pleasure of meeting him at the World Economic Forum (WEF) in Davos, Switzerland in January 2023.

When I met him, I expressed my sympathy for the challenges the United Kingdom was facing with Brexit. To my surprise, he shared his admiration for Korea and couldn't praise it enough. He stated, "Korea boasts incredibly strong consumer brands. Electric cars from Hyundai and Kia are selling remarkably well in the United Kingdom. The popularity of K-pop is also immense among young people. Korea is firmly establishing itself as a dynamic, innovative, and highly intriguing country."

This book is comprised of five parts. Part 1 delves into the 'Korean life' that captivates foreigners. While many Koreans have ventured into global markets and formed a network known as 'Korean Merchants,' there are also numerous foreigners who have come to Korea and settled here. Among them, a considerable number have an astonishing command of the Korean language. In my view, some of these foreigners not only speak Korean fluently but also possess a deeper knowledge of Korea than some Koreans who have lived in the country for over 60 years. Many of them have explored every nook and cranny of Korea's tourist attractions, are adept at using buses and subways, and have no trouble ordering food for delivery.

Have you ever wondered what aspects of Korea surprise them the most? An example that was shared with me was, "I left my wallet on the bus, and no one touched it." Such a level of trust, which is genuinely a remarkable characteristic of Koreans, is, in my opinion, an invaluable asset that sets us apart. It is something that could be hard to find in foreign countries, even in those we admire as developed nations.

Part 2 delves into the success stories of Koreans on the global stage. It is not limited to BTS; there are many Koreans who have made their mark globally. I explore the phenomenon of K-culture, which has gained significant attention from foreigners, in Part 3. Parts 4 and 5 feature the narratives of Korean companies, some of which were previously introduced in my book, *The Korea We Don't Know: A 70-year Miracle of Korea*. In this edition, I have updated and expanded these stories.

And then there are notable incidents that could not be overlooked in the context of this book. One of these incidents involves a series of random stabbing attacks that occurred in the heart of Seoul, despite my assertion that Korea is a safe country. The other incident pertains to the scandal surrounding the World Scout Jamboree held in Saemangeum, Buan-gun, North Jeolla province. The initial stabbing attack occurred near Sillim Subway Station in Seoul during the summer of 2023, followed by another attack at a department store in Seongnam City, resulting in the tragic deaths of two innocent citizens. The nation was gripped by fear, concerned that similar crimes might proliferate. However, it is remarkable that within a space of five days, the police mobilized local cybercrime investigation units nationwide, leading to the arrest of approximately 30 individuals who had posted messages indicating their intent to harm others. This incident showcased the strength of Korea as a digitally adept powerhouse with a low crime rate. While a few similar incidents have occurred since then, it is fair to say that Korea remains a safe country compared to many others.

Furthermore, the '2023 Saemangeum 25th World Scout Jamboree,' that took place, in August, was fraught with a multitude of problems and challenges. The event began amid a severe heatwave, and within a few days, numerous participants voiced complaints about various inconveniences. The organizers also faced criticism for their poor management. Ultimately, due to an approaching typhoon, participants were forced to conclude their camping experience earlier than originally planned. However, it was through the collective efforts of the government, businesses, and citizens that the Jamboree event was salvaged, ultimately triumphing over the crisis. The solidarity of the Korean people left a lasting impression on the world as it always does. Despite initial concerns and complaints from teenagers and parents worldwide, it is undeniable that they discovered another facet of Korea's charm and came under the influence of the Korean Wave.

As always, I find myself contemplating many additional topics to write about once I've completed a book. When I begin writing, I often tell myself, "This is more than enough material," but invariably, a multitude of additional stories emerge after I've finished. I must eventually, regrettably draw a line, as I cannot continue indefinitely. I also hope readers will understand this limitation. Nevertheless, I promise to seek out and present more and enhanced content whenever the opportunity arises.

I must express my gratitude once again to the employees who

assisted me in bringing this book to fruition. I would like to extend my thanks to editorial writer Park Bong-kwon and editorial staff members Won Ho-seop and Song Kyeong-eun. Their diligent efforts included extensive research and idea exploration. My fervent hope is that the Republic of Korea will continue to be recognized as a 'miracle country' and be a source of pride, both to ourselves and to people around the world.

Chang Dae-whan
Chairman of Maekyung Media Group

# CONTENTS

# PART 2
## KOREANS MAKING THEIR MARK IN THE WORLD

# PART 3
## THE POWER OF CULTURE

PART 4

# KOREA, A COUNTRY
# THAT NEVER GOES DARK

PART 5

# KOREAN COMPANIES
# THAT MADE THE IMPOSSIBLE, POSSIBLE

PART 1

# KOREAN IDIOSYNCRACIES THAT FASCINATE FOREIGNERS

In April 2023, two Russian women entered the Seosomun Police Station in Jung-gu, Seoul. It was their first visit to Korea, and they appeared visibly distressed. In somewhat limited English, they told the officer that one of them lost her purse and sought assistance in locating it. Upon receiving their report, the police officer discovered that one of the Russian women had inadvertently left her purse with approximately ₩3 million in cash in it on the bus that had transported them from Incheon Airport to their hotel. Without delay, the officer contacted the bus company.

In a stroke of luck, the bus company had found the purse that the woman left behind and was holding it in an effort to return it to its rightful owner. The item's quick return left the Russian women overjoyed and surprised, as recounted by the police officer. They expressed their amazement because, had this occurred in Russia, recovering the purse would likely have been almost impossible.

The TV entertainment program "Hankook Saram" (translated as "Korean People," 2021), which showcases the allure of Korea from foreigners' perspectives, conducted a social experiment to investigate whether Koreans would take another person's belongings. In this experiment, hidden cameras were strategically placed to observe the reactions when a purse or smartphone was left unattended on a table in various business establishments, such as cafes.

Remarkably, the purse was left untouched for four hours, even as customers passed by. Although there were patrons sitting at the adjacent table, none showed any interest in the unattended purse. Eventually, a male customer did pick up the purse, but his intentions were revealed as benign when captured on the hidden camera: he merely carried it to the counter and left it there. The foreign guests featured on the show expressed their astonishment at the lack of interest displayed by Koreans toward the purse left on the table.

One guest on the show, Joachim from Sweden, reacted in disbelief and said, "If this situation happened in Sweden, someone would have taken it right away." Kimiya, an international student from Iran, remarked, "Koreans are so accustomed to this (not stealing other people's belongings) that they are surprised when foreigners find this cultural norm shocking." While it may be challenging to comprehend in foreign countries, Koreans regard it as a given that one should not touch other people's belongings. This particular trait on display in the episode garnered significant interest when it was introduced as 'K-Conscience' on social media.

Mushtaq Majid, a Pakistani YouTube traveler who is well-known for his videos about Korea, said, "I have traveled to 22 countries around the world, and Korea was the safest among them." He further emphasized, "Koreans refrain from touching other people's belongings, and theft is virtually nonexistent. Even if you leave your belongings unattended in a cafe while you use the restroom or step away, you will find them undisturbed upon your return. It's the same on the subway." He found this truly remarkable.

# Koreans Don't Take
# Unattended Wallets

The Overseas Culture and Public Relations Service, operating under the Ministry of Culture, Sports, and Tourism, conducted a survey involving 12,500 individuals aged over 16 residing in 24 countries and the results were published in the *2021 National Image Survey Report*. According to this report, a substantial 80.5% of respondents had a positive impression of Korea. The primary factors contributing to this favorable view included modern culture (22.9%), products and brands (13.2%), economic prosperity (10.2%), cultural heritage (9.5%), national character (8.6%), and social systems (7.8%).

When respondents were questioned about the aspects of Koreans they admired, the most common responses were kindness, trustworthiness, sincerity, and openness, in that order.

Korea, historically labeled as the "land of courteous people in the East," has long been recognized for its compassionate and polite population by people from other cultures. Many foreigners are taken aback when they observe young passengers willingly giving up their seats to the elderly and other less abled individuals on public transportation such as subways and buses. Korea's unique culture of humility and national character is closely tied to its consideration for others. The cleanliness of public restrooms, subway stations, parks, and streets is also deeply rooted in Korea's culture of etiquette.

## BASIC KOREAN ETIQUETTE UNFAMILIAR
## TO MOST FOREIGNERS

- When engaging in a formal greeting, lower your posture by bowing your head, instead of waving your hand.
- When shaking hands politely, support the wrist of the shaking hand with your other hand and bow your head slightly.
- Younger people should not initiate handshakes.
- When receiving an item, accept it with both hands.
- When served food, express your gratitude by saying "Thank you for the food" before eating, and after the meal, say "Thank you, I enjoyed the meal."
- In a formal dinner setting, ensure that the oldest member of the group takes the first bite before starting the meal.
- When drinking with an older person, turn your head slightly and hold the glass with both hands while taking a sip.
- When pouring a drink for an older person, use both hands to hold the bottle.

# LOWEST CRIME RATE IN THE WORLD

Korea boasts one of the world's lowest crime rates. According to the 'Crime Rate by Country 2023' report published by the American data analysis agency World Population Review, Korea recorded a crime index of 26.68, ranking 116th out of 136 countries globally. In comparison, the United States ranked 56th, Germany ranked 95th, and Japan ranked 129th. The crime index represents the number of reported crimes per 100,000 people, with smaller numbers indicating lower crime rates. Despite recent incidents of random "unprovoked stabbing attacks," Korea and Japan are evidently safer when compared to many other countries. Korea also boasts one of the world's lowest murder rates. According to data from the UN Office on Drugs and Crime (UNODC), Korea's murder rate in 2020 stood at 0.6 per 100,000 people, or 83rd out of 96 major nations worldwide.

The low crime rate in Korea can be attributed to various institutional and environmental factors. Firstly, the possession of dangerous weapons such as guns is strictly prohibited. Additionally, CCTVs are installed extensively throughout the country to prevent crime, and they are believed to play a significant role in deterring criminal acts. Criminals are less likely to commit crimes when they are aware of the presence of surveillance cameras. According to the Korea Internet & Security Agency, as of the end of 2021, approximately 16 million CCTVs are installed and operated in Korea, both by private and public institutions. This translates to 0.31 CCTVs installed per person, which is three times the world average.

Seoul particularly boasts a more comprehensive surveillance network. British cybersecurity information research company

Comparitech counted the number of public surveillance cameras in 150 major cities across the globe, and the results showed that Seoul has a total of 77,564 surveillance cameras, equivalent to 332 units per square mile (2.6 km$^2$). In terms of the number of surveillance cameras per unit area, Korea ranks first in the world.

The black box installed in virtually every vehicle in Korea also functions as a mobile CCTV system. According to data compiled by market research firm Embrain Trend Monitor, the black box installation rate for domestic vehicles stood at 88.9% in 2019. This is a remarkably high installation rate, especially when compared to rates in Europe and Japan, which were in the 10-20% range.

Korean black boxes are equipped with various technologies designed to improve video stability, algorithms to reduce image noise, and AI technologies capable of facial recognition as well as identifying forged images. All this places Korea at the forefront of technology, making it a country where criminals cannot even dream of committing crimes unnoticed. Additionally, it is common in Korea to apprehend criminals through digital forensics, an investigative technique that secures evidence for a crime by collecting and analyzing data from digital devices or the Internet. The smartphone ownership rate among Korean adults is an impressive 95%. Notably, during investigations such as the tracking of international cannabis traffickers in 2011 and the Burning Sun Gate investigation in 2018 (a scandal in the Korean entertainment industry that began with an assault incident at Club Burning Sun in Itaewon, Seoul, in late November 2018), many suspects were identified through KakaoTalk, the ubiquitous Korean messenger service app, and their chat records.

According to crime statistics from the National Police Agency, Korea's arrest rate (the ratio of arrests to the number of crimes committed) in 2022 stands at 79.5%, and in murder's case, is an impressive 94.7%.

# K-food Extravaganza

In May 2023, CJ CheilJedang, Korea's largest food company, introduced 'K-Street Food,' a product line featuring six popular street food items including tteokbokki, hot dogs, gimbap, seaweed rolls, Bungeo-ppang (fish-shaped pastry stuffed with sweetened red bean paste), and hotteok. This initiative was driven by the increasing popularity of Korean dishes such as bulgogi and kimchi, prompting the company to expand Korean street food offerings in major global markets.

The global fascination with Korean tastes is a surprising phenomenon. Korean food has been steadily expanding its presence worldwide, with traditional dishes like bibimbap, kimchi, and bulgogi becoming more familiar to people in other countries thanks to the Korean food globalization project that began in the early

2010s. Today, Korean favorites such as Korean-style hot dogs, fried chicken, 'chimaek' (a portmanteau of 'chicken' and the Korean word for 'beer'), and 'Korean food culture' are rapidly gaining traction in the global market. The New York Times commented on this trend in October 2022, stating, "Korean food has become a cultural export." Additionally, various Korean processed foods like ramen, instant rice, dumplings, and convenience items are quickly gaining popularity, with even foreign food companies offering Korean-labeled products due to their popularity.

The number of tourists visiting Korea to explore Korean cuisine is also on the rise. They travel to renowned restaurants in Korea, where they can savor a wide variety of Korean dishes 24 hours a day. Traditional Korean markets offer an array of delectable treats, from tteokbokki, deep-fried delights, and sundae (blood sausage) to green onion pancakes. Streets are lined with restaurants that stay open late into the night. Foreign visitors are also captivated by the convenience of having a diverse range of food delivered to their doors at any time and place. In Korea, you can easily purchase and enjoy ready-to-eat meals at over 50,000 convenience stores, which can be found on practically every street corner in any neighborhood.

Korea's seaweed products hold a commanding 70% share of the global market and are exported to 114 countries. In 2022 alone, the export of seaweed products amounted to $655.7 million, surpassing all other agricultural, fishery, and food products in Korea. The annual production of dried seaweed worldwide stands at 25 billion sheets, of which Korea produces 12.4 billion, significantly more than Japan (8.3 billion sheets) or China (4.4 billion sheets). Seaweed has gained popularity not only in Asian countries but also in regions such as North America and Europe. Korean seaweed products are readily available in major city supermarkets worldwide, as well as in small and medium-sized stores. Some of the largest importers of Korean seaweed products include the United States, Japan, China, Thailand, and Russia. Additionally, the consumption of snacks like seaweed bugak (seaweed coated with glutinous rice and then fried) is on the rise.

## K-FOOD EXPANDS ITS PRESENCE OVERSEAS: NUMBER OF KOREAN RESTAURANTS QUADRUPLES IN 8 YEARS

According to the Korea Food Promotion Agency (KPFA) under the Ministry of Agriculture, Food and Rural Affairs, there were 33,499 Korean restaurants operating in 90 countries around the world as of 2017. This signifies a nearly fourfold increase in the number of Korean restaurants overseas in just eight years since 2009, when there were 9,253. The agency also revealed that 70% of the patrons dining at these establishments were local residents, not

Koreans. In the United States alone, there are approximately 7,000 Korean restaurants.

The number of Korean restaurants earning Michelin stars is also increasing steadily. Data analyzed by food scientist and NYU professor Krishnendu Ray indicates that the '2022 Michelin Guide New York' featured four times as many Korean restaurants as it did in 2006. The average cost of dining at a Korean restaurant is one-fourth that of Japanese sushi restaurants ($235), which are well known for their high prices in the United States, but it is comparable to the cost of dining at French restaurants ($63). This suggests that Korean cuisine is perceived as a somewhat upscale dining option by local residents.

According to the *Overseas Korean Food Culture and Industry Big Data Analysis Report* published by the KFPA, some of the most globally popular Korean menus include not only well-known dishes such as kimchi, bulgogi, and bibimbap, but also items such as soju, kimchi stew, ribs, hotteok, pork belly, tteokbokki, Korean-style fried chicken, and Korean-style barbecue. Additionally, Korean-style gimbap, dalgona coffee, Korean snacks, and even ramen have gained popularity.

Korean ramen is particularly popular overseas, with the industry celebrating 60 years since the first ramen product was introduced and produced in Korea in 1963. It has grown tremendously over those 60 years, with half of its total sales coming from overseas.

The popularity of Korean ramen products in global markets has led to the proliferation of counterfeit products mimicking the design of Korean ramen in China and Southeast Asia. There have even been reports of a food company in Japan, the birthplace of ramen, copying Korea's 'Buldak Bokkeummyeon' (spicy chicken ramen), thus demonstrating the influence of Korean ramen on the world stage.

The growing K-food fever has also led to an increased demand for spicy food in overseas markets. The KFPA analyzed monthly reviews of Korean food-related products from Walmart and Amazon, and the results showed that Samyang Food's 'Buldak Bokkeummyeon' accounted for 239 (8.3%) of the total 2,863 reviews of K foods, making it the highest-rated single product.

# KOREAN FOOD FEVER
# FUELED BY KOREAN CONTENT

The popularity of Korean food has rapidly increased in recent years, even gaining attention overseas. This surge in popularity is largely attributable to the exceptional taste of Korean cuisine and Korea's unique food culture. According to the *2022 Overseas Korean Wave Survey* published by the Ministry of Culture, Sports, and Tourism, 33.8% of foreigners who love Korean food cited "taste" as the primary factor contributing to the popularity of Korean cuisine. This was followed by "indirect experience of Korean food culture" (15.1%) and "use of healthy food ingredients" (9.6%).

Social media has also played a significant role in this phenomenon. As a platform where unique content attracts viewers' attention, videos showcasing relatively unfamiliar aspects of Korean food culture have garnered interest. Many social media users developed an interest in Korean food through word of mouth from individuals who initially tried Korean food for fun but then acquired a taste for it. Curiosity about Korean food culture, as depicted in videos featuring Korean pop stars, Korean movies, and Korean dramas, has also contributed to the increasing popularity of Korean cuisine. Notable examples include "Chapaguri," a ramen dish created by mixing Chapagetti (instant black bean noodles) and Neoguri (instant udon noodles), which was featured in the film "Parasite"

(2019)—the first Korean film to win an Academy Award for Best Picture—as well as the lunch boxes and dalgona coffee featured in "Squid Game" (2021), a Korean drama series that gained global popularity on Netflix. Following the U.S. release of "Parasite," the number of Amazon and Walmart reviews for Chapagetti and Neoguri doubled compared to before. Other common Korean dishes such as tteokbokki, kimbap, and hotteok also received attention after videos of BTS members enjoying the treats went viral.

Additionally, Korean seasonings and condiments, such as gochujang (fermented chili paste), gochujang-based seasoning sauce, and soy sauce-based bulgogi sauce, are gaining popularity. Health supplements containing Korean red ginseng ingredients and Korean food-related kitchenware, such as ramen cooking pots and makgeolli bowls, are also in demand. For instance, food company Daesang is selling Jongga Kimchi in over 5,000 stores, including major retailers such as Walmart and Costco in the United States, where global food companies battle it out. Gochujang produced by Daesang under its Chung Jung Won's global brand O'food is currently available in over 20,000 stores in the United States. This demonstrates that an increasing number of non-Koreans are stocking their refrigerators with Korean staples such as gochujang, kimchi, and frozen dumplings.

Sempio Gochujang by Sempio Foods Company also received three stars (exquisite) at the 'Great Taste Awards', a prestigious

British food and beverage awards ceremony, in September 2021. Out of the 14,000 products submitted, only 1% reportedly received three stars. Additionally, in May 2020, Sempio's soy sauce brand Yeondu won the Innovative Product of the Year Award at the Food & Beverage Awards (FABI Awards) ceremony in the United States. Yeondu is a nearly clear soy sauce made from 100% fermented soybeans, and it received high praise for adding a deep umami flavor to food that complements not only Korean but also Western cuisine.

## THE ADVANCE OF KOREAN FRANCHISES

Korean restaurant franchises are also expanding overseas thanks to the K-food fever. A notable example is Korean seasoned fried chicken brands. There have been reports of KFC, the American chicken franchise with a 70-year history, facing an intriguing experience in the United States: Some consumers are visiting KFC to order sweet and spicy Korean seasoned fried chicken, as they mistakenly think KFC is an abbreviation for Korean Fried Chicken rather than Kentucky Fried Chicken. It was even reported that some KFC stores have gone as far as spelling out "KFC" on their signs or displaying the full name alongside the abbreviated brand name.

Korean franchise BBQ entered the U.S. market and was ranked

second among the fastest-growing restaurant brands in the United States, according to industry magazine *Nations Restaurant* in June 2022. BBQ has ambitious plans to increase its number of U.S. stores to 1,000 within the next two years. Other Korean franchises, including Kyochon Chicken, Goobne Chicken, and Mom's Touch, are also expanding in the U.S. market.

Korean bakery franchises Paris Baguette and Tous Les Jours are also gaining popularity in overseas markets. It is said that the number of foreigners looking for various Korean breads, such as red bean bread and pizza bread, is rapidly increasing. Paris Baguette is actively expanding its business in the North American and European markets, with 120 stores in the United States alone. Paris Baguette started with its first store in Gwanghwamun, Seoul in 1988 and opened its first overseas store (Châtelet store) in Paris, France in July 2014. It now operates approximately 450 global stores in 10 countries, including Singapore and Malaysia. Tous Les Jours has also expanded into six countries, including the United States, China, Vietnam, and Indonesia.

Convenience food products such as meal kits, which have recently become popular in the Korean market, are also making inroads overseas. As the kit includes pre-made ingredients and seasonings, one can easily prepare a meal at home in about 15 minutes. There is a wide variety of Korean dishes to choose from, ranging from tteokbokki and stir-fried pork to pasta and mille-feuille nabe. A leading Korean meal kit supplier, Presage, is exporting its products to countries including the United States, Canada, Australia, Hong Kong, Vietnam, and the United Arab Emirates.

Customers enjoy Korean-style fried chicken at a BBQ branch
in Manhattan, New York, USA

# Deliveries at The Speed of Light

'Ppalli ppalli(빨리빨리)' is one of the phrases that Koreans use frequently. Literally meaning "chop chop," Koreans exclaim "ppalli ppalli" when ordering food in a restaurant or in the workplace. For this reason, some foreigners who visit Korea complain that it is distressing to watch Koreans because they always seem to be in a rush and never take things easy. But there are also many foreigners who believe that this "ppalli ppalli" culture is what made the Korea's miracle possible and transformed Korea from one of the poorest countries in the world into an advanced country that successfully industrialized and democratized itself in just 70 years. They claim that quick business processing and promptness have become Korea's foundation as it grew to become a country that ranks 8th on the list of the most powerful countries in the world today.

Today, many foreign companies that have entered the Korean market are quickly assimilating into this culture because they are fascinated by the speed of business that would likely not be possible in their countries. This "ppalli ppalli" culture, which has become part of the Korean identity, is also behind the country's booming delivery business. Literally everything can be delivered, and the speed of delivery is beyond imagination in other countries. In Korea, speed itself translates into competitiveness.

It is common in Korea to see a food delivery driver looking for 'the customer who ordered Jjajangmyeon' somewhere in Hangang Park in Seoul, people ordering food for delivery in the middle of the night, and items purchased online on the way home from work arriving ahead of the person who ordered them. Korea's unique "ppalli ppalli" culture has created a delivery industry where the delivery time grows shorter and shorter from 'second-day delivery' to 'same-day delivery,' and even deliveries within just a few hours.

Furthermore, as platforms whose focus was food orders and delivery expand their business into distribution and sales sectors, it is now possible for customers to receive almost any item, including fresh food, in the comfort of their home within 30 minutes to 1 hour after ordering.

# EVERYTHING AVAILABLE FOR DELIVERY, FROM LUNCH BOXES AND COFFEE TO PASTA AND PORK BELLY

The food delivery industry showcases just how much delivery services have evolved. Practically everything is available for delivery—fried chicken, pizza, steamed pig trotters, lunch boxes, coffee, pasta, and grilled pork belly to name a few. Foreigners find it particularly amazing that you can even have food delivered to outdoor locations without a specific address or even in the middle of the night or early morning. A video titled "Ordering Korean Delivery Food 24 Hours a Day" on the DianainKorea YouTube channel run by an international Korean-American couple, went viral and recorded 4.72 million views, more than 20 times the number of the channel's subscribers at the time (230,000).

Even before the COVID-19 pandemic, Korea's food delivery market had been growing exponentially. The growth was expedited in 2019 when Coupang Eats introduced a 'single-order delivery service' that significantly reduced delivery time from around 1 hour to 30 minutes. The service involved one delivery driver delivering only one order at a time instead of bundling three to four orders. Baedal Minjok also launched the single-order delivery service 'Baemin 1' in response to the "single order delivery market," and a third food delivery platform. For its part, Yogiyo introduced its 'Yogi

Delivery' service for single order delivery.

According to *Online Shopping Trends* published by Statistics Korea, the online food delivery market grew from ₩2.7 trillion in 2017 to ₩26.594 trillion in 2022 during the COVID-19 pandemic, a nearly tenfold growth in five years. As of February 2023, mobile orders accounted for 98% of all online food delivery orders, an indicator that almost all orders are placed through mobile phones.

The remarkable growth rate of the food delivery market in Korea becomes even more evident when compared to similar markets in other countries. According to research published in the international journal *Science* in August 2022 by a team led by Eva-Marie Meemken, professor of Food Systems Economics and Policy at ETH-Zurich, and Marc F. Bellemare, professor of Applied Economics at the University of Minnesota, the global food delivery market grew rapidly, increasing from $90 billion in 2018 to $294 billion in 2021, a 227% growth. But during the same period, the Korean food delivery market recorded a whopping 385% growth. According to big data analysis company Mobile Index, the number of monthly active users (MAU) on the three domestic delivery ordering platforms (Baedal Minjok, Yogiyo, and Coupang Eats) was 29.22 million as of February 2023.

# QUICK COMMERCE KICKS OFF
# WITH 30-MINUTE DELIVERY SERVICE

The online penetration rate (the proportion of online transactions out of total consumption) in the Korean consumer market, as surveyed and announced by Statistics Korea, was 48% as of 2021. When analyzed by item, home appliances accounted for 58.1% of all online orders, followed by books at 54.8%, furniture at 48.8%, cosmetics at 39.4%, fashion at 31.7%, and food and beverage at 25.2%.

Supermarkets such as E-Mart, Lotte Mart, and Homeplus offer same-day delivery services, ensuring delivery on the same day if orders are placed in the morning and the next day if orders are placed in the afternoon. Online-based platforms such as Coupang, and Market Kurly have introduced an 'early morning delivery service,' guaranteeing delivery by 7 a.m. the next day if the order is placed before 11 p.m. to 12 a.m. This early morning delivery is possible because distributors have urban logistics centers in each region where they purchase products directly and ship them out immediately when the order is placed. In 2022, Naver also launched an integrated quick commerce platform, "Naver Shopping," which guarantees same-day delivery for all orders. As competition intensifies in the delivery industry, it has become commonplace for Koreans to receive products they order precisely when they want them.

Platforms that had primarily focused on food ordering and delivery also ventured into the e-commerce sector, ushering in the era of 'quick commerce' where orders are delivered to your doorstep within 30 minutes to an hour. Even established large retailers have joined the competition, introducing quick commerce services of their own. Among them are Shinsegae Group's 'Sseuggo' and Homeplus' 'Immediate Delivery.' Sseuggo was launched in 2022 as a service that delivers products from Shinsegae Group brands, including Starbucks, E-Mart, Wine & More, and No Brand, within one hour. You can order a wide range of items for quick delivery, including meal kits and pet supplies. Homeplus' Immediate Delivery service, initiated at the end of 2022, delivers orders to customers from 253 'Homeplus Express' stores throughout the country.

**Online Penetration Rate by Product Group**

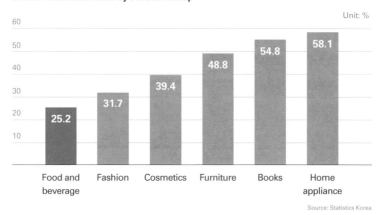

Source: Statistics Korea

# PRODUCTS ORDERED ONLINE FROM OVERSEAS DELIVERED WITHIN THREE DAYS

In the past, it typically took more than a week to receive products ordered from overseas shopping platforms after customs clearance. However, this timeframe has recently been significantly reduced to as little as three days. This remarkable change can be attributed to Korea's emergence as a fiercely competitive battleground for global e-commerce giants such as Amazon, AliExpress, and iHerb, all because the country's e-commerce market has grown to a value exceeding ₩1,000 trillion and fast delivery has become the norm.

Global companies are accelerating their efforts to target the Korean market by forging partnerships with local logistics providers and prioritizing rapid delivery. AliExpress grabbed Korean consumers' attention by offering a 'Choice' service that guarantees delivery within 3 to 5 days, with some areas even offering same-day or next-day delivery. Amazon, in collaboration with Korea's leading e-commerce platform, 11th Street, operates the Amazon Global Store, enabling Korean customers to receive their orders of U.S. products within an average of 4 to 8 days from the time of purchase on Amazon.

# Jeonse, Korea's Unique Housing Solution That Even Angelina Jolie has Used

The jeonse system is a distinctive housing rental system that is unique to Korea. While similar rental solutions exist in India and some African countries, nowhere is it as widely utilized as in Korea. Due to its unique nature, the English word for jeonse is often spelled phonetically as it sounds in Korean, appearing as either "Chonsei" or "Jeonse."

In 2019, Hollywood actress Angelina Jolie garnered attention when she entered into a jeonse lease agreement for a luxurious residential-commercial complex apartment in Sajik-dong, Jongno-gu, Seoul. This decision coincided with her son Maddox, whom she had adopted from Cambodia, enrolling at Yonsei University that year.

Jeonse is a unique lease contract in which the lessee (tenant) pays a substantial deposit, typically ranging from 40% to 80% of the house price, to the landlord. The landlord refunds this deposit to the tenant at the end of the lease term, which is typically two years. Unlike traditional rental systems in many other countries, jeonse does not involve monthly rent payments after the initial deposit. While coming up with the initial lump sum deposit can be challenging, it provides a stable housing arrangement for tenants without the burden of ongoing monthly rent payments.

In contrast to rental systems prevalent in most other countries, including the United States, where people generally pay monthly

rent or take out mortgage loans for 20 to 30 years to purchase a house, the jeonse system offers a distinct alternative.

According to a survey conducted by KB Financial Group Management Research Institute, jeonse accounted for 15.5% of all types of residential contracts in 2020. Within the rental housing market, jeonse constituted 50%, and when considering reverse jeonse (a hybrid between jeonse and monthly rent, involving a partial deposit and reduced monthly rent), the proportion rose to nearly 92%.

## JEONSE, A PATH TO HOMEOWNERSHIP

In Korea, the jeonse system has served as a pathway for individuals to become homeowners, even when they may not have sufficient cash on hand to purchase a house outright. Through this system, one can acquire a home and subsequently rent it out to collect the jeonse deposit. Over time, as the interest from the tenant's deposit accumulates, one can eventually own the house.

While immediate residence in the house may not be possible, the primary goal is to accumulate sufficient funds to reimburse the tenant's jeonse deposit. Alternatively, moving into the house is an option if a housing mortgage loan is obtained from a bank for an amount equivalent to the deposit for reimbursement. Given the consistent long-term rise in real estate prices in Korea, engaging in such an investment strategy, often referred to as "gap investment," has proven to be an effective means of accumulating assets.

Tenants also tend to favor the jeonse system, as it allows them to entrust a lump sum of money to the landlord, akin to a form of savings, rather than making monthly rental payments. Many tenants find this arrangement financially advantageous, as they receive their full deposit back at the end of the lease term.

© Maeil Business DB

Panoramic view of apartment complexes in Apgujeong, Gangnam-gu, as seen from Namsan, Seoul

In Korea, it is a common practice for lease tenants to eventually purchase a house by combining the deposit received at the end of the lease term with their savings. As long as it aligns with the interests of both the landlord and the tenant, jeonse continues to be a popular housing lease format in Korea.

## JEONSE IS NOT A GUARANTEED SOLUTION

But recently, jeonse has run into some challenges. Housing prices fell due to rising interest rates, causing a situation where they fell below the jeonse deposit amount. This has raised significant concerns, as it raises the possibility that landlords will face difficulties in returning the jeonse deposit to their tenants under these circumstances.

In certain areas, housing prices have dipped below the deposit amounts, creating a predicament where landlords struggle to return deposits to their tenants. This situation has brought significant financial stress to many tenants. Reuters has reported on the vulnerability of the jeonse system, noting that it has been especially favored by individuals in their 20s and 30s who may not have the means to purchase a house. The report also highlights the plight of landlords who, after extensive real estate investments, have gone bankrupt and are unable to refund the jeonse deposits to their tenants, leaving young tenants in financial distress. Analysts suggest that the possibility of another housing price surge, like those seen in the past, may diminish due to the demographic shifts in Korean society. Jeonse, which thrived on the premise of steadily rising house prices, may face reduced demand, with rental contracts based on monthly rents becoming more common, mirroring trends in other countries.

# Fast Wi-fi Everywhere!

Koreans joke that if you want to showcase Korea's charm to foreigners, you should take them to a PC room. An episode of reality show "Welcome. Is This Your First Visit to Korea?" featured three visitors from Finland exploring PC rooms in Korea. While Koreans are well-acquainted with PC rooms, the Finnish visitors were amazed, as there is no equivalent in Finland. The state-of-the-art computers, diverse snacks, and comfortable chairs in the PC rooms clearly impressed them. They were also astonished by the lightning-fast Internet speeds, where web pages loaded instantly with a click, enabling uninterrupted gaming throughout their visit.

In Korea, the Internet is as essential as air. Wi-Fi is nearly ubiquitous, available in restaurants, cafes, buses, subways, outdoor parks, squares, and more, and is usually free of charge. You can

Free public Wi-Fi is available at 2,320 bus stops in Seoul

browse the web, stream music, and watch videos anywhere, any time. Unlike in many other countries where hotels may offer Wi-Fi to guests either for free or a fee, in Korea, where "customers always come first," hotels routinely provide free Wi-Fi to all guests.

## 95% OF THE POPULATION HAS A SMARTPHONE: THE WORLD'S HIGHEST PENETRATION RATE

In Korea, accessing the Internet is not difficult, whether you're at sea, atop a mountain, or on an island. It's no exaggeration to say that Koreans are virtually always connected to the Internet, and their "accessibility to information technology" is among the world's highest. According to the '2022 World Internet Usage Statistics' released by Internet World Stats, Korea boasts an Internet usage rate of 97% of the total population. This places it 4th out of 230 countries globally, trailing behind only Iceland (99.0%), Kuwait (98.3%), and Denmark (97.8%), and surpassing the United Kingdom (94.9%), Taiwan (94.8%), Japan (93.3%), and the United States (90.3%). For context, China stood at 69.8%, and the world average was 65.6%.

Furthermore, a 2022 survey conducted by Gallup Korea Research Institute among 1,000 people aged 18 and older nationwide found that the smartphone penetration rate among Korean adults was an impressive 95%. In a global survey of 27 countries conducted by U.S. market research firm Pew Research Center, Korea emerged as the country with the highest proportion of smartphone users, and was the only country with a 100% mobile phone penetration rate among the adult population, with 95% of them using smartphones. The average smartphone penetration rate across the 27 countries was 76%.

According to the Ministry of Science and ICT's 'Wireless Communication Service Statistics Status' report, there were approximately 73.81 million domestic mobile phone subscription lines as of the end of May 2022, of which 53.89 million were smartphone lines. Considering that the total number of residents registered by the Ministry of Public Administration and Security in the same month was 51.58 million, the number of smartphones in use exceeds the entire population of Korea. This high rate of Internet use and smartphone penetration is closely linked to the significant prevalence of mobile shopping in Korea.

The age at which children first use smartphones is steadily decreasing. In 2020, Yonsei University's Bareun ICT Research Institute conducted a survey of 602 parents with children under the age of 6 and published the results in a report titled 'Analysis of Smart Media Use by Infants and Toddlers and Parental Perception.' According to this report, 59.3% of participating parents stated that their children were using smart media devices such as smartphones. Notably, the average age at which children first used a smartphone was 1.8 years old, marking a significant shift from the previous study conducted in 2014, which reported an average age of 3 years old for initial smartphone use. This indicates that children are becoming familiar with smartphone technology before they even develop language and writing skills.

# IT POWERHOUSE KOREA BEATS
# THE WORLD TO 5G COMMERCIALIZATION

As an IT powerhouse, Korea serves as a global testbed for IT technology. It was in Korea that Google's subsidiary, DeepMind, tested its artificial intelligence technology, 'AlphaGo,' in a historic match against the 9-dan Go player Lee Sedol in March 2016.

During the 2018 Pyeongchang Winter Olympics, KT made headlines by giving the world's first 5th generation (5G) mobile communication a test run. Korea became the first country in the world to commercialize 5G when the country's top three mobile communication providers, KT, SK Telecom, and LG Uplus, simultaneously launched 5G services in April 2019. This achievement came 23 years after Korea introduced 2nd generation mobile communication (2G CDMA) in 1996.

Around the same time, U.S. mobile communication provider Verizon also commercialized 5G services, but its maximum speed was only half of that offered by the Korean companies. Most European countries began 5G commercialization in earnest, but not until after the second quarter of 2020, placing Korea's adoption more than a year ahead in comparison. Korea also boasts the highest number of 5G subscribers in the world. According to a study released by the UK market research firm OpenSignal in July 2022, Korea ranked first in various aspects, including 5G mobile communication download speeds, when measuring perceived 5G quality.

The 5G technology makes mobile communications up to 70 times faster than before. In a 5G mobile communication network, one million devices within a 1km radius can be connected through IoT, and seamless communication is possible even when you are on high-speed trains traveling at 500km per hour . It not only allows you to download a 1GB video within 10 seconds but also enables you to experience augmented reality (AR) or virtual reality (VR) content in real-time.

# K-medical Service Wins
# the Hearts of Foreigners

Former Korean national soccer team coach Guus Hiddink, who led the team to the semifinals at the 2002 Korea-Japan World Cup, underwent umbilical cord blood stem cell knee cartilage regeneration surgery in Korea in 2014 and 2022. He had surgery on his right knee in January 2014, and 8 years later, he underwent surgery on his left knee as well. It is reported that more than 90% of the cartilage in Hiddink's right knee was regenerated a year after his first surgery. In an interview with Korean media, Hiddink said, "After my first surgery eight years ago, I was really happy to be able to enjoy high-intensity tennis, golf, and even simple soccer again. It was a natural decision for me to entrust my other knee to Korean medical staff, who have the best medical technology in the world."

According to the *2021 Life Table* published by Statistics Korea, the average life expectancy of Koreans is 83.6 years, significantly higher than the average in OECD member countries, known as the 'club of advanced countries.' Korean men have an average life expectancy of 80.6 years, which is 2.9 years longer than the OECD average of 77.7 years. Korean women, on the other hand, have an average life expectancy of 86.6 years, surpassing the OECD average by 3.5 years (83.1 years). Among 38 OECD member countries, Korean men's life expectancy ranks 9th, tied with Italy, while Korean women's life expectancy ranks 2nd globally after Japan, a country famous for its longevity.

In the 1970s, life expectancy for Korean men and women was only 58.7 years and 65.8 years respectively, well below the OECD average of 66.3 years for men and 72.6 years for women. Keeping this in mind, it is remarkable that Korea's life expectancy has increased by more than 20 years in just 50 years. Korea joined the OECD in 1996, and seven years later in 2003, Korean women's life expectancy exceeded the OECD average, with Korean men's life expectancy following suit in 2005. Korea holds the distinction of experiencing the fastest increase in life expectancy among OECD member countries over the past 30 years.

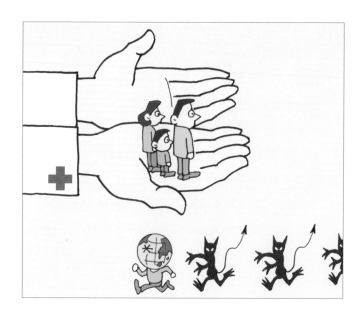

## UNPARALLELED ACCESS
## TO QUALITY MEDICAL CARE

Why is the life expectancy of Koreans higher than that of major developed countries such as the United States, Germany, and France? The contributing factors are believed to be extensive health insurance coverage, low medical costs, and excellent medical technology. In the case of the United States, health insurance is mostly offered by private insurance providers, and people often avoid visiting hospitals for minor illnesses like colds due to the high cost. But in Korea, anyone with a common cold can receive treatment for a co-pay of just ₩3,000, thanks to the mandatory National Health Insurance for all citizens. Foreigners are amazed by Korea's health insurance system, which grants easy access to quality medical services at affordable prices.

The number of outpatient treatments per person in Korea is 14.7 times per year, significantly surpassing the OECD average of 5.9 and the highest among OECD member countries. This is possible thanks to the Korean health insurance system, which keeps medical expenses affordable. While affordable medical costs have led to social issues including "medical shopping" and people seeking excessive medical services, the advantage of unparalleled medical accessibility, envied by countries worldwide, outweighs these disadvantages.

'Deaths that can be prevented through disease prevention measures' and 'deaths that can be prevented through timely treatment' are referred to as 'avoidable deaths.' Korea's high accessibility to medical care is credited for the low avoidable death rate, which stands at 147 per 100,000 people. This rate is much lower compared to the OECD average of 215 people, indicating that Korea performs well in minimizing avoidable deaths.

The annual health checkup services provided by companies in Korea to their employees and spouses are also believed to significantly contribute to the increased life expectancy of Koreans.

The widespread availability of medical procedures, including gastroscopies, has led to a significant decrease in the probability of death from stomach cancer among men, which dropped from 5.1% in 2001 to 2.4% in 2021. During the same period, the number for women also declined by more than half, from 2.8% to 1.3%.

Korea's overall healthcare is excellent. According to 'OECD Health Statistics 2022,' a database of OECD member countries' national health and medical statistics, Korea's public health indicators (life expectancy, avoidable death rate, etc.), as well as healthcare utilization and medical equipment ownership, are much higher than the OECD average. Korea boasts a wealth of medical resources, including magnetic resonance imaging (MRI) and computed tomography (CT) machines, with the number of hospital beds at 12.7 per 1,000 people, which is approximately three times the OECD average of 4.3 beds per 1,000 population.

However, the number of clinical doctors, including traditional Korean medicine doctors, is relatively small at 2.5 per 1,000 people, which is lower than the OECD average of 3.7. The number of nursing staff is also lower at 8.4 per 1,000 people, compared to the OECD average of 9.7. Despite this manpower shortage, easy access to hospital infrastructure contributes to Korea's excellent health indicators. Primary hospitals are densely located throughout the city, and secondary and tertiary hospitals are evenly distributed across regions.

# ATTRACTING FOREIGN CLIENTS

In November 2022, when the world's richest man, Saudi Arabia's Crown Prince Mohammed bin Salman, visited Korea, he rented Lotte Hotel in Sogong-dong, Jung-gu, Seoul, in it entirety. Typically, when a foreign leader like the prince visits Korea, the government designates a large hospital in the city center as an emergency treatment facility for potential emergencies. However, the Saudi delegation chose St. Mary's Hospital in Gangnam, Seoul, which is somewhat removed from the city center, as the emergency treatment hospital. This decision was rather unconventional but was believed to be influenced by the hospital's stellar reputation, and it is a facility often frequented by Middle Eastern doctors for training.

Seoul St. Mary's Hospital opened a robotic surgery center in 2010 and offers training opportunities to overseas doctors. In April 2022, Intuitive Surgical, an American Silicon Valley medical company leading the global robotic surgery market with its surgical robot 'Da Vinci,' attracted public attention when it selected the hospital as the first Total Observation Center (a robotic surgery program education center) outside the United States.

Previously, in April 2021, Seoul National University Hospital achieved the world's first liver transplant via laparoscopic surgery using a robot. The accomplishment was a significant milestone for the Korean medical team, as liver transplantation using this method, as opposed to open surgery, had long been considered impossible.

Korean medical technology ranks among the top in major developed countries. According to the Korea Health Industry Development Institute's *2022 Healthcare Industry Technology Level Evaluation Expert Survey and Result Analysis* report, Korea's healthcare and industrial technology level was evaluated at 79.4%

compared to the United States, the country with the world's leading medical technology. The technology gap with the United States was found to be 2.5 years. In comparison, Europe scored 88.4%, Japan 81.7%, and China 74%. Notably, while Japan's medical technology level decreased by 3.8% compared to 2016, Korea's level of medical technology increased by 3.3% during the same period, narrowing the technological gap with the United States.

Korea has consistently adopted cutting-edge medical technologies quickly, largely due to the nation's receptiveness to new IT and bio technologies such as robotic surgery and stem cell treatment. Robotic surgery has particularly gained substantial popularity in Korea, and is currently used in laparoscopic surgery, thoracic surgery, and ENT surgery.

The use of adult stem cells in medical treatments is recognized as being on a par with advanced countries. In 2011, Korea achieved a significant milestone by gaining approval for the world's first adult stem cell treatment. Currently, among the nine stem cell-based treatments approved in various countries worldwide, Korean pharmaceutical companies have developed four (Hathicellgram-AMI, Cartistem, Cupistem, and Neuronata-Rju), the highest number by any individual country. The enactment of the 'Advanced Regenerative Bio Act' in August 2019 further accelerated technology development and industrial growth in this field. The Ministry of Health and Welfare anticipates that the domestic regenerative medicine treatment market will expand more than sixfold from 2016 to reach $320 million by 2026.


## COVID-19 MEASURES THAT WON WORLDWIDE RECOGNITION

In early 2020, as the COVID-19 pandemic swept across the globe, countries faced the challenge of implementing effective quarantine measures. During this critical period, the K-quarantine model, which prioritizes openness, democracy, and transparency, garnered international acclaim. The Korean government swiftly identified confirmed COVID-19 cases through the widespread distribution of free test kits, without resorting to border closures or lockdowns (imposing restrictions on movement). Quarantine efforts were further refined by classifying confirmed patients into mild and severe cases. The systematic tracing of transmission routes was made possible thanks to smartphone apps and various data sources. The government developed and distributed COVID-19 diagnostic kits in just three weeks in a feat that caught the world's attention.

The most significant contributing factor to the success of Korea's quarantine system was the cooperation of its citizens. During the same period, the United States and European countries saw protests against authorities' quarantine measures, such as border and city-

COVID-19 Testing Center at Incheon International Airport Terminal 2

© Maeil Business DB

"The success of COVID-19-related quarantine regulations in Korea is largely credited to widely available COVID-19 tests. This was made possible because a Korean biotech company developed diagnostic kits that were pre-ordered by health authorities ahead of the spread of COVID-19 and distributed them within three weeks. Korea has successfully contained the spread of COVID-19 without resorting to all-encompassing quarantine measures, thanks to drive-through diagnosis, tracking infection routes using big data, and categorizing and separating patients according to the severity of their conditions."

_CNN, March 13, 2020

"Korea responded effectively to the COVID-19 crisis thanks to a health insurance system that applies to all citizens. As the number of confirmed cases increased, additional medical personnel were deployed. The nation also implemented strategies such as tracking individuals suspected of being infected, conducting widespread diagnosis, securing a sufficient number of hospital beds relative to the population, offering drive-through diagnoses, and establishing a management system for patients with mild symptoms."

_Organization for Economic Co-operation and Development, Department of Employment, Labor and Social Affairs, March 20, 2020

"Korea's successful containment of the COVID-19 virus is credited to the citizens who accepted a surveillance system for the public interest. Tracking the infection route and preventing transmission through the extensive collection of information—such as CCTV footage, card transaction history, and smartphone location data—played a major role in mitigating the spread of the disease."

_The Conversation, March 23, 2020

"Korea played a pioneering role in mass COVID-19 testing. Moreover, Korea successfully tracked the virus's spread by constructing an integrated database (DB). This DB incorporated advanced technology, the movement paths of individuals infected with COVID-19 and their close contacts through mobile phone location tracking functions, credit card payment records, public transportation usage records, and CCTV records. Korea's strategy, which did not enforce a lockdown, is lauded for minimizing losses to the economy and society while being based on transparency and democracy."

_Asia Times, July 17, 2020

"The Korean government is promoting non-contact services to prevent the spread of COVID-19 while simultaneously stimulating the economy. As non-contact consumption becomes a daily experience, Korea has coined a new term, 'untact'. The government plans to revitalize 'untact' industries, including online shopping, video conferencing, and remote medical services, as part of the Digital New Deal."

_World Economic Forum, August 11, 2020

wide lockdowns, temporary business closures, and the isolation of confirmed cases. In contrast, Koreans were willing to endure personal inconveniences for the public good and were receptive to the government collecting various types of personal information for quarantine purposes. Consequently, Korea successfully slowed the number of confirmed cases without implementing an extreme lockdown policy.

## TRADITIONAL MEDICINE
## FOR A MODERN AUDIENCE

Eastern medicine, considered the most systematic among traditional medical practices, recently showcased its allure at the International Asian Traditional Medicine Conference (ICTAM) held in Korea. During the conference, small groups of international attendees experienced Eastern medical practices, such as acupuncture and moxibustion treatments tailored to individual constitutions, in person. Repeated exclamations of "wonderful!" could be heard as participants underwent these therapies. After receiving 'Smile Facial Acupuncture'—a procedure aimed at relaxing facial muscles and enhancing expressions—some playfully remarked to their colleagues, "Who are you?" or "Why do you look so radiant all of a sudden?"

At the core of Eastern medicine lie the concepts of meridians and yin and yang. Meridians refer to the orderly cellular composition of the human body acting as pathways through which blood and energy circulate. Meanwhile, yin and yang represent the harmonious balance observed in nature. Viewing the human body as a microcosm, Eastern medicine approaches physiological phenomena in alignment with natural laws, aiming to restore health by ensuring a smooth flow of energy and maintaining harmony among all bodily elements.

For many foreigners, Eastern medicine remains an intriguing and enigmatic field. However, ongoing efforts are being made to scientifically validate its effectiveness. In the United States, over 30 medical schools are actively researching the principles and effects of various Eastern medical practices, including acupuncture and moxibustion. Furthermore, there is a growing group of patients undergoing Eastern medical treatments alongside modern therapies. For example, Johns Hopkins University Hospital not only has an acupuncture clinic within its cancer center but has also expanded its range of Eastern medical treatments. Collaborating with Kyung Hee University's School of Oriental Medicine, the Johns Hopkins University Hospital Center for Complementary and Integrative Medicine offers acupuncture as a treatment option for ailments such as pain, nausea, insomnia, and depression, broadening the acceptance and application of these ancient practices.

In October 2021, a study led by Qiufu Ma, a professor of neurobiology at Harvard University Medical School, was published in the international academic journal *Nature*. The study demonstrated that the application of electroacupuncture to the hind limbs of rats reduced inflammation throughout their bodies. Another set of research results indicated that stimulation of an acupuncture point located above the malleolus on the leg—known as the 'Gwangmyeong' in Eastern medicine—effectively improved vision. This particular point, part of the foot and limb meridian, is traditionally used to treat eye diseases and enhance visual brightness.

Recently, there has been significant progress in the development of electronic medicines that utilize neural control, a concept bearing similarities to the scientific principles underlying acupuncture in Eastern medicine. Electronic medicine introduces a novel type of medical device that relies on physical stimulation—such as electricity, electromagnetic waves, light, or ultrasound—rather than pharmaceuticals. These devices stimulate nerve signals (or circuits) influencing nerves, cells, tissues, and organs, subsequently regulating metabolic functions. Such advancements are anticipated to aid in disease diagnosis, support the maintenance of bodily homeostasis, and alleviate symptoms associated with various diseases.

# Korea: The World's Fastest Aging Country

Korean subways offer designated seating for elderly individuals and disabled passengers. Each train car features between three to six seats situated at either end, reserved exclusively for elderly passengers, the disabled, children, and pregnant women. But conflicts over these seats have been escalating in recent years due to the country's rapidly aging population, resulting in the demand for these seats far outpacing their availability. Furthermore, with Koreans over 65 eligible for free subway rides, this mode of transportation has become crucial for the elderly population. Instances have been reported where pregnant women in their early stages have been reprimanded by older individuals for occupying these reserved seats. Additionally, disputes among elderly passengers over seating availability occasionally escalate into significant altercations.

Elderly individuals seated at Tapgol Park in Seoul

# ON THE BRINK OF BECOMING
# A SUPER-AGED SOCIETY

As of April 2023, the Ministry of Public Administration and Security's resident registration statistics reveal there are 9,432,919 individuals aged 65 or older in Korea. Given the total population of 51,408,155, this means the elderly constitute 18.3% of the population. If the current trend persists, Korea is projected to transition into a super-aging society by 2024, with the elderly making up more than 20% of the population. With baby boomers born between 1955 and 1963 increasingly joining the ranks, the rate of aging in Korea is set to accelerate further.

Korea's progression towards becoming a super-aging society is occurring at an unparalleled pace. The UN designates a society as "aging" when 7% of its population is 65 or older, "aged" when the percentage is more than 14%, and "super-aging" when it tops 20%. Out of all the OECD member countries, eleven, including Japan, Germany, and Italy, have already achieved super-aging status. Remarkably, Korea is anticipated to join these ranks in 2024, a mere six years after it was categorized as an aging society in 2018, in an unprecedented global phenomenon.

Korea's elderly population is growing rapidly due to a combination of factors: the nation's advancement, increased average life expectancy (a result of rising per capita income, as well as improvements in medical and welfare services), and a significant drop in birth rates. The latter is attributed to individuals increasingly avoiding childbirth, a decision often driven by concerns the economic costs of raising a child and potential career interruptions. Consequently, the proportion of elderly individuals in the population is inevitably set to increase amid declining birth rates.

A low birth rate is defined as a total fertility rate (TFR)— the average number of births a woman is expected to have in her lifetime—of 2.1 or lower, with an "ultra-low" birth rate characterized by a TFR of 1.3 or lower. However, as of 2022, Korea's TFR is at a mere 0.78. This figure is less than half of the average TFR of the 38 OECD countries, which was recorded at 1.59 in 2020. Notably, Korea is the only country worldwide with a TFR of less than 1. The nation has been grappling with the issues of a very low birth rate since 2017 when the TFR was 1.05, and the rate has consistently remained below 1 since 2018. Should this trend persist, Korea will inevitably experience a significant decline in its overall population, making the low birth rate one of the most pressing challenges facing Korean society.

According to data from the National Statistical Office, the total population of Korea—including both Korean citizens and foreign residents—was 51,738,000 in 2021, marking the first recorded population decline in the country's history. This figure is nearly 100,000 less than the total population in 2020, which was

51,829,000. While the COVID-19 pandemic led to a decrease in the number of individuals moving to Korea from abroad, 2021 is the first year to see a population decline since records began in 1949.

## CONSUMPTION TRENDS
## IN AN ELDERLY POPULATION

In Korea, consumption trends are swiftly evolving to accommodate the rising elderly population, with the 'care food' market serving as a prime example of this shift. Care foods are specialized dietary options designed for specific demographics, such as the elderly, pregnant women, and patients requiring targeted nutritional management for disease prevention and control. This category includes soft diets for individuals who struggle with chewing harder foods and customized nutritional plans designed to help manage various health conditions.

These care foods are not only easy to prepare but also manufactured to be easily chewable and digestible, even for those with dental issues, while at the same time ensuring that consumers receive the necessary nutrients. The product range is wide, featuring not only simple options like porridge but also everyday items like grilled mackerel, chicken, and stir-fried pork, all prepared using methods that make them easier to chew and consume.

The care food market in Korea is experiencing rapid growth as more domestic food companies enter the space with new care food brands and product lines. Data from the Korea Agro-Fisheries & Food Trade Corporation's Food Industry Statistics Information System anticipates that the domestic care food market will expand from ₩2.5 trillion in 2022 to ₩3 trillion by 2025. With a broadening product range and increasing market demand, care foods are becoming an essential component of the consumption landscape in Korea's era of a burgeoning elderly population.

'Active seniors' in their 50s and 60s, who are edging towards the elderly demographic, are emerging as a pivotal consumer group in Korean society. Although consumer market trends are traditionally driven by individuals in their 20s and 30s, active seniors are increasingly making their mark, particularly within leisure sports markets—including golf courses, vacation resorts, and fitness centers—and high-end product markets, such as automobiles and luxury goods. These active seniors, enjoying greater financial stability than younger generations and boasting a "younger" physical age than their predecessors, are active consumers.

According to a study conducted by the market study Kaizuyu Data Research Institute, between January and April 2023, individuals in their 50s and 60s accounted for 34.5% of new car purchases. This figure surpasses the 31.3% of purchases made by those in their 30s and 40s during the same period. While new car buyers were predominantly in their 30s and 40s until 2022, this trend has reversed. A five-year analysis of age-specific purchase trends for new and used cars reveals a declining trajectory for buyers in their 30s and 40s, which contrasts with the consistent upward curve for those in their 50s and 60s.

# Getting Around Smartly with Korea's Public Transportation

Nothing is more taxing than waiting for a bus on a hot summer day or a chilly winter morning. However, the experience for citizens using buses in Korea is slightly different. In major cities across the nation, especially within the metropolitan areas, passengers are treated to cooling chairs in the summer and heated chairs in the winter while awaiting public transportation at bus stops. Some of these stops are constructed as smart shelters that adjust automatically according to external temperatures. It is rare to find another country that boasts such temperature-controlled public transportatioin facilities outdoors.

The cutting-edge smart shelter debuted in Seongdong-gu, Seoul. Not only is it equipped with an ultraviolet (UV) sterilizer that eliminates 99% of airborne viruses, but it also boasts an AI-based

CCTV system. This system allows passengers to track approaching buses in real time. Additionally, it can detect suspicious activities and sounds such as screams around the bus stops and relay this information to the Seongdong Police Station and Fire Department, ensuring prompt responses to any possible criminal activities. Buses and subways in Korea also incorporate smart technology. They feature display screens offering daily life information, power supplies that harness solar panels on the ceiling for internal power, and automatic screen doors that regulate entry and exit using thermal imaging cameras. Such technologically advanced bus stops are a rarity outside of Korea.

# THE WORLD'S MOST ADVANCED SUBWAY SYSTEM

The Seoul subway system is an integral part of the lives of its citizens, with an average of 7 million people using it daily. The system is not only user-friendly for locals but also for foreigners, owing to its extensive reach throughout the city. The interiors and accompanying facilities offer world-class convenience. Almost all subway stations are equipped with elevators and escalators. Additionally, there are 131 wheelchair lifts and 24 moving walkways available across 64 and 8 stations, respectively.

In 2023, the Seoul subway nabbed the top spot in "The World's Best Subway Systems," a survey measuring user satisfaction across the ten busiest cities worldwide. This study was conducted by Essential Living, a British real estate development company. Trailing Seoul on the list were Shanghai, Tokyo, Mexico City, and London. Rankings were based on a thorough evaluation of multiple factors, including: Accessibility that emphasizes facilities that allow the disabled to use the subway without relying on stairs; Convenience, which takes into account service hours, non-contact payment systems, and more; Pet-friendly Environment; Connectivity that indicates the availability of Wi-Fi wireless internet services; Comfort that indicates the presence of air conditioning and restroom facilities; Cost-effectiveness that evaluates aspects such as single-journey ticket fares and monthly fees; and Infrastructure that assesses the age and condition of facilities, including trains.

As of January 2023, Seoul operates 12 subway lines that include Lines 1 to 9, the Uisinseol Line, and the Sillim Line. Out of a total of 337 subway stations, 123 stations facilitate transfers between lines, which represents 36.5% of all subway stations. The Seoul subway system accommodates an average of 7,175,300 passengers daily, amounting to approximately 2.6 billion people annually. It is fourth in the world in terms of the number of passengers after Beijing, Shanghai, and Tokyo. However, when considering track length, Seoul tops the list with a staggering 940 km.

One significant advantage Seoul offers is the seamless use of mobile communication devices, whether one is waiting for or riding the subway, thanks to the free Wi-Fi available at every station. In comparison, in cities like New York, communication speeds noticeably decrease when passengers transition from the station to the platform. Furthermore, accessing the internet, sending text messages, or making calls becomes challenging once the train departs for the next station. In contrast, Seoul's passengers can freely browse the web, stream music and videos, and communicate via smart devices while on the train, enjoying the same convenience they would above ground.

Subways in Seoul are renowned for their comfortable indoor environments and the non-contact smartphone payment system. This system allows passengers to pay for their ride using credit cards or transportation cards. CNN reported, "The Seoul subway system is unique in offering both mobile phone service and Wi-Fi.

Almost every train is equipped with TVs, and during the winter, the indoor temperature is adjusted automatically based on the outdoor temperature."

Despite these top-notch amenities, the fares remain affordable. As of July 2023, the basic fare for a single ride on the Seoul subway stands at ₩1,250, while a monthly pass costs ₩55,000. In terms of cost-effectiveness, it ranks fourth globally, coming after Mexico City, Shanghai, and Moscow. The lines serve not only Seoul but also the Incheon and Gyeonggi metropolitan areas, and cities like Busan, Daegu, Gwangju, and Daejeon have their own networks. Furthermore, seniors aged 65 and above can ride the subway for free.


## TRANSFER DISCOUNTS
## WITHIN THE TRANSPORTATION NETWORK

Korea's transportation system radiates from the metropolitan center. Major subway stations in the metropolitan area, city and intercity bus transfer hubs, express bus terminals, train stations— including high-speed rails like the KTX and SRT—, Gimpo and Incheon International Airports, and the city airport terminals, are all intricately interconnected. This comprehensive network ensures that public transportation can effortlessly ferry you to any desired location.

Even residents in remote islands and mountainous regions have access to village buses. All subways and buses in the metropolitan area benefit from an integrated transfer system that offers passengers a discount when transitioning between buses and subways.

The bus system caters to various passenger needs, offering an array of options tailored to different budgets and travel preferences. This system is segmented into village buses, city buses, metropolitan and trunk express buses, intercity buses, express buses, and airport buses. To facilitate uninterrupted travel, there are designated bus lanes on highways nationwide. Express buses, with their smaller number of stops, have notably reduced commute times for many office workers.

Another notable benefit of the Korean public transportation system is the convenience of accessing train schedules, real-time bus locations, and anticipated wait times via a mobile website or smartphone apps. It's uncommon to see people waiting long periods at bus stops in Korea; with a smartphone, anyone can track the current location of their bus and determine how many minutes remain until its arrival, regardless of where they are in the country. For buses such as the metropolitan ones, passengers can even check the availability of empty seats in real-time. Major city bus stops also feature electronic boards displaying bus arrival information.

Moreover, smartphones streamline the process of ticket reservations and payments. Tech-integrated taxi call services are on the rise, with Kakao Taxi standing out as a prime example.

Upon entering your destination, the app immediately informs you of the estimated travel time and fare, dispatching a cab within approximately 5 minutes. As the vehicle approaches, you can monitor its real-time location. Once onboard, the "Share" function allows you to notify family or friends about essential ride details and your current location, as well as the expected time it will take to reach your destination and the actual arrival time.

## INCHEON BRIDGE, A COMBINATION OF THE WORLD BEST BRIDGE TECHNOLOGIES

Incheon Bridge is a 12.34km-long bridge that opened in 2019 with a total of six lanes in both directions. It connects Songdo International City in Incheon—a city that has quickly emerged as a hub in Northeast Asia—and Incheon International Airport in Yeongjong Island, shortening the travel time from the southern metropolitan area to Incheon Airport by 40 minutes. The length of the bridge is 12.34km for the marine bridge section alone, and when including the access road, its total length is a staggering 21.27km. It is the longest bridge in Korea and the 6th longest in the world. The height of the two pylons rising in the middle of the bridge is 238.5m, which is equivalent to the height of the 63 Building (249m). As of 2023, the tallest building structure in Korea is the Lotte World Tower in Jamsil, Songpa-gu, Seoul (555.65m).

Panoramic View of Incheon Bridge

PART 2

# KOREANS MAKING
# THEIR MARK
# IN THE WORLD

On May 24, 2006, at 12:30 p.m., the Notre Dame Cathedral near Geneva Central Station in Switzerland buzzed with activity. activity, with over 1,000 people gathered for a funeral mass. The service was in memory of a Korean: Lee Jong-wook, the former Director-General of the World Health Organization (WHO), who served in the position for three years. Among the vast assembly paying their respects were leaders of international organizations affiliated with the United Nations, representatives from health ministries of various countries, and diplomatic envoys.

Condolences flooded in globally, and the WHO staff's mourning echoed through the hallowed halls of the Notre Dame Cathedral. Even North Korea, typically adversarial towards South Korea, displayed an unexpected response. North Korean Ambassador Ri Chol remarked, "He was a man of integrity, embodying the morals and faith of the Korean people and held in high regard within the diplomatic community in Geneva," adding, "He always treated our staff with human decency." Upon learning of the passing of Lee, often referred to as Asia's Schweitzer, a man of action, and the "vaccine emperor," then-UN Secretary-General Kofi Annan lamented, "Today, the world has lost a great man."

In the 2000s, Korea captured global attention by swiftly overcoming the Asian Financial Crisis and subsequently emerging as the world's 10th largest economy. But it faced criticism for not asserting its presence in international organizations as prominently as it could have. Pioneers who helped transcend these constraints include the likes of former WHO Director-General Lee Jong-wook and former UN Secretary-General Ban Ki-moon. More recently, Um Woo-jong, born to immigrant Korean parents and previously the director of ADB's Sustainable Development and Climate Change Department, made headlines with his appointment as the Secretary-General of the Asian Development Bank (ADB).

# Korean Leaders at
# International Organizations

## 'LITTLE GIANT' LEE JONG-WOOK

In January 2003, Lee Jong-wook, then the director of WHO's Stop Tuberculosis (TB) Department, was elected as the organization's sixth Director-General, besting around 80 candidates nominated from various countries. He was the second Asian to assume the role, and elevated Korea's stature on the global stage by becoming the first Korean to lead an international organization.

Lee graduated from Seoul National University College of Medicine and went on to earn a master's degree in public health and medical sciences from the University of Hawaii. Before joining WHO in 1983, he served as the head of a leprosy eradication team in Fiji, located in the South Pacific, and upon joining the

organization, he took on roles such as the head of WHO's Global Program on Vaccines and Immunization and executive secretary of the Children's Vaccine Initiative. He also championed a worldwide polio eradication project and facilitated the distribution of meningitis and Haemophilus influenzae type B vaccines to developing countries.

In 1995, while serving as the head of WHO's Global Program on Vaccines and Immunization, he was recognized for his significant contribution to reducing the prevalence of polio to less than 1 in 10,000 globally. The esteemed American science magazine, *Scientific*

*American*, even dubbed him the "Vaccine Czar."

In 2000, as director of the Stop Tuberculosis (TB) Department at WHO, Lee broadened the tuberculosis eradication program to encompass developing countries. In 2001, he visited North Korea, supplying the country with 60,000 treatment doses. This tuberculosis eradication initiative is attributed with significantly lowering the tuberculosis infection rate beginning in 2004.

One of his most fervent pursuits after ascending to the role of WHO Director-General was the fight against AIDS. He initiated the '3by5' campaign, which aspired to treat 3 million AIDS patients by 2005. To finance this endeavor, he personally met with then-U.S. President George W. Bush and the Bill Gates Foundation to win their support for the cause. This initiative culminated in the treatment of 3 million AIDS patients by 2008, and the AIDS-related mortality rate started to decline subsequently. This endeavor is hailed as one of the most momentous feats in the annals of public health. In 2004, he founded the Strategic Health Operations Center (SHOC), which was envisioned to serve as a central hub during global public health emergencies. Despite traveling for over 150 days annually, he consistently chose to fly economy class and was accompanied by only a small entourage.

Lee, who was always dedicated to his work, tragically passed away from a cerebral infarction on May 20, 2006. George W. Bush honored him by saying, "As the world's leading health official,

Dr. Lee worked relentlessly to enhance the health of countless individuals."


## COMPASSIONATE LEADER BAN KI-MOON


In October 2006, then-Minister of Foreign Affairs and Trade Ban Ki-moon was elected as Secretary-General at the UN General Assembly. Though Korea was once unable to even join the UN due to its partition, it drew global attention by producing a UN Secretary-General just 15 years after its admission to the body.

Ban's relationship with the United Nations began in 1956 when he was an elementary school student. As a national uprising took place in Hungary, he sent a petition to the UN Secretary-General at the time, Dag Hammarskjöld, on behalf of his school's students, urging him to champion freedom and peace. Later, during his high school years, he was chosen to represent Korea in a program sponsored by the U.S. Embassy in Korea and had the opportunity to meet President John F. Kennedy. A well-known story from this meeting recounts that when Kennedy asked him, "What is your dream?", Ban replied, "To become a diplomat." From that moment, he aspired to become a diplomat and in 1970, he achieved this dream as the second runner-up in the 3rd Foreign Service Examination.

After ascending to the position of UN Secretary-General, he played an instrumental role in finalizing the Paris Agreement, culminating in a global climate change accord that had been elusive for nearly a decade since the Kyoto Protocol in 1997. In the wake of the 2014 Ebola outbreak in Africa, he responded promptly by summoning the UN Security Council. Furthermore, through his mediation during the South Sudanese civil war, he facilitated the path to independence for South Sudan. Recognizing his efforts, he was re-elected and served a second term, which he concluded in 2016.

In 2011, the British BBC characterized Ban as "a diligent and earnest leader who has demonstrated remarkable ability in fostering harmony." The British Daily Telegraph also noted, "During his term, there was a significant reduction in infant mortality rates among the most impoverished families, and the education rate for girls reached an all-time high." In 2016, Forbes lauded him as a "human and strong leader."


## HERO OF THE EXTREME POOR, KIM YONG


Kim Yong, who migrated to the U.S. with his Korean family during his childhood, is the former president of Dartmouth College. He was nominated and then appointed as president of the World Bank in 2012, outperforming notable contenders including former U.S. Secretary of State Hillary Clinton. His appointment made Kim the first Asian to hold the title. After earning his bachelor's degree from Brown University in 1982, he pursued further studies at Harvard University Medical School, where he received both a doctorate in medicine and a Ph.D. in anthropology. From 2004 to 2006, he led the WHO's AIDS Department and collaborated closely with then-Secretary-General Lee Jong-wook in the fight against AIDS. His accomplishments were further acknowledged in 2009 when he became the first Asian to lead an Ivy League institution in the United States, Dartmouth College.

While serving as the president of the World Bank, Kim achieved numerous milestones, including securing a $500 million fund for global pandemics, and was reappointed in 2017. However, he unexpectedly resigned in 2019, with nearly three years remaining in his term. International media speculated that the resignation stemmed from clashes with then-U.S. President Donald Trump, who criticized the international aid initiatives that Kim was championing.

## UM WOO-JONG, SECRETARY-GENERAL OF THE ASIAN DEVELOPMENT BANK

In February 2021, Um Woo-jong, who was serving as the Administrative Director of the Asian Development Bank (ADB) at the time, was appointed its Secretary-General. This marked the first time in 15 years that a Korean had been appointed as Secretary-General at the bank, the last being Secretary-General Lee Younghoe in 2006. Um moved from Korea to the Philippines with his parents in 1975 when he was 11 years old.

He attended the Manila International School for his middle and high school education before moving to the United States in 1982 for college. He graduated from the Department of Computer Science at Boston College in 1986 and worked as a programmer in the United States. He returned to the Philippines in 1993 and joined the Asian Development Bank, where he began to showcase his leadership skills.

In 2014, 21 years after joining the institution, he was acknowledged for his expertise and became the youngest administrative director in the history of the Asian Development Bank, making him the first Korean to assume this position. He was then appointed as Secretary-General and accomplished many feats during his tenure. He was instrumental in increasing the Asian Development Bank's clean energy investment from $500 million to $2 billion, as well as conceptualizing and spearheading the Asian Development Bank's $80 billion climate change program.

As the stature of Koreans in the international community grows, there is a notable increase in the number of Koreans heading international organizations. According to data from the Ministry of Foreign Affairs, the head count of Koreans (at the professional level P or above) working in international organizations such as the UN has sharply increased from 193 (in 26 organizations) in 1999 to

1,039 (in 81 organizations) in 2021. The number holding 'Level D' positions or higher, regarded as senior roles, rose from 10 in 1999 to 63 in 2021.

# From a Sports Periphery to a Powerhouse

In April 2023, the British BBC published an article about Son Heung-min, captain of the English Premier League's Tottenham Hotspurs FC, alongside his picture. The article extolled his achievements, dubbing him "Asian soccer's first global superstar." The article went on to praise him and said his milestone as the first Asian to net his 100th Premier League goal was set to be etched in history.

Son achieved this remarkable feat with a right-footed strike in the initial 10 minutes of the 2022-2023 Premier League match against Brighton at Tottenham Hotspur Stadium in London, England. He is the first Asian and the 34th player globally to achieve the feat. The BBC marveled, "Since his transfer from Leverkusen, Germany, to Tottenham in 2015, Son Heung-min has risen to become one of the best players in the world." The article added, "His humility and affable demeanor endear him to those around him."

Korean sports have always symbolized the dreams and aspirations of its people. During the period when the nation grappled with poverty and actively campaigned to lift itself out of it, watching athletes elevate the nation's prestige with their dedication and passion was an emotional experience for many. The victories felt personal. When Yang Jeong-mo came home with the nation's first-ever Olympic gold medal from the 1976 Montreal Games, tens of thousands took to the streets in celebration, proudly waving Korean flags. Korea-Japan matches in particular were intense clashes symbolizing the pride and honor of both nations. Ahead of the 1954 Swiss World Cup, during a match against Japan, Lee Yu-hyung, the national soccer team coach at the time, was so fervent about winning that he declared, "If we don't triumph over Japan, we will jump into the Korean Strait."

The prominence of sports often mirrors the stature of a nation. As the Korean economy witnessed rapid growth, Korean sports rose in prominence, aligning with the nation's ascending status.

Son Heung-min, who plays for Tottenham Hotspur FC in the Premier League

# FROM ASIA'S TIGER
# TO A GLOBAL SOCCER POWERHOUSE

Once upon a time in Korea, the question "Do you know Ji-sung Park?" became a trending meme, along with the other question, "Do you know PSY?" Korean soccer began its ascent when the team reached the semifinals of the 2002 World Cup. Yet, even with this accomplishment, many perceived Korean soccer as a dominant force only within Asia.

Several exceptional Korean players found opportunities in soccer leagues in the Netherlands, Japan, and France. But breaking into and excelling in top-tier leagues like those in Spain, England, Italy, and Germany has historically been a challenge for Asian players. Cha Bum-geun, viewed as a pioneering figure in Asian soccer, shone brightly in the German Bundesliga during the 1980s. Yet, successors matching his caliber were few and far between. A brief glimmer of hope was provided when Korea's star striker, Hwang Seon-hong, found the back of the net in the Japanese J-League during the 1990s.

During this period, the Korean soccer community beamed with pride as Park Ji-sung donned the Manchester United jersey, playing alongside global sensations including Wayne Rooney and Cristiano Ronaldo. Following Park's lead, other Korean talents such as Lee Young-pyo, Seol Ki-hyun, and Ki Sung-yong made their mark in top-tier English leagues. Amid this wave, Son Heung-min emerged, crafting a success narrative unmatched by his peers.

Son, who also captains the Korean national soccer team, has been a beacon of excellence from his early days. He inaugurated his Bundesliga journey with a goal for Hamburg SV in 2010. Sensing his potential, German club Leverkusen procured him for an unprecedented transfer fee. In 2015, his journey took him to Tottenham for a staggering 30 million euros (about ₩40.8 billion)—a record for an Asian player until Kim Min-jae's 2023 move to FC Bayern Munich. Celebrated as the Premier League's top scorer for the 2021-2022 season and nominated for the illustrious Ballon d'Or, Son has transcended boundaries. His achievements, such as recording the most goals and assists for an Asian player in both the Premier League and UEFA Champions League, have solidified his position as a global soccer icon, garnering acclaim not just in Korea but worldwide.

Historically, Korean players who have excelled in European leagues have predominantly been strikers and midfielders. Yet defender Kim recently echoed Hong Myung-bo, the renowned 'Asian sweeper', by making waves in Italy and Germany. In his debut year following a transfer, Kim spearheaded his team to an Italian league championship before making a move to Bayern Munich, one of Germany's elite soccer clubs.

Standing tall at 190 cm and weighing 88 kg, Kim boasts an imposing physique. Initially a striker, his rise to prominence began in high school when he transitioned to a defensive position, dominating most games thereafter. While it is stikers who typically grab the limelight, Kim consistently shone thanks to his relentless agility, expansive coverage, and enduring stamina. Such was the caliber of his gameplay that it became commonplace for commentators to fervently chant, "Kim Min-jae, Kim Min-jae, Kim Min-jae."

Upon joining Jeonbuk Hyundai Motors in 2017, he swiftly claimed the starting center back position. His outstanding performance soon earned him a spot on the national team, marking him as a future stalwart. Choi Kang-hee, the Jeonbuk Hyundai Motors coach at the time, frequently lauded him, asserting to reporters, "I wouldn't want to face Kim Min-jae as an opponent. He's destined for European success."

Kim played in China before gracing the European scene by joining Türkiye's Fenerbahce SK in 2021. His next move was to Italian club Napoli in 2022, when it won a league title for the first time in 33 years. Kim was the Italian League's Player of the Month in September 2022, becoming the first Asian player to receive this honor. In July 2023, he made a high-profile transfer to Bayern Munich in Germany. The transfer fee was set at 50 million euros, roughly equivalent to ₩71 billion. This topped Son Heung-min's fee, setting a record for an Asian player. The sports community eagerly anticipates Kim's forthcoming performances, with many declaring, "Today's price is a bargain for his potential."

## ARE ALL SOUTHEAST ASIAN SOCCER COACHES KOREAN?

Korean players aren't the only ones shining on the global stage; Korean coaches are also gaining international attention. Respect for Korean coaches surged notably when Park Hang-seo sparked a new Korean Wave in Vietnam. Four countries advanced to the semifinals of the 'Southeast Asian Football Championships' in January 2022, sometimes referred to as the World Cup of Southeast Asia: Indonesia, Vietnam, Malaysia, and Thailand. It is a testament to the influence of Korean coaches in Southeast Asia that they coached three of these four teams: Vietnam by Park Hang-seo, Malaysia by Kim Pang-gon, and Indonesia by Shin Tae-yong.

Park Hang-seo took charge of the Vietnamese national soccer team in October 2017. Under his leadership, the team reached the semifinals of the Jakarta-Palembang Asian Games a year later and clinched the 2018 ASEAN Football Federation (AFF) Championship, also known as the Suzuki Cup. The successes continued in 2019 when the team was victorious in the Southeast

Vietnam national soccer team coach Park Hang-seo greets attendees
at the Pony Chung Innovation Award ceremony

Asian Games and qualified for Vietnam's first appearance at the
World Cup. These accomplishments heightened the demand for
Korean coaches. In October 2019, Shin Tae-yong assumed the
coaching role for the Indonesian national team, guiding them to a
runner-up finish in the 2020 ASEAN Football Federation (AFF)
Championship.

# PARK SE-RI, CHOI GYEONG-JU, KO JIN-YOUNG, AND KIM SI-WOO

For nearly two decades, people have pondered, "Why are Korean women golfers so dominant?" International media attributes Korean women golfers' phenomenal performance to factors such as parental dedication, extensive practice, a well-organized national team system, and an exceptional junior development program.

The 1998 US Women's Open took place at Black Wolf Run, USA, on July 7. During a playoff, Park Se-Ri's tee shot on the 18th and final hole landed in a pond. Eager to clinch her first major tournament win, after her ball landed in the water, Park removed her shoes and socks, waded into the pond, and executed a remarkable shot. While the shot itself was memorable, what resonated deeply with many was the stark contrast between Park's pale feet and the sun-tanned hue of her legs from countless hours of training on the courses.

Park propelled the match into overtime with that remarkable pond shot, ultimately securing her place in history as the first Korean to win the competition. Her triumph in the US Open came during a challenging period for Koreans in the aftermath of the Asian financial crisis. It resonated with many and became synonymous with the lyrics from Yang Hee-eun's song "Evergreen Tree" which states, "I will triumph in the end." Park's success paved

the way for the emergence of "Se-ri's Kids"—a group of Korean female golfers such as Kim Mi-hyun, Park Ji-eun, Shin Ji-ae, Park In-bee, and Choi Na-yeon. They dominated the LPGA, drawing admiration and envy from competitors worldwide. In the 2015, 2017, and 2019 seasons, Korean golfers, including Ko Jin-young, Park Sung-hyun, and Kim Hyo-joo, bagged 15 victories, accounting for nearly half of the LPGA tour.

But outstanding achievements are not limited to the LPGA. Choi Kyung-Joo clinched the top spot at the PGA Tour held in New Orleans, Louisiana, USA in 2002, marking his place as the first Korean to win the PGA Cup. He maintained his momentum with a total of 8 victories up until 2011. Following in his footsteps, Yang Yong-eun and Noh Seung-yeol also secured wins in the PGA, underlining the prowess of Korean male golfers on the global stage. In 2022, 20-year-old golfer Kim Joo-hyung emerged victorious in the Wyndham Championship, making the player born in the 2000s the youngest winner of the tour to date, beating Tiger Woods by eight months.

No one could have imagined the incredible success of Korean players on the LPGA and PGA tours until Park Se-Ri and Choi Kyung-Joo emerged on the scene. Currently, Korean players on the LPGA and PGA tours outnumber those from the United States, Australia, the United Kingdom, and South Africa.

## FOLLOWING IN KIM YUNA'S FOOTSTEPS

For a considerable period, Korea remained on the outskirts of the figure skating world. In 2004, Kim Yuna boarded a flight with just ₩700,000 in her pocket to compete in the World Junior Grand Prix. Without a coach, she choreographed her own routines and despite facing these challenges, she won the gold medal. During a time when there were no dedicated figure skating rinks in Korea, Kim practiced alongside the public at venues like Lotte World and Gwacheon Ice Rink.

Her prowess on the ice was undeniable. Between 2002 and 2006, she won five consecutive national titles. In 2002, Kim was merely 11 years old when she showcased exceptional performances previously unseen by Koreans. Her accomplishments include winning the Novice (Under 13) category of the Triglav Trophy in 2002, emerging victorious in the Junior Grand Prix in September 2004, and winning the Junior World Championships in March 2006. In March 2007, Kim scored an unprecedented 71.95 points in the short program at the World Championships. She was also the first skater to top the once-thought unattainable 200-point mark at the 2009 World Championships. Her crowning achievement came when she won the gold medal at the 2010 Vancouver Winter Olympics, affirming her status as the queen of figure skating.

In March 2023, Lee Hae-in was the silver medalist at the ISU World Championships, becoming the first Korean figure skater to achieve the honor 10 years after Kim. From a young age, Lee has been touted as a Kim's potential successor, and has already set multiple records along her journey. In October 2018, at just 13 years old, she became the youngest Korean skater to secure a medal at the ISU Junior Grand Prix. By 2019, she matched Kim's accomplishment by winning two consecutive ISU Junior Grand Prix events. At the ISU World Championships in March 2022, she tallied a score of 196.55 points, securing a 7th place finish. This marked her second consecutive year in the 'top 10', after placing 10th in 2021. She is the first Korean figure skater to maintain a spot in the world's top 10 for two consecutive years since Kim's retirement.

## KOREANS MAKING WAVES IN THE MAJOR LEAGUES

For the older Korean generations, Jang Hoon is often the first name that comes to mind when discussing Korean baseball players who have shone on the global stage. Jang graced the baseball field prior to the inception of Korean professional baseball, making him a potentially unfamiliar name to contemporary Korean baseball enthusiasts. Nevertheless, in the 1960s, he was an iconic 'legendary hitter' in Japan, which was then considered the world's premier professional baseball league, second only to the United States.

Jang was named Rookie of the Year in 1959, his Japanese professional league debut. He continued to play in the Japanese league until 1981, participating in 2,752 games and achieving a remarkable career batting average of 0.319. His hit tally stands at

3,085, placing him at the top of the all-time list. He was renowned as a formidable hitter in the Japanese professional league, with 228 intentional walks (instances where a pitcher deliberately throws in a manner resulting in a walk to prevent a hit), ranking him second in the historical records. Such was his legendary status that he was dubbed "the hit maker." In recognition of his stellar career, Jang was inducted into the Japanese Professional Baseball Hall of Fame in 1990. After the establishment of Korean professional baseball in 1982, he returned to Korea, serving as a special assistant to the president of the Korea Baseball Organization (KBO) and playing a pivotal role in advancing the stature of Korean professional baseball.

In 1994, Park Chan-Ho was signed by a U.S. major league team. During the Asian financial crisis in 1997, which had a huge impact on Korea, every pitch he threw symbolized hope. Park achieved 14 wins in 1997, 15 wins in 1998, and 18 wins in 2000, establishing himself as one of Asia's premier representatives in the MBL alongside Japan's Hideo Nomo. Following Park, pitchers Kim Byung-hyun and Kim Sun-woo also joined the major leagues. In 2013, "monster" Ryu Hyun-jin joined the LA Dodgers, securing 14 wins in his debut season. Clayton Kershaw, known to be one of the best pitchers in the major leagues, lauded Ryu, saying, "He's the kind of player who can deliver any pitch as a strike, the moment he wakes up." Recently, Korean batters like Kim Ha-seong and Bae Ji-hwan have been delivering impressive performances, following the path paved by Choo Shin-soo.

# VOLLEYBALL PRODIGY KIM YEON-KYUNG

When asked whether there is a Korean athlete who is perceived as a world star, many Koreans mention volleyball player Kim Yeon-kyung. In 1994, Kim Se-jin, while studying at Hanyang University, topped the offense category at the Volleyball World League and was subsequently honored with the 'Best Male Offensive Award' by the International Volleyball Federation. From that moment on, Kim Se-jin was frequently referred to as a 'world star.' However, it is noteworthy that he never played in overseas leagues. On the other hand, Kim Yeon-kyung earned her title as a top global volleyball star by displaying exceptional skills in international leagues.

Kim Yeon-kyung holds the distinction of being the first Korean player to venture overseas since the inception of professional volleyball in the country. After her stint in the Japanese Premier League, she transferred to Fenerbahce SK in Türkiye. In her debut season, she won the league title, was named the top scorer, and was awarded the league MVP. The women's volleyball league in Türkiye is regarded as one of the world's premier leagues, paralleling England's Premier League and Italy's Serie A in soccer. Her achievements are akin to a Korean soccer player entering the English Premier League and securing the team championship, top scorer, and league MVP in their first year.

At the 2012 London Olympics, she was the top scorer, amassing

207 points in 8 games. Although the Korean women's volleyball team ranked 15th in the world, Kim Yeon-kyung's exceptional performance propelled the national team to the semifinals at both the London and Tokyo Olympics, and for that the International Volleyball Federation christened her the 'Volleyball Hero.'

## LEE SEDOL TRIUMPHS OVER ARTIFICIAL INTELLIGENCE

On March 13, 2016, a momentous Go match took place between Google's artificial intelligence, AlphaGo, and Korea's 9-dan Go player, Lee Sedol, in Seoul. It was their fourth encounter. Having been defeated in the previous three matches, few held hope for a victory by Lee Sedol, expecting AI to nab another win.

"The chances of making that move were one in 10,000."

"We couldn't even come up with this strategy."

"It was pure genius."

However, in this fourth game, Lee Sedol executed a groundbreaking move that AlphaGo could not counter. Demis Hassabis, CEO of DeepMind which developed AlphaGo, commented, "AlphaGo had the upper hand in the initial phase. But due to the pressure and ingenious tactics employed by the 9-dan player Lee Sedol, AlphaGo erred."

© Maeil Business DB

Demis Hassabis, CEO of DeepMind, the developer behind AlphaGo,
and 9-dan player Lee Sedol

Since the 1990s, Korean Baduk has solidified its reputation as
the best in the world. While it appeared to waver momentarily due
to China's rise in the mid-2010s, Korea's longstanding prominence
in baduk was reaffirmed when Google selected 9-dan player Lee as
AlphaGo's opponent in 2016.

The growth of Korean baduk can be traced back to the 1950s,
reaching a pinnacle when 9-dan player Cho Hun-hyun won the
World Professional Baduk Championship in 1989. In the 1980s,
9-dan player Jo Chi-hoon made waves on the Japanese Baduk scene,
elevating the stature of Korean Baduk players on the global stage. Jo
Hoon-hyun's success paved the way for a new generation of Korean
baduk players who left an indelible mark on the sport. Among them

was 9-dan Lee Chang-ho, often referred to as the 'God of Baduk'.

At 14, Lee Chang-ho earned the distinction of being the youngest champion in Korea by winning the King of Baduk Tournament. At 16, he won a world championship title, making him the youngest player ever to do so. Throughout his career, Lee Chang-ho redefined the game, solidifying his reputation as one of the most formidable players. Following in his footsteps was Lee Sedol, who bested Lee Chang-ho in 2003. Baduk made its debut at the 2010 Guangzhou Asian Games, where a team led by Lee Sedol won three gold medals and one bronze for Korea.

As of May 2023, Shin Jin-seo holds the top spot in world baduk rankings, followed by Park Jung-hwan in 2nd place, and Byeon Sang-il in 5th. Three of the game's top ten players are Korean, while the remaining seven hail from China.

# Riding the Korean Wave With
# BTS, B-boys, Dancers, and Musicians

NBC's "America's Got Talent" is regarded as one of the world's premier open audition programs. Similar to Korea's "Superstar K", the show provides a platform for ordinary individuals to showcase their unique talents. What sets "America's Got Talent" apart from most audition programs is its lack of genre restrictions. Anyone with a unique skill—be it singing, dancing, magic, or vocal mimicry—can enter and compete. The winner walks away with a grand prize of $1 million.

In June 2021, a sizable Korean group graced the stage of America's Got Talent. Dressed in taekwondo uniforms, they were members of the World Taekwondo Federation demonstration team. The group, consisting of 22 members, performed Taekwondo group dances, including a breaking demonstration, for 3 minutes and 30

© Just Jerk

Just Jerk on "America's Got Talent"

seconds, earning a standing ovation from all the judges. It is said that the team's appearance on "America's Got Talent" was facilitated after the show's production crew saw the video of their performance in the finals of "Italy's Got Talent" in January 2020. By April 2023, the Taekwondo demonstration video from "America's Got Talent" had accumulated over 35 million views.

Earlier, in June 2017, the renowned Korean dance crew 'Just Jerk' showcased their skills on "America's Got Talent," earning a standing ovation from both the judges and audience with their synchronized dance that blended Eastern and Western styles. Before dancing, they confidently declared, "We will show you a dance you have never seen before," and they indeed delivered a show-stopping performance. It is noteworthy that Just Jerk clinched the top spot at 'Body Rock 2016', a global hip-hop dance competition held in San Diego, USA, in June 2016.

The global sweep of K-pop and the Korean Wave is not just powered by a few well-known celebrities like BTS and Blackpink. Many Koreans are enthralling global audiences with their songs, music, and dance. Consequently, it's not surprising to occasionally see the Korean national flag, the Taegeukgi, on "America's Got Talent."

## CHOPIN CHO SEONG-JIN AND THE TIME TRAVELER LIM YUN-CHAN

The 2015 International Chopin Piano Competition heralded the first Korean winner, Cho Seong-jin. Born in 1994, Cho's performances are so remarkable that many have dubbed his performances as 'the return of Chopin.' Given that the Chopin Competition is among the most prestigious in the world, Cho Seong-jin's victory became a sensation not only in Korea but also internationally. He began playing the piano at the age of 6 and gained attention by securing first place at the Chopin Junior

Competition in Russia in 2008 and at the Hamamatsu International Competition in Japan in 2009. In 2011, he placed third at the Russian Tchaikovsky Competition.

In March 2022, Cho's brilliance once again captured the world's attention. He performed at Carnegie Hall in New York, stepping in for a Russian artist who had to withdraw following Russia's invasion of Ukraine the month before. Despite the tight schedule that allowed him only 75 minutes for rehearsals with the Vienna Philharmonic before the concert, Cho delivered a flawless performance.

The New York Times was lavish in its praise, stating "He demonstrated exceptional performance skills," and adding, "It was his inaugural appearance on the Carnegie Hall stage, and even more notably, playing a concerto with the Vienna Philharmonic. Yet, Cho Seong-Jin's performance was remarkable."

Renowned Polish pianist Christian Zimmerman, often regarded as one of the preeminent pianists of the 20th century, also lauded his performance, saying, "From this point forward, the name Cho Seong-Jin will resonate widely. He continues to evolve year after year."

But Cho is not alone in receiving such accolades. On June 18, 2022, fellow Korean pianist, Lim Yun-chan, born in 2004, won the 16th Van Cliburn International Piano Competition. At just 18, Lim became the youngest winner in the competition's 60-

'Time Traveler' Lim Yun-chan

year history. After playing both Beethoven's Piano Concerto No. 3 and Rachmaninoff's Piano Concerto No. 3 during the finals, Lim received a standing ovation. Previously, at the age of 14, he placed second at the Cleveland Youth Competition in the United States in 2018, and a year later, won the Isang Yoon International Competition. These accomplishments earned him the moniker, 'monstrous rookie.' His instructor, the pianist Son Min-su, affectionately refers to him as a 'time traveler' because, "The way he immerses himself in music is reminiscent of someone living in the 18th or 19th century."

## B-BOYS, THE FORERUNNERS OF K-POP ICONS

Before K-dramas and K-pop songs took the world by storm, there were Korean performers who made a global impact as early as the 2000s. They were the B-boys, dancers so skilled and dynamic that onlookers often marveled, "How can a human move like that?" The term B-boy, synonymous with break dancing, is believed to have originated in New York, USA, in the 1970s.

In 2001, a group of talented Korean B-boys formed a team called 'Visual Shock' and won the 'Best Show' award at the 'Battle of the Year' competition in Braunschweig, Germany. The following year, a united group of B-boys named 'Project Korea' triumphed at the 'UK

B-Boy Championship,' making them the first Korean team to taste victory at an international B-boy contest.

In the same year, a collaborative Korean B-boy team named "Expression" won in the 'Battle of the Year,' enhancing the global reputation of Korean B-boys. Korea was the first Asian country to achieve this honor, and subsequent Korean teams displayed unparalleled dominance in the 'Battle of the Year,' securing victories nine times up until 2021—this includes placing second in 2003, emerging as winners in 2004 and 2005, and runners-up again in 2006.

In 2005, Korean B-boy teams pioneered the world's first genre, termed the 'B-boy storytelling musical.' It was during this time that productions such as "The Ballerina Who Loved a B-Boy" and "Marionette" were staged and gained international acclaim. Such innovative ventures helped transform the earlier, somewhat negative image of B-boying as a dance associated with wayward youth. It soon became an esteemed art form, finding expression across various platforms, including broadcasting, advertising, and video games.

According to B-Boy Rankings—a website that tabulates scores for break dancers—the United States leads the B-boy national rankings, with Korea a close second place as of April 2023. Japan and Canada were third and fourth respectively. In the individual rankings, 'Menno' from the Netherlands holds the top position, while Korea's 'Wing' is in second place, and Canada's 'Phil' is in third. In the team rankings, Korea's esteemed 'Jinjo Crew' ranks third. Notably, B-boying has been chosen as a demonstration sport for the 2024 Paris Summer Olympics and given Korea's stellar reputation in the B-boying world, it is anticipated that the nation's participants will win medals.

# KOREAN WINNERS AT
# INTERNATIONAL COMPETITIONS

While they are not well known to the general public, many Koreans have achieved commendable results in various international competitions worldwide. A prime example is Lee Seung-Hoon, the champion in the acrobatic flying category of 'Red Bull Paper Wings'. This paper airplane competition took place in Salzburg, Austria, in May 2022. In the aerobatic flying segment, contestants demonstrate the creativity and performance of their paper airplanes for a duration of 60 seconds, and Lee won with his exceptional skills. Initiated in 2006, the Red Bull Paper Wings competition takes place once every three to four years, earning it the moniker, 'Paper Airplane Olympics'.

Approximately 61,000 individuals from 62 countries worldwide participated in this event. During the competition, Lee displayed remarkable acrobatic flight maneuvers, such as simultaneously throwing and catching a boomerang paper airplane and spinning a 'screw paper airplane' like a tornado. His performance was so captivating that, breaking convention, four judges awarded him scores of 11 and 12, which topped the perfect score of 10. Lee Seung-hoon's aggregate score of 46 surpassed the "perfect" score of 40, and was the highest score in the competition's history.

In the same year, Choi Mina Sue became the first Korean to

win 'Miss Earth', one of the world's top four beauty pageants. Competing against participants from Colombia, Palestine, and Australia, Choi ultimately came out on top. Although Koreans have previously secured respectable positions in various beauty pageants, none had secured a win until Choi. Notable achievers include 1998's Miss Universe 2nd runner-up Jang Yoon-jung, 1988's Miss World 2nd runner-up Choi Yeon-hee, 2000's Miss International 2nd runner-up Son Tae-young, 2009's Miss International 2nd runner-up Seo Eun-mi, and 2013's Miss Earth 4th-placer, Choi Song-i.

Before this, in 2018, Lee Seung-hwan made history by becoming the first Korean to secure the top spot at the 'Mr. International Contest' held in Myanmar. Participants in the Mr. International Contest have won preliminary rounds in various countries, and it is the male counterpart to Miss Universe, which is acknowledged as the most esteemed women's beauty pageant.

# Did We Miss the Nobel Prize?
# Fear Not, We Have the Fields Medal!

On November 17, 2010, Walter de Heer, a professor of physics at the Georgia Institute of Technology, penned a letter to the Nobel Committee stating: "An oversight exists in the 'Scientific Background' document featured on the Nobel Committee's website concerning the 2010 Nobel Prize in Physics. Professor Philip Kim should also be awarded the Nobel Prize."

In the letter, he argued that there were significant inaccuracies in the data provided by the Nobel Committee when detailing the new material graphene, which was the basis for the 2010 Nobel Prize in Physics. The academic journal Nature covered this in depth, leading to a flurry of articles in Korea claiming, "Professor Philip Kim lost out on the Nobel Prize due to an error by the Nobel Prize Committee." While Kim is undeniably a distinguished scientist deserving of the Nobel Prize, stating that he was overlooked solely because of a committee mistake might be an exaggeration. Even though he ultimately did not win the Nobel Prize, there is no doubt that Kim stands as a foremost Korean-born expert in the field of 'graphene'.


## PHILIP KIM: THE KOREAN SCIENTIST WHO ALMOST WON A NOBEL PRIZE

Walter de Heer raised concerns with the materials posted by the Physics Department of the Royal Swedish Academy of Sciences and the Nobel Committee on their website. Instead of displaying a photo of graphene, the featured image was of thin graphite from a paper published by Professor André Geim in 2004. de Heer pointed out that a separate paper discussing the physical properties of graphene was published in 2005, and criticized the Committee for conflating the two distinct achievements.

Here is where Kim comes into the picture. In 2005, both Professor Kim and Kim and Geim's teams published papers in *Nature* that confirmed the physical properties of graphene. Although the teams did not collaborate, their papers bore striking similarities, leading them to be published in the same academic journal. In academia, this occurrence is often referred to as a 'Back to Back' publication, akin to consecutive home runs hit by two batters in baseball.

Speaking to *Nature*, de Heer argued, "It's premature for graphene to be awarded the Nobel Prize, but if it were to be recognized, the paper from *Nature* in 2005 should be the basis. Therefore, Professor Philip Kim deserves to share the accolade." In response, Geim said, "I would have been more than pleased to share the award with Professor Philip Kim."

The Nobel Committee acknowledged the concerns raised by de Heer. But this acknowledgment pertained only to the academic issue that he highlighted. There was no discussion regarding Kim's omission from the list of Nobel Prize recipients. Given the Nobel Prize's emphasis on pioneering discoveries, the Committee attributed greater importance to the discovery of graphene by Geim and his research team. In light of these nuances, Korean media framed the situation as though "a Korean missed the chance to secure the country's first Nobel Prize in Science because of an oversight by the Nobel Prize Committee," a representation that was not entirely accurate.

Indeed, given the hight hopes in Korea of securing a Nobel Prize in Science, the outcome was understandably disappointing. If Kim had presented his paper on the properties of graphene before Geim and his team, he might have been in contention for a joint accolade. However, it is clear that his introduction to graphene came later, and the paper confirming graphene's properties was a collaborative publication.

Currently, Kim is both teaching and conducting research at Harvard University's Department of Physics. He graduated from Seoul National University's Department of Physics with a master's degree in 1990, later moving to the United States and earning a doctorate from Harvard University's Department of Physics in 1999. He joined Columbia University as a professor in 2001, and his research on graphene has established him as one of the preeminent scholars of his era.

While Kim missed out on the distinction of being the 'first to discover graphene', he has since made significant strides in its commercialization. Five years after graphene's discovery, in 2009, Kim, in collaboration with his student, Professor Hong Byeong-hee of Seoul National University, published the world's first method for large-scale synthesis of graphene in *Nature*. Until that time, no scientist had successfully mass-produced graphene. However, Kim and Hong pioneered a method to produce high-purity graphene on a large scale. Their technique made it feasible to produce graphene sheets the size of a TV screen. Typically, it takes 20 to 30 years from the discovery of a new material to its commercialization and subsequent Nobel Prize recognition. But in the case of graphene, the scientist behind its discovery received the Nobel Prize in Physics in a mere six years. This rapid recognition was due in part

to quick advances in research that nudged graphene closer to commercialization. Dr. Konstantin Novoselov, who shared the 2010 Nobel Prize in Physics, sent a note of gratitude to Hong, crediting his large-area graphene synthesis research by saying, "Your work on commercialization paved the way for my early receipt of the Nobel Prize."

# FROM AN ORDINARY STUDENT
# TO THE FIELDS MEDAL WINNER

On July 5, 2022, the International Mathematical Union (IMU) selected Professor Huh June of Princeton University, USA, as winner of the Fields Medal. The Fields Medal is the most prestigious award in mathematics, awarded to mathematicians under the age of 40 who have achieved the most outstanding accomplishments. Since the Nobel Prize does not have a category for mathematics, the Fields Medal is often dubbed the 'Nobel Prize of Mathematics.' The IMU highlighted Huh's achievements by stating, "Huh June solved several combinatorics problems using the tools of algebraic geometry," adding, "in recognition of his contribution to developing geometric combinatorics, we award Professor Huh June, the Fields Medal." The announcement that Huh won the Fields Medal was celebrated in Korea, a country eager for international recognition in the sciences. It particularly resonated in the country as Huh was a high school dropout and did not major in mathematics in college.

Huh was born in the United States but completed his elementary and middle school education in Korea. His father, Huh Myung-hoe, a former professor of statistics at Korea University, encouraged his son to work on math problems from a young age. Despite this, the younger Huh did not show much enthusiasm for mathematics and would often resort to secretly copying from the answer sheet.

Frustrated by this lack of interest, his father eventually stopped trying to teach him mathematics.

In middle school, when Huh expressed an interest in participating in a math competition, his teacher discouraged him, suggesting it was "too late," leading Huh to abandon the idea. Dreaming of becoming a poet, Huh subsequently dropped out of high school, and later taking an examination equivalent to a high school, diploma as well as attending a cram school. His efforts culminated in his admission to the Department of Physics at Seoul National University, a top university in Korea. However, his time at the university was challenging. He struggled with the physics curriculum, receiving numerous 'F' grades. It took him eleven semesters, three more than usual, to finally earn enough credits to graduate.

A pivotal moment in Huh's life occurred when he attended a lecture by Heisuke Hironaka, a Japanese professor emeritus at Harvard University and a Fields Medal recipient. At that time, Huh was passionate about writing and harbored a dream of becoming a science reporter. Motivated by the idea of possibly interviewing Hironaka one day, he started attending advanced math lectures. Huh later pursued further studies at Seoul National University's graduate school in the Department of Mathematics and went on to apply to 12 American colleges for a doctorate program, and was accepted by just one of them, the University of Illinois, due to his poor college grades.

However, Huh's talent quickly shone once he delved deep into mathematics. In the first year of his doctoral program, he gained global recognition in the mathematics community by solving the 'Reed Conjecture', a long-standing and challenging problem. International media praised his accomplishment, drawing parallels by saying, "It's akin to someone who began playing tennis at 18 and then won the Wimbledon tournament before hitting 20." Huh subsequently transferred to the University of Michigan, where he completed his doctorate and rapidly won widespread recognition in the scientific world. He clinched several major awards at a young age, including the Blavatnik Young Scientist Award in 2017, the New Horizons Award in 2019, and the Samsung Ho-Am Award in 2021.

The Fields Medal was first awarded in 1936 and 64 individuals have received the medal from then until 2022. Among these laureates, 9 are of Asian descent, and 6 of these 9 pursued their college education in Asia. In the past 30 years, only two Asians have been awarded the medal, one of whom is Huh.

# Koreans Featured in Time Magazine

*Time*, an American weekly current affairs magazine, is the world's largest weekly publication and ranks among the most influential magazines globally. In 1999, the magazine garnered widespread attention by featuring the '100 Most Influential People of the 20th Century', and has annually published its list of the 'World's 100 Most Influential People of the Year' since 2004. This list celebrates a diverse range of individuals, including artists, businesspeople, politicians, and religious leaders, all acclaimed as notable figures in the 21st-century international community. As of 2022, Koreans have been featured on this list a total of 15 times.

# THE LATE LEE KUN-HEE,
# CHAIRMAN OF GLOBAL COMPANY SAMSUNG

The late Chairman of Samsung Group, Lee Kun-hee, had the distinction of being the first Korean businessman to be featured in *Time*'s list of the top 100 influential people in 2005. *Time*, explaining their choice, stated, "...thanks in part to Lee Kun Hee, chairman of South Korea's Samsung Electronics, which has stormed from obscurity to challenge Sony as the world's premier consumer-electronics company." Notably, during that period, Lee was the sole Korean to be recognized as one of the 'Respected World Business Leaders' by the British business daily, Financial Times.

Samsung Electronics' meteoric ascent caught the world's attention as it transitioned from a modest domestic appliance company to an international behemoth, boasting a net profit of $10 billion and a brand valuation of $12.6 billion. This growth was fueled by its diverse and high-value product portfolio, encompassing TVs, mobile phones, and semiconductors. Highlighting this transformation, The New York Times reported, "The standing of Sony and Samsung Electronics has now decisively flipped."

Lee assumed the role of the second chairman of the Samsung Group in 1987, following the passing of his father and founder Lee Byung-cheol. Under his leadership, Samsung flourished, transforming into a leading global enterprise by the time he

stepped down in early May 2014. Lee's tenure is often lauded as a "second founding" of the company, a task many believe is even more challenging than maintaining the original business. Following his ascension to the chairmanship, the company skyrocketed to the top, nabbing the top spot in global market shares across various sectors.

Under his aegis, Samsung climbed to the top of the global market across a plethora of products. This impressive lineup includes DRAM semiconductors, which was the world's number one in 1992, followed by SRAM (1995), large LCDs (1999), NAND flash memory (2002), solid-state drives (2005), flat TVs (2006), monitors (2006), and smart card ICs (2006). In the IT sector alone, 11 Samsung products topped global market shares, with approximately 20 products from the broader Samsung Group achieving a similar distinction.

The global community was taken aback when Samsung managed to outpace tech titan Sony. In 2001, with a vision to "surpass Sony within five years," Lee proactively sought out talent, traveling to Japan, renowned for its advanced technology. Samsung's office in the Kasumigaseki Building in Tokyo virtually served as Lee's residence. On multiple occasions, Japanese engineers were invited to Korea, sometimes only for weekends, to provide additional training to Samsung employees, and many were even recruited. By 2002, the compensation for Sony's executives had dwindled to half that of their counterparts at Samsung Electronics. That same year, Samsung's market capitalization overtook Sony's and in 2006, Samsung outpaced Sony to secure the top spot in the global TV market.

When Lee assumed leadership of the company in 1987, Samsung Group reported sales of ₩17.39 trillion, a net profit of ₩206 billion, and a market capitalization of ₩1 trillion. By 1988, as Samsung celebrated its 50th anniversary, sales surged past ₩20 trillion and the company's sales are projected to skyrocket to an impressive ₩500 trillion by 2023.

In 2013, *Time* magazine recognized another luminary from the Samsung Group as part of its '100 Most Influential People in the World': Vice Chairman Kwon Oh-hyun, the Samsung Electronics CEO who spearheaded the global success of the Samsung 'Galaxy' smartphone series. Former Apple CEO John Scully heaped praise on Kwon, likening him to a "business titan" akin to Steve Jobs, and credited him with achieving unparalleled success thanks to the Samsung Galaxy.

Lee Jae-yong, Samsung Electronics Chairman and eldest son of Chairman Lee Kun-hee, also earned a spot, ranking 18th on Bloomberg's '50 Most Influential People in the World' list in 2016. Bloomberg highlighted his decisive move to recall Samsung Electronics' Galaxy Note 7 after a battery ignition issue developed upon its release, a decision that risked $2 billion. Lee Boo-jin, president and CEO of Hotel Shilla and the eldest daughter of Chairman Lee Kun-hee, stands out as the only Korean to grace *Forbes*' list of '100 Most Influential Women in the World.'


## K-POP AND K-FILMS INCREASE
## KOREA'S GLOBAL INFLUENCE


Korea has recently cemented its status as a cultural powerhouse, producing influential figures not only in politics and business but also in culture and the arts. A prime example is BTS, the boy group recognized as one of the '100 most influential people in the world' in 2019. They are the first K-pop artist group to clinch the #1 spot on the U.S. album chart and have been dubbed the '21st century pop icon' as well as 'The Beatles of the 21st century'. BTS set a new

Figure Skating Queen Kim Yuna

standard in the global K-pop scene by holding a record-breaking spot on the U.S. Billboard's 'Hot 100' chart longer than any other K-pop artist. Earlier, in 2006, dancer and singer Rain made waves in the United States, the epicenter of pop music, thanks to the Korean Wave and was subsequently recognized as one of *Time*'s '100 most influential people in the world'.

Bong Joon-ho, director of the movie "Parasite," earned a spot on the '100 most influential people in the world' list in 2020. "Parasite" distinguished itself by being the first Korean film to nab four Academy Awards, including Best Picture, Best Director, Best Screenplay, and Best International Feature Film. It also won the prestigious Golden Lion Award at the Cannes International Film Festival, one of the world's three major film events. With these significant accolades, the film is credited with rewriting the history of world cinema.

In 2021, Yoon Yeo-jung made history as the first Korean actress to win an Academy Award for Best Supporting Actress for her portrayal of Sunja in the film "Minari" (2020). In addition, she became the first Korean actress to be featured on the '100 Most Influential People in the World' list. By 2022, another Korean, director Hwang Dong-hyuk, graced the list. He is celebrated for helming the globally popular Netflix series "Squid Game," which topped viewership charts in 94 countries.

Former figure skater Kim Yuna earned a spot on the '100 Most

Influential People in the World' list in 2010. Often referred to as the 'figure skating queen', Kim shattered the world record for women's figure skating. Her graceful performances and impeccable technical prowess garnered admiration from global audiences. Kim Yuna won the gold medal at the 2010 Vancouver Winter Olympics, further elevating her to international prominence. Notably, she ranked second in Time's Hero category, just behind former U.S. President Bill Clinton.

The trailblazers who became the first Koreans to grace *Time*'s '100 Most Influential People in the World' list were former Seoul National University Professor Hwang Woo-seok—known for his groundbreaking embryonic stem cell research in 2004—and WHO Secretary-General Lee Jong-wook, who made significant strides in eradicating poverty, addressing AIDS, and combatting avian influenza.

PART 3

# THE POWER OF
# CULTURE

Recently, platforms like Netflix and other global over-the-top (OTT, online video streaming service for broadcast programs, movies, etc.) services have transcended borders, experiencing tremendous growth. As a result, Korean content, including dramas, movies, entertainment, and animation, has been enchanting viewers across the globe.

As per Flix Patrol's 'Top TV Show' chart, in 2022, Korea ranks second among the countries represented on the list with 16 shows in the 'Top 100' popular shows on Netflix, the world's premier OTT platform. The country placed just behind the United States, which has 48 shows on the list. Notably, Korea's position is unparalleled among non-English content. Furthermore, Netflix data reveals that in 2022, 60% of its global subscribers tuned into Korean movies or TV programs. A diverse array of genres like zombies, horror, crime, and narratives spanning from human-centered and historical dramas to entertainment shows, won international audiences over. Such widespread appeal underscores the burgeoning potential of K-content.

The Netflix drama series "The Glory" chronicles the journey of a woman who endured bullying and subsequently stakes her life on a ruthless quest for revenge. This series skyrocketed to global attention by securing the top spot in the OTT combined content rankings for three consecutive weeks following its premiere in December 2022. Through its candid and poignant depiction of school violence, "The Glory" resonated profoundly with international audiences, offering a compelling narrative that unmasked raw human emotions and desires.

"Extraordinary Attorney Woo" (2022) is yet another Korean drama that took the top position among non-English TV series on Netflix. This series depicts the lives of ordinary individuals, as narrated by a lawyer diagnosed with autism spectrum disorder. The film "JUNG_E," which premiered on Netflix in January 2023, quickly climbed to the apex of the global Netflix movie rankings soon after its debut. Similarly, "Physical: 100" (2023), a riveting survival entertainment show that pits participants against each other based on sheer physical prowess without considering gender, ethnicity, or age, achieved the zenith in global Netflix TV series rankings. Significantly, this is a pioneering achievement for Korean entertainment content on the global stage.

# From Squid Game to The Glory, K-Content Captivates Viewers Worldwide

During President Yoon Seok-yeol's state visit to the United States in April 2023, his meeting with Netflix co-CEO Ted Sarandos was followed by a significant announcement: Netflix would invest $2.5 billion in K-content over the next four years. This investment nearly doubles the amount that Netflix has poured into the Korean market since it entered the market in 2016. This surge in investment comes amid the global acclaim for and popularity of K-content, exemplified by the Korean drama series "Squid Game," which holds the record as Netflix's most profitable drama to date.

"Squid Game" unveils the harrowing tale of individuals from society's underbelly, compelled to risk their lives in a high-stakes survival game with a tantalizing prize of ₩45.6 billion. Upon its release in September 2021, the series secured the top spot in 'Today's

Top 10' in 94 countries. Moreover, it shattered a Netflix record, with over 100 million accounts streaming at least two minutes of "Squid Game" within a 28-day span. Over these 28 days, the series accumulated a staggering 1.65045 billion hours of global viewership, setting an unprecedented benchmark for Netflix.

The "Squid Game" phenomenon did not end with its viewership; it sparked a worldwide trend of parodies and spin-offs. Pop-up stores and themed experience centers cropped up everywhere, capitalizing on the show's fame. The gym uniforms donned by the game's participants and the distinctive attire of the game hosts became sought-after costumes for events, notably during Halloween in the United States. Moreover, Korean delicacies like dalgona and ramen, showcased in the series, soared in popularity. Recognizing the profound influence and impact of "Squid Game" on American pop culture, the city of Los Angeles, USA, commemorated the series' release date, September 17th, as 'Squid Game Day'.

## SQUID GAME IN NUMBERS

- Cumulative worldwide viewing time hit 1.65045 billion hours within the first 28 days of its release, setting a new all-time record.
- It ranked first worldwide for 53 consecutive days, the longest duration in Netflix's history. Notably, 95% of its total viewing time came from outside Korea.
- As of November 2021, there were 129,000 YouTube-related videos created about the show that have accumulated a staggering 17 billion views within just 8 weeks after its release.
- According to Bloomberg, by October 2021, the series had generated over $900 million in profit against a production cost of $21.4 million (approximately ₩30 billion).

## KOREAN SLANG TRENDING GLOBALLY

With the surge in global viewership of Korean dramas on OTT platforms, Korean slang has become increasingly popular among international audiences. This rising trend is both fascinating and indicative of the significant influence that Korean content exerts in the global market.

Bloomberg highlighted the case of one Mr. Thompson, an American who has never been to Korea nor studied the Korean language. However, he's now frequently using Korean slang terms like "Aish" (trans. "damn") and "Jenjang" (trans. "dang") in moments of frustration. This habit developed after he became engrossed in the hit Korean drama "The Glory" on Netflix. Thompson admitted to repeatedly watching the show and shared that he has been favoring Korean dramas over American ones for the past decade, attributing his preference to the compelling storylines.

The Korean drama sensation is believed to have originated from the historical drama "Dae Jang Geum," which aired from 2003 to 2004. Actress Lee Young-ae portrayed the lead role, Seo Jang-geum, in this series inspired by historical events. The drama chronicles the triumphs and romance of Seo, who begins her journey as a court lady after the tragic death of her parents in a political conspiracy, a fallout where Lady Yun, one of the king's concubines, was deposed. Ultimately, Seo rises to the position of personal physician to King Jungjong.

"Dae Jang Geum" achieved a staggering viewership rating of 57.8% in Korea, and its international export to territories including China, Taiwan, Japan, Hong Kong, the United States, Canada, Russia, Turkmenistan, and Iran marked the beginning of the Hallyu, or Korean Wave. Such was its immense popularity that Japan's NHK network aired reruns of the series. Furthermore, former Uzbekistani President Shavkat Mirziyoyev was such an ardent fan of "Dae Jang Geum," Lee received a dinner invitation during his 2017 state visit to Korea. In Sri Lanka, the drama recorded an astonishing 99% viewership rating. In India, there is even a touching account of a man who found renewed hope in life after watching this beloved Korean series.

## KOREAN MOVIE 'PARASITE' REWRITES FILM HISTORY AGAINST ALL ODDS

Korean dramas have not only achieved sensational popularity but have also been recognized as artistically brilliant. Some argue that Korean content has shattered long-standing biases, winning awards that had been dominated by English-language productions. One example is "Squid Game," directed by Hwang Dong-hyuk and starring lead actor Lee Jung-jae, which made history by being the first non-English-language drama to secure the Best Director and Best Actor Awards at the Emmy Awards in September 2022. Hosted by the American Academy of Television Arts and Sciences (ATAS), these awards are considered the Oscars of the television world.

"Squid Game" began its winning streak earlier on. Both Lee Jung-jae and Jeong Ho-yeon became the first Korean actors to win the SAG Best Actor and Actress Awards at the Screen Actors Guild Awards. Additionally, the show clinched accolades including the Guest Award, Stunt Performance Award, Visual Effects Award, and Production Design Award at the Creative Arts Primetime Emmy Awards, which honor the invaluable contributions of technicians and support staff. These achievements underscore the widespread acclaim the series has garnered across various sectors.

Korean films are steadily gaining prominence on the international stage. Consider the Korean movie "Parasite." Directed by Bong Joon-ho, this dark comedy delves into the starkly different lives of two families—one affluent and the other impoverished. In 2019, the film earned the distinction of being the first Korean movie to win the Palme d'Or—the highest accolade—at the Cannes International Film Festival, which ranks among the world's top three film festivals. In 2021, Bong became the first Korean director to chair the jury at the Venice International Film Festival, overseeing the screening of films in the competition section.

"Parasite" is celebrated for its groundbreaking achievements in

Poster for the movie "Parasite"

film. It was nominated in seven categories at the 2020 Academy Awards (or Oscars) and triumphed in four, including Best Picture, Best Screenplay, Best International Feature Film, and Best Director. This made it the first Korean film to ever receive an Academy Award. "Parasite" also stands out as the first non-English language film to win Best Picture.

"··· When I was in school, I studied Martin Scorsese's films. Just to be nominated was a huge honor. I never thought I would win. When people in the U.S. were not familiar with my films, Quentin [Tarantino] always put my films on his list. He's here, thank you so much. Quentin, I love you. And Todd [Phillips] and Sam [Mendes], great directors that I admire. If the Academy allows, I would like to get a Texas chainsaw, split the award into five and share it with all of you."

_Excerpts from Director Bong Joon-ho's acceptance speech at the 92nd Academy Award ceremony

The international media was effusive in its praise for both "Parasite" and Bong's gracious acceptance speech. The New York Post, in an article headlined 'Bong Joon-ho was a saint,' observed, "While it's customary for winning directors to acknowledge their fellow nominees, when was the last time you saw a victor move even those who didn't win to tears of joy?" Meanwhile, The New York Times emphasized, "A foreign language film has finally conquered the Oscars." CNN chimed in, stating, "This historic night was dominated by 'Parasite'." The Associated Press summed up the sentiment, noting, "Parasite's win marked a turning point in the Academy Awards."

"Parasite" achieved the rare honor of winning both the Cannes Film Festival's Palme d'Or and the Academy Award for Best Picture. This accomplishment had only been matched once before, and it was the first time in 64 years since director Delbert Mann's "Marty" won the honors in 1955. Bong became the first Asian director to win the Academy Award for Best Director since Taiwanese director Ang Lee nabbed the Best Director award for both "Brokeback Mountain" and "Life of Pi." Furthermore, "Parasite" took center stage in the film industry by becoming the first Korean film to garner the Golden Globe Award for Best Foreign Language Film, the British Academy Award for Best Original Screenplay and Best Film Not in the English Language, and France's César Award for Best Foreign Film.

As per Box Office Mojo, "Parasite" raked in $253.51 million in global box office sales. Its cumulative earnings in North America totaled $52.78 million, making it the fourth highest-grossing foreign language film ever released in the region. The record for the top-grossing foreign language film in North American box office history belongs to "Crouching Tiger, Hidden Dragon" (2000) with earnings of $128.1 million, followed by the Italian film "Life is Beautiful" (1997) at $57.2 million, and the Chinese movie "Hero" (2002) at $53.7 million.

At the 2021 Academy Awards, actress Yoon Yeo-jung made history by becoming the first Korean actor to win the Best Supporting Actress Award for her portrayal of Sunja in the film "Minari." The movie narrates the inspiring journey of a Korean immigrant family building a new life in Arkansas. Yoon's acceptance speech garnered worldwide acclaim for its wit and humility.

The New York Times remarked, "This is the best acceptance speech. She should be the host of next year's Oscars." The British newspaper, The Guardian, also offered praise, stating, "Youn Yeo-jung is the star of the night, showcasing her immense talent." Reuters hailed her as "a witty and sensational actress," while the Washington Post observed, "A charismatic grandmother has captured the hearts of countless people." Yoon also starred in the American Apple TV drama series "Pachinko" (2022) and returned to the red carpet as a presenter at the 2022 Academy Awards.

"Mr. Brad Pitt, finally. Very nice to finally meet you. Where were you when we were filming in Tulsa···. I don't believe in competition. How can I win over Glenn Close? ··· So, all the nominees, five nominees, we are the winners of different movies, we played a different role, so we cannot compete with each other tonight ... have just a little bit luck, I think. Maybe I'm luckier than you."

_Yoon Yeo-jung's acceptance speech
at the 93rd Academy Award ceremony

# K-Content: Soft Power Superstar

The British lifestyle magazine, *Monocle*, featured the Korean national flag on the cover of its December 2020 issue, heralding Korea as a 'soft power superstar.'

Each year, Monocle assesses nations' competitiveness in the realm of soft power and unveils its list of the top ten countries in this sector and in 2020, Korea ranked second after Germany. *Monocle* observed, "Korea has set the benchmark for other nations in entertainment and innovation." The magazine also noted, "Entertainment content is now the cornerstone of Korea's soft power, with Korean movies, TV dramas, and music making waves internationally." France, Japan, and Taiwan were the 3rd, 4th, and 5th respectively.

K-content has captivated audiences globally, emerging as Korea's primary export product. According to the 2021 Standard Content Industry Survey released by the Korean Ministry of Culture, Sports, and Tourism, the industry's exports amounted to $12.4 billion in 2021. This figure surpasses the export values of other significant Korean export products such as home appliances ($8.67 billion) and electric vehicles ($6.99 billion). K-content encompasses TV programs, movies, K-pop, and webtoons.

The surging popularity of K-content overseas can be largely attributed to Korea's escalating global prominence. Hwang Yi-hang, a professor at the Business School of the University of Hong Kong, and his research team presented their findings on the explosive growth of Korean content at the 'International Comprehensive Arts, Culture, and Communications Conference (CACC)' held in Wuhan, China, in April 2022. The research highlighted several contributing factors: the Korean Wave that began in the 2000s; global recognition of leading Korean brands such as Samsung, LG, and Hyundai Motor Company; and the advanced content competitiveness and production creativity stemming from the evolution of entertainment sectors like music (K-pop), drama, and film.

In Korean dramas and movies, viewers are captivated by the unique worldviews present in Korean narratives, the portrayal of realistic events that resonate with real life, and the intricate emotional arcs. CBR, an American media outlet specializing in comics, movies, and TV content boasting over 60 million subscribers, dissected the global success of "Squid Game." Their analysis highlighted, "A survival game where life hangs in the balance is a concept familiar in science fiction, yet 'Squid Game' plunges this concept firmly into the realm of reality, eliciting intense empathy." CBR further noted, "More than half the participants meet their end in the first game alone. If one were to describe 'Squid Game' in a single word, it might be 'shocking.'"

Other enthralling elements include characters that are relatable and approachable; the unsettling incorporation of traditional Korean children's games like 'The Rose of Sharon Has Bloomed' (Korea's version of Red Light, Green Light) and 'Dakjichigi'; Jo Sang-woo, the protagonist who starts with noble intentions but becomes increasingly consumed by his desires, slowly morphing into a monstrous figure; the sheer sadism exhibited by the "VIPs" who revel in watching the brutal life-or-death contest; the illicit organ trafficking scheme carried out by the Squid Game staff; and the complex character of the initial participant, Oh Il-nam. Similarly, the "Parasite" garnered global empathy by humorously yet poignantly addressing the desires and class struggles inherent not just in Korean society but in communities worldwide.

In the past, films and dramas predominantly centered on themes of social achievement and economic advancement. However, recent smash hits like "The Glory" and "Extraordinary Attorney

Woo" delve into a broader spectrum of societal issues. Industry experts attribute the evolution of the content industry to a shift in the Korean mindset. While there is a significant pride in Korea's economic ascent, there is also an acute awareness of its societal underbelly, particularly those who are marginalized and deprived of its benefits.

In the realm of entertainment programs, Korea particularly excels in real variety, reality, and survival show, all of which limit the intrusion of production crews. Beginning with "Infinite Challenge" and "2 Days & 1 Night," reality-focused entertainment programs have been at the forefront of Korean entertainment since the 2000s. The 2010s witnessed a surge in the popularity of survival audition programs, such as "Superstar K," "K-Pop Star," and "Produce 101," all tailored to unearth the next K-pop sensations, further elevating the quality of content. As Netflix's survival observational entertainment shows "Solo Hell" and "Physical: 100" garner global acclaim, such entertainment programs are being exported in what is coined as the 'K format'.

The format package of tvN's observational reality show "Grandpas Over Flowers," in which aging celebrities travel around the world, was exported to NBC, one of the four major TV networks in the USA. NBC premiered the American version titled "Better Late Than Never" in 2014, which topped the viewership ratings for its time slot among all U.S. broadcast networks. KBS's "The Return

**Major awards in the Korean film industry**

| | |
|---|---|
| Actress Kang Soo-yeon | The first Asian actress to win an acting award (Best Actress) at the Venice International Film Festival for her role as Ok-nyeo in The Surrogate Womb (1986) |
| Chihwaseon (2002) Directed by Im Kwon-taek | First Korean film to win Best Director at Cannes Film Festival in 2002 |
| Samaria (2004) directed by Kim Ki-deok | First Korean film to win the Silver Bear Award (Best Director) at the Berlin International Film Festival in 2004 |
| Actress Jeon Do-yeon | The first Korean actress to win the Best Actress Award at the Cannes Film Festival in 2007 for her role as Lee Shin-ae in Secret Sunshine (2007) |
| Pieta (2012) Directed by Kim Ki-deok | First Korean film to win the Golden Lion Award (Top Prize) at the Venice International Film Festival in 2012 |
| Actress Kim Min-hee | The first Korean actor to win the Berlin International Film Festival Acting Award (Best Actress) in 2016 for her role as Young-hee in On the Beach at Night Alone (2016) |
| Parasite (2019) Directed by Bong Joon-ho | First Korean film to win the Palme d'Or at the Cannes Film Festival (Top Prize) in 2019 The first Korean film to win four Academy Awards (Oscar Awards): Best Picture, Best Original Screenplay, Best International Feature Film, and Best Director in 2020 |
| Actress Yoon Yeo-jung | The first Korean actress to win an Academy Award in 2021 (Best Supporting Actress) for her role as Sunja in Minari (2020) |

of Superman," which offers a glimpse into fathers managing daily childcare routines, inked a format licensing deal with CSSPR in the U.S. in 2015. Additionally, tvN's mystery game survival entertainment show "The Genius" exported its entertainment format to the Netherlands, France, and the United Kingdom, subsequently leading to adaptations produced and aired in these countries, spreading its influence across Europe.

Global content companies are taking note of the rapidly expanding Korean market. From 2016 to 2022, Netflix reportedly invested over ₩1.85 trillion in Korea, and the streaming giant aims to produce 23 new series in the country in 2023. Furthermore, Netflix has plans to allocate an additional $2.5 billion to Korean content production over the next four years, which breaks down to an average annual commitment of about ₩825 billion.

Disney Plus also recognized the significance of the Korean market, choosing Korea as the first Asian country to launch its service in November 2021. Designating Korea as a strategic business hub, Disney Plus expressed immense confidence in Korean content, stating, "Korea acts as a 'trend setter', captivating global audiences with the compelling force of K-culture."

# Getting to 64.3B K-pop Content Views

Global K-pop sensation BTS released a slew of hits, with "Butter" reigning atop the Billboard Hot 100 chart for 10 weeks. Despite being nominated for a Grammy Award for three consecutive years, the group has yet to win the coveted prize. This omission incited disappointment from BTS's fan club 'ARMY', which boasts an official membership of 18 million, and numerous international media outlets also criticized the Academy. Forbes in America observed, "While not every talented musician has secured a Grammy, it's evident that BTS has been overlooked." The Associated Press also voiced its surprise, noting the conspicuous absence of "Butter." These reactions underscore BTS's profound influence.

K-pop heralded the onset of the Korean Wave and has firmly entrenched itself as a standalone music genre. Notably, groups like BTS and Blackpink have skyrocketed to global stardom, amassing fans from all corners of the globe. Other notable Korean musicians, including TWICE, Stray Kids, ITZY, SEVENTEEN, aespa, IU, and PSY, also command an international following.

According to the '2022 K-Pop Global Map' published by the K-pop data analysis agency, K-pop Radar, a total of 64.315 billion views were amassed from YouTube videos of 229 K-pop artist teams over the space of a year until July 2022, which is a 2.5-fold increase over the past three years. Leading the charts were BTS, accounting for 18.7% of the views, and Blackpink with 11.3%. K-Pop Radar attributes this success to the rise of 4th generation Korean idols including aespa, ENHYPEN, and IVIVE, who debuted during the COVID-19 pandemic, building on the foundation established by BTS and Black Pink.

## '21ST CENTURY BEATLES' BTS HOLDS 28 GUINNESS WORLD RECORDS

BTS, a seven-member boy group comprised of Jin, Suga, J-Hope, RM, Jimin, V, and Jungkook, debuted in Korea in 2013. For the first few years, BTS did not command a significant fandom, but their trajectory shifted dramatically with the release of their 5th mini album "Love Yourself." Their popularity skyrocketed, with the music video for the title track, "DNA", topping global YouTube views and marking their first entry into the U.S. Billboard main singles chart 'Hot 100'.

With these achievements under its belt, BTS has shattered numerous records both domestically and internationally. By the close of 2022, BTS had etched 28 world records into *the Guinness Book of World Records*. These accolades include: 'The first K-pop artist to top the US album chart' (2018); 'Highest-earning K-pop group' ($50 million in 2020); 'Live concert with the most tickets sold' (756,000 tickets in 2020); 'Artist with the highest album sales in Korea' (4.44 million copies in 2021); and 'Artist with the longest tenure on the U.S. Billboard Hot 100 chart with K-pop music' (32 weeks in 2021). Additionally, in 2021, BTS was inducted into the Guinness World Records 'Hall of Fame'.

BTS played a pivotal role in expanding K-pop's reach to America and Europe, which earned them the moniker '21st Century Beatles.' They garnered a nomination for the Best Pop Duo & Group Performance Award at the Grammy Awards, which is hosted by the globally esteemed Academy of Recording Arts and Sciences, and they delivered a standout solo performance. Their song "Life Goes On" distinguished itself by becoming the first Korean song to ascend to the top of Billboard's 'Hot 100' in its 62-year history.

BTS, one of the most popular and influential pop stars in the world

While BTS has yet to win a Grammy Award, they have dominated both domestic and international award ceremonies for several years. As of January 2023, BTS has amassed a staggering total of 382 awards. The group won the grand prize at the 'Mnet Asian Music Awards (MAMA)' for five consecutive years from 2016 to 2020. At the 'Billboard Music Awards', BTS clinched titles including the 'Top Duo & Group Award', 'Top Social Artist Award' (from 2017 to 2021), 'Top Song Sales Artist Award', and 'Top Selling Song'. In 2020, BTS was heralded as a 'Music Innovator' at the '2020 Innovator Awards' presented by the *Wall Street Journal* magazine in the United States. Moreover, the boy group was celebrated as the 'Artist of the Year' at the 2021 'American Music Awards'. With their track "Dynamite," they carved a new record in domestic music history, reigning supreme on a total of 161 music shows.

BTS's meteoric rise to global superstardom in the 21st century can be attributed to their exceptional performance skills, catchy songs, diverse group dynamics, and captivating looks. However, these factors alone do not account for their unique position, as numerous K-pop groups in Korea possess comparable talent and backgrounds. Consequently, experts emphasize the significance of the themes and messages woven into BTS's music. Unlike many artists who predominantly explore romantic love, BTS's music resonates with the evolving zeitgeist.

Analysts postulate that the appeal of BTS lies in their lyrical themes—dreams, rebellion, anxiety, hope, and diverse interpretations of love—which deeply resonate with young students and adults alike. These profound messages have distinguished BTS from their peers and solidified their unique identity. In their early albums, BTS poignantly depicted the struggles and growth of contemporary youth. Through their "Love Yourself" series, they voiced the concerns and emotions of young people experiencing love. Moreover, they endeared themselves to their international fanbase by sharing messages of solidarity and hope during the challenging times of the COVID-19 pandemic.

BTS has garnered attention for various activities beyond just their music. Notably, they became the first Korean pop artists to address the General Assembly on behalf of the younger generation. In 2018, at the General Assembly held at the UN Headquarters in New York, USA, the group's leader, RM, delivered a heartfelt message: "My name is Kim Nam Jun, also known as RM, the leader of BTS... I am who I am, with all my faults and mistakes... Love me for who I am, who I was, and who I hope to become." BTS was also invited to speak at the UN General Assembly in 2020 and 2021.

During the opening ceremony of the 2021 UN 'Second High-Level Meeting on the Sustainable Development Goals (SDG Moment)', BTS captivated the audience by conveying a message of hope to young people worldwide in the midst of the COVID-19 pandemic, speaking in Korean. RM reflected, "I once thought the world had stopped, but it continues to move forward, step by step. I believe that every decision we make isn't the end but rather the dawn of change." Following their address, they unveiled a special performance video of "Permission to Dance", which was pre-recorded at the UN headquarters. This performance resonated globally, as it integrated choreography that utilized international sign language to signify 'fun', 'let's dance', and 'peace'. In May 2022, they further distinguished themselves by becoming the first Korean artists to visit the White House in the United States, using their platform to advocate for the elimination of anti-Asian hate crimes.

# Blackpink Boasts the Most YouTube Subscribers Among Artists Worldwide

Blackpink, which debuted in 2016, is a four-member girl group comprising Jennie, Lisa, Rosé, and Jisoo. Their unique name mirrors their dual identity: 'Black' represents their robust hip-hop style and confident allure, while 'Pink' epitomizes elegance and beauty. The name also conveys messages such as "Don't just perceive us as pretty faces" and "There's more to us than meets the eye." Blackpink's hallmarks include music that seamlessly blends power with delicate emotional nuances, show-stopping performances, catchy choruses complemented by signature dance moves, and cinematic music videos that vividly showcase each member's distinct style.

The members' diverse backgrounds and individual characteristics also fuel their global appeal: Jennie, born in Korea but educated in New Zealand; Jisoo, a native Korean; Rosé, who holds dual citizenship in Korea and New Zealand; and Lisa, who hails from Thailand.

"Hit you with that ddu-du, ddu-du, du"

The hand gesture, reminiscent of a shooting gun, seen in the chorus of the hit song "Ddu-Du Ddu-Du," catapulted Blackpink to global stardom and sparked a worldwide meme phenomenon. With the "Ddu-Du Ddu-Du" music video, they became the first K-pop group to amass 2 billion views on YouTube by January 2023, just four years after its debut, setting an unparalleled record in K-pop history. According to YouTube, Blackpink's "Pink Venom" music video set a new milestone with 90.4 million views within the first 24 hours of its release, and it topped the popularity charts in over 40 countries globally.

Blackpink turned heads when they made a splash on the global stage by becoming the first K-pop girl group to be invited to America's premier music festival, 'Coachella Valley Music and Arts Festival,' in 2019. They performed hit songs including "Ddu-Du Ddu-Du," "Boombaya," and "Kill This Love." During their 2019-2020 world tour, "Blackpink in Your Area," the group held 36 performances in 26 cities in 17 countries, spanning North America, Europe, Asia, and Oceania. A total of 452,183 spectators attended their sold-out shows, generating $56.76 million in ticket sales. The group's meteoric rise and behind-the-scenes stories were showcased to the world in the documentary "Blackpink: Light Up the World" released in October 2020.

Since their debut, Blackpink has achieved numerous records, including several "bests", "firsts", and "shortests" with the release of new songs. To date, the group has released about 30 songs, and ten of these tracks—including title songs—rose to the top spot on major music charts globally. In 2021, Blackpink made history by becoming the first girl group to rank #1 on the Billboard 'Artist 100' chart. A year later, in 2022, they became the first K-pop girl group to be invited to the renowned American awards show, 'MTV Video Music Awards (VMAs)', where it won the 'Best Metaverse Performance' accolade. The girl group also secured the same award at the '2022 MTV Europe Music Awards (EMA)', and member Lisa was honored with the 'Best K-Pop' award for her solo effort, 'LALISA'.

Their second full-length album, "Born Pink," released in September 2022, climbed to the top spot on the iTunes album chart in 54 countries, including the United States and the United Kingdom. Additionally, it secured the number one position on the Apple Music album chart in 60 countries. Notably, the album topped the charts on China's premier music platform, QQ Music, with each track from the album also hitting the top—further cementing Blackpink's global dominance.

Blackpink performing at Coachella

To celebrate Blackpink's achievements, YG Entertainment illuminated several world-famous landmarks with pink lights, underscoring the group's status as global superstars. Iconic landmarks that were illuminated include N Seoul Tower in Seoul, Tokyo Tower in Japan, Brooklyn Bridge in New York, Santa Monica Ferris Wheel in Los Angeles, and the Eiffel Tower in Paris, France. Their second world tour, "Born Pink" (2022-2023), expanded in scale, attracting 1.5 million fans across 22 countries. At the 2023 Coachella Valley Music and Arts Festival, the girl group set a significant milestone by becoming the first Korean artists to be chosen as headliners.

As of June 2023, Blackpink boasts 89 million YouTube subscribers, making it the artist with the most subscribers worldwide. By August 2023, their collective Instagram followers surpassed 383.72 million. The individual breakdown is as follows: Lisa with 96.88 million, Jennie with 80.9 million, Jisoo with 75.16 million, Rosé with 73.61 million, and Blackpink's official account with 57.17 million.

## MEDIA PRAISE FOR BLACKPINK

- "Blackpink is recognized and acclaimed as the world's premier girl group, having achieved unparalleled success in the contemporary music market." _Guinness World Records, Jan. 26, 2023

- "Entertainers of the Year 2022." _Time, Dec. 5, 2022

- "With their record-breaking album, 'BORN PINK', the four-member group not only cemented their status as K-pop superstars but also earned the title of 'the greatest girl group in the world.'" _US Grammy Awards, Aug. 13, 2022

- "The girl group with the largest global fan base in 2020." _Forbes, Dec. 7, 2020

- "Blackpink is making a splash worldwide! They are the most influential pop stars of their time." _Bloomberg, Nov.10, 2020

Jennie also made a foray into Hollywood, making her Hollywood debut by appearing in the HBO series "Idol (2023)", co-starring with pop star The Weeknd. She had a grand entrance as an actress on the red carpet when "Idol" was uniquely selected as an official invitee in the non-competitive section at the 76th Cannes International Festival in May 2023, a rare distinction for a drama series.

## MAKE ME PRETTY WITH K-BEAUTY

In the past, Korean beauty products were primarily concentrated in the Asian market. However, they have recently garnered significant attention in North America and Europe. Many consumers are first attracted to Korean-made beauty products due to their quality and competitive prices. After trying them and appreciating their superior quality, they often become loyal customers, repeatedly purchasing products from Korean cosmetic giants including Amore Pacific, LG Household & Health Care, and Aekyung Industrial. As per the 2022 Cosmetic Production, Import, and Export Statistics disclosed by the Ministry of Food and Drug Safety, domestic cosmetic exports surpassed ₩10 trillion for the second consecutive year. This places Korea 4th globally in terms of cosmetics export volume.

Owing to the global influence of K-pop and K-culture, K-beauty is emerging as a 'trendy consumption' choice, especially among the younger generation in the United States. It is now commonplace that 70 to 80% of nail salons in New York City, seen as the modern hub of nail art, are owned by Koreans. Korean nail technicians are renowned for their meticulous attention to detail and exceptional service, commanding salaries that are 10 to 15% higher than technicians of other nationalities in the local job market.

Recently, the Korean beauty market has emerged as a sought-after testing ground for global beauty products. A prime example is Amway's skincare device, 'Dermasonic', which was launched in 2015 and enjoyed immense global popularity. However, its origins trace back to Korea, from where it was then exported to countries like Japan, China, Southeast Asia, Russia, and Europe. Products such as mask sheets, freeze-dried collagen and hyaluronic acid balls, sunblock (often referred to as sunscreen), and facial lift patches produced by Korean firms are also winning over international consumers. Within the beauty industry, there's a prevailing sentiment: "If you succeed in Korea, you'll thrive worldwide." This is not just a testament to Korea's expanding influence in the global market, but also a reflection of the discerning nature of Korean consumers, who are attuned to the latest trends and meticulously evaluate every facet of a product before making a purchase.

## LUXURY BRANDS TAP KOREAN STARS AS MODELS

Global luxury brands are increasingly turning to Korean stars, particularly K-pop icons, as 'Global Ambassadors'. A 'Global Ambassador' represents the brand on an international scale. Blackpink stands out because each member of the group serves as a global ambassador for a distinct luxury brand. Jennie, often dubbed

'Human Chanel', is an ambassador for Chanel; Rosé for Saint Laurent and Tiffany; Jisoo for Christian Dior; and Lisa for Celine and Bulgari.

Chanel has several Korean global ambassadors besides Jennie. These include top global model Suju, GD from the boy group Big Bang, and actress Kim Go-eun. Both Suju and GD were also chosen as muses inspiring Chanel. For Christian Dior, other Korean global ambassadors include Jimin of BTS and figure skater Kim Yuna, who is widely acclaimed for her stunning performances. BTS has been representing Louis Vuitton as global ambassadors for a while now. Additionally, model and actress Bae Doo-na, as well as actress Jung Ho-yeon, are global ambassadors for Louis Vuitton.

IU is a renowned Korean singer who has consistently topped various music charts with her mesmerizing voice and deeply emotional lyrics. She is also garnering attention as a global star, with her influence being especially pronounced in Southeast Asia. Gucci chose IU as one of their global ambassadors, along with several other notable Korean singers and actors, including Hani, a Thai member of the girl group NewJeans, often referred to as a 'monster rookie', Kai from the boy group EXO, and actors Lee Jung-jae and Shin Min-ah. Model and actress Kim Da-mi serves as Fendi's global ambassador, while Prada appointed K-pop boy group NCT's Jaehyun to the same role.

Louis Vuitton's pre-fall fashion show was held at Jamsu Bridge
in Seoul in May 2023

In May 2023, Seoul became the epicenter of global fashion as
Louis Vuitton and Gucci presented iconic fashion shows in the
Korean capital. These showcases were enhanced by contributions
from 'Squid Game' director Hwang Dong-hyuk and music director
Jeong Jae-il in shaping the concept and design. Seamlessly blending
tradition with modernity, these events cemented Korea's position in
the luxury goods industry.

Louis Vuitton staged its inaugural pre-fall fashion show on
Jamsu Bridge, overlooking the Han River. 'Pre-Fall' denotes the

inter-seasonal collection preceding the autumn season. Notably, Jeong Ho-yeon, who rose to global fame through "Squid Game," electrified the audience by opening the show on the 795m-long submarine bridge, which had been transformed into a runway for the event. The show, set to the tunes of Sanullim's "No, already?", Pearl Sisters' "First Love", and Han Dae-su's "To the Land of Happiness", was complemented by the natural backdrop of the Han River's wind and waves, alongside the distant night views of Gangnam and Namsan. The event was broadcast live worldwide via social media.

In the same month, Gucci collaborated with the Korea Cultural Heritage Administration to stage the '2024 Cruise Fashion Show' at Gyeongbokgung Palace in Seoul. The 235m-long pavilion of Geunjeongjeon Hall, constructed in 1935 within Gyeongbokgung Palace, was repurposed as a runway for the event. Gucci has a reputation for hosting shows in historic locales globally, including Westminster Abbey in London, England; Pitti Palace in Florence, Italy; and Promenade des Alyscamps in Arles, France.

## FINANCE INCREASINGLY ATTENTIVE TO K-POP

Global investors, major conglomerates, and Silicon Valley venture capital (VC) firms are increasingly turrning their attention to the K-pop market, and committing to significant investments. Their interests span entertainment companies, fan platforms, and the metaverse. Kakao Entertainment, a prominent Korean content company, nabbed an investment of ₩1.2 trillion from Saudi Arabian and Singaporean funds in early 2023. Such sizable investments from globally recognized investors underscore the worldwide popularity of Korean culture and its burgeoning potential. Notably, Kakao Entertainment became the largest shareholder of SM Entertainment, securing a 39.87% stake in the company in March 2023.

Investment in K-pop-related startups has been notably robust. Levoist, the startup behind the K-pop platform 'WeX', secured an initial investment in 2022 from Rogers Holdings Chairman Jim Rogers, who is often ranked alongside renowned investors like Warren Buffett and George Soros. Notably, Rogers' two daughters are avid Blackpink fans.

WeX, a K-pop music investment platform, saw participation from over 2,000 investors spanning more than 50 countries worldwide. Additionally, K-pop commerce platform 'Ktown4u' secured an investment worth ₩50 billion from three investment firms in 2022. WeX has effectively linked 5,200 K-pop fan clubs globally to shopping portals and has flourished into a community boasting 200 million members with annual sales exceeding ₩200 billion.

# Korea: The Birthplace of Webtoons

In January 2023, Japan's major broadcaster, TV Asahi, showcased a drama series adapted from the popular Naver webtoon, "Guide to Proper Dating". This webtoon, revolving around the college students' lives and romances, stands as one of Naver Webtoon's most cherished intellectual properties (IP) with a significant fan base in Korea. Webtoons are essentially comics serialized online. This marks the first instance of a Korean webtoon being adapted into an overseas drama before being aired by a domestic broadcaster, heralding a new era in webtoon exports.

This particular webtoon underscores the global appeal of diverse Korean content—from music, film, and dramas to webtoons and games—that burst onto the scene as Korean IPs. Successive dramas and films based on webtoons are becoming blockbusters, reinforcing

the notion that webtoons, crafted by Koreans, are joining the ranks of K-pop as pivotal drivers of the Korean Wave's global resonance. Prominent Korean drama series adapted from Naver webtoons and subsequently making waves on global OTT platform Netflix include titles like "Sweet Home", "Hell", "All of Us are Dead" and "The Sound of Magic: Annarasumanara".

Webtoons exert an influence that transcends traditional comics. They are coveted content sources because, relative to drama scripts, pivotal scenes are vividly illustrated. Moreover, webtoons that have already cultivated a loyal online fandom guarantee a measure of box office success. Consequently, Korean webtoons are emerging as a goldmine for the next wave of Korean drama scripts.

The global monthly user base for Naver Webtoon has seen explosive growth, soaring from 46 million at the time of its spin-off from Naver in May 2017 to over 180 million by March 2022. This surge in users prompted a staggering 337% jump in sales, climbing from ₩240 billion in 2017 to ₩1.05 trillion in 2021.


## K-WEBTOONS CHALLENGE
## JAPANESE DOMINANCE


"There was a time when it was universally acknowledged that Japan reigned supreme in the realm of comics. That perception might be shifting."

As Korean webtoons increasingly captured the imagination of Japanese fans—in a nation traditionally celebrated as the bastion of comics—prominent Japanese media outlets began spotlighting this trend. In August 2022, the Nihon Keizai Shimbun (Nikkei) highlighted how Korea was seizing a prime position in the Japanese comics app market, equipped with 'webtoons' that feature vibrant illustrations and a vertical-scrolling format optimized for smartphone users. Nikkei portrayed Korea as a formidable 'rival', with the publication analyzing that the traditional Japanese comics production system, which mirrors a cottage industry and revolves around publishers and editors, is being rivaled by Korea's adept use of information technology, positioning it to lead the global market.

The Japanese comics application market has long been dominated by Korean webtoon portals, namely Naver's 'Line Manga' and Kakao's 'Piccoma'. According to MMD Research Institute, a market research company specializing in Japanese publishing, while major Japanese companies such as 'Mecha Comic' and 'Shonen Jump' have performed well, they still lag behind these two Korean giants. Besides these top Korean webtoon portals, two other platforms, 'Comico' (ranked 5th) and 'eBook Japan' (ranked 7th), also rank in the top 10 in terms of Japanese comics application usage. Korea's Naver and Kakao, which operate the first and second largest comics applications in Japan, are rapidly expanding their reach into Europe and the United States.

Nikkei also suggests that the rise of Korean webtoons can be traced back to the 1997 foreign exchange crisis. According to the newspaper, the financial crisis had a crippling effect on publishers, prompting young and talented webtoon creators to publish their works online. The success of the webtoon market hinges on the open nature of online culture, where creators can "publish anything freely and as they see fit. Once a work gains popularity, revenue and distribution channels naturally follow." Some observers also note that the Japanese comics market system, which relies on editors to discover and nurture artists until their debut, may not align well with the inherent nature of the webtoon market system.

# KOREAN CONTENT CREATORS: MASTERS OF CREATIVITY

Naver and Kakao stand as titans in the webtoon production landscape, dominating the global webtoon market. Together, these companies garner annual sales of ₩1 trillion from webtoons and web novels alone. Capitalizing on the "K-content" wave, they are broadening their portfolios to encompass not only webtoons but games and character merchandise as well.

Another segment of the Korean content industry experiencing meteoric growth is gaming. Korea boasts prominent game developers such as Krafton and Smilegate, alongside the '3Ns'—Nexon, NCSoft, and Netmarble. As of 2023, the domestic game market is valued at approximately ₩18 trillion, with annual exports accounting for ₩8 trillion. These figures underscore the pivotal role game companies play in exports, rivaling traditional manufacturers. Notably, companies like Smilegate generate more revenue overseas than they do domestically.

In November 2022, game developer Nexon showcased its global prowess and potential as an entertainment juggernaut by becoming the largest shareholder of respected Hollywood film production company AGBO. Hybe, although primarily recognized for propelling K-pop sensation BTS to global stardom, has also leveraged its coveted artist assets—often referred to as 'killer intellectual property (IP)'—to bridge the divide between K-pop and K-games, subsequently venturing into the gaming arena.

Nexon has been intensifying its push into foreign markets, including Hollywood, while concurrently bolstering its competitiveness in film and TV drama IPs alongside other content forms. Some industry observers speculate that Nexon might be emulating Disney's business model, which saw the entertainment giant diversifying into comics, movies, and games, all grounded in the Marvel Universe. To achieve its aim, Nexon formed 'Nexon Film & Television' in 2021, aiming to augment the influence and valuation of its existing IPs.

Hybe is broadening its business portfolio, incorporating games, webtoons, the metaverse, and non-fungible tokens (NFTs) into its foundational music business, which has been heavily reliant on BTS. In a strategic move back in 2019, Hybe acquired rhythm game developer Superb and subsequently spun off a gaming division that became 'Hybe IM' in early 2023. By June 2023, the company had developed and released the mobile game titled 'BTS Island: In the SEOM'.

In a separate development, game producer Krafton garnered attention in 2021 with the release of the film "Ground Zero," featuring actor Ma Dong-seok, and the documentary "Mystery Unknown: The Birth of Battleground," which delves into the Battleground origin story. Additionally, Krafton collaborated with webtoon production firm YLab to release a webtoon leveraging its game IP.

Meanwhile, NCSoft is venturing into character-based business strategies, introducing 'Doguri', a character inspired by the 'thief raccoon' from its game 'Lineage 2M'.

## SEOUL: EMERGING GLOBAL ART HUB

Korea is currently experiencing a surge in world-class galleries and art fairs. This influx serves as compelling evidence that Korea, and Seoul in particular, are emerging as significant hubs in the global traditional art landscape. In September 2022, the renowned U.K.-based Frieze art fair, which stands among the world's top three art events alongside Art Basel in Switzerland and FIAC in France, chose Seoul for its venue.

'Frieze Seoul' marked Frieze's inaugural art fair in Asia and its fifth globally, following events in Los Angeles, New York, London, and the specialized 'Frieze Masters.' Beginning in 2022, Frieze Seoul intends to co-host the annual 'Frieze Seoul' in partnership with 'KIAF (Korea International Art Fair) Seoul,' the premier art fair in Korea organized by the Korea Gallery Association.

In 2021, Thaddaeus Ropac, which boasts galleries throughout Europe, and Berlin's Konig Gallery opened branches in Seoul. For Thaddaeus Ropac, the Seoul branch is its first in Asia. Other galleries, including Peres Projects from Berlin, as well as Gladstone and Two Palms from New York, not only participated in Art Busan in 2022 but also launched branches in Seoul within the same year. German-based Sprüth Magers and Switzerland's Hauser & Wirth, which are among the world's top three galleries, are actively considering establishing a presence in Seoul. Earlier entrants to Korea include Pace Gallery and Lehman Maupin, who have relocated to Hannam-dong, expanding their gallery spaces.

As numerous world-renowned galleries make their way into Korea, there is growing anticipation that Seoul will emerge as a pivotal hub in the Asian art market, following in the footsteps of Hong Kong. This surge in the Korean art scene is largely attributed to the enthusiasm of the MZ generation, which is propelling the market to rapid growth. Many believe Korea's strategic geographical position, particularly in terms of aviation and logistics, means it is primed to become a central hub. Data from the Arts Management Support Center indicates that the size of the domestic art market surged to ₩1.4618 trillion in 2022, or an approximately threefold growth in just two years.

Korean artists are also making significant inroads overseas, receiving invitations to showcase their work in museums and galleries globally and signaling the rise of the 'Korean art wave'. Notably, a special exhibition dedicated to Korean art graced the Venice Biennale in 2015. A year later, in 2016, artist Park Seo-bo, a pioneer of Korean monochrome painting, made history as the first

The KIAF Seoul and Frieze Seoul art fairs were jointly held
at COEX in Seoul in 2022

Korean to curate a solo exhibition at the White Cube Gallery in
London, the U.K.'s largest. His exhibition, featuring 16 pieces from
his Art series spanning from 1967 to 1981, sold out, making him
an instant sensation. Additionally, Gallery Pérotin in Paris, France,
hosted a grand solo exhibition by Lee Bae, a Korean artist based in
France, in March 2022.

# A Nation that Distinguishes Itself
# in Global Sports

The Summer Olympics, Winter Olympics, FIFA World Cup, and World Athletics Championships are collectively referred to as the four major global sporting events. With the staging of the 2018 Pyeongchang Winter Olympics, Korea became only the fifth nation globally to have hosted all four of these prestigious events. This achievement places Korea in the distinguished company of France, Germany, Italy, and Japan. To refresh our memories, Korea hosted the Summer Olympics in Seoul in 1988, co-hosted the Korea-Japan World Cup in 2002, and organized the World Athletics Championships in Daegu in 2011. Following in Korea's footsteps, the United States became the sixth nation to join the ranks after hosting the 2022 World Athletics Championships in Oregon.

In the realm of the Olympics alone, only nine countries have had the honor of hosting both the Summer and Winter Games. France paved the way, hosting both in 1900, followed by the United States in 1932, Germany in 1936, Italy in 1960, Japan in 1972, Canada in 1988, and Russia in 2014. Korea joined this exclusive list as the eighth nation with the 2018 Pyeongchang Winter Olympics, and China became the ninth with the 2022 Beijing Winter Olympics. By hosting two Olympic events, Korea also stands joint-eighth in terms of nations having hosted the most Olympic Games.

Korea proudly hosted the 2019 World Aquatics Championships and was the stage for the Asian Games in 1986, 1999, 2002, and 2014. Additionally, the country welcomed athletes for the Summer Universiade in 1997, 2003, and 2015, and is set to do so again in 2027. Korea also showcased the 2024 Youth Winter Olympics and is preparing a bid to host the Summer Olympics in 2036, cementing its reputation as a sports powerhouse.

## HOSTING THE WORLD'S SECOND-LARGEST NUMBER OF INTERNATIONAL CONFERENCES

Korea stands tall among nations that have hosted a significant number of international conferences. A report by the United International Association (UIA) revealed that Korea organized 473 international conferences in 2021, placing Korea at the forefront in Asia and second globally. The United States leads the global tally with 512 events, followed closely by Japan in third place with 408 events. Notably, prior to the COVID-19 pandemic, Korea outshone the United States for two consecutive years, securing the top position with 997 events in 2016 and an impressive 1,297 in 2017. Such feats are commendable, especially when considering disparities such as land size and population between Korea and the U.S. International conferences are now not just confined to Seoul but have become commonplace in other cities, with Busan being a notable example.

According to the criteria set by the UIA, an "international conference" is defined as a conference sponsored by an international organization with a participation of more than 50 attendees. An event is also defined as an international conference if it is organized by a domestic branch or group of an international organization; includes more than 300 participants (and may be accompanied by an exhibition); has attendees from over 5 different countries; foreign participants make up more than 40% of the total attendance; and runs for a duration exceeding 3 days.

In the year 2000, Seoul was the host city for the 3rd Asia-Europe Summit (ASEM). Korea was pivotal in the formation of the G20, which comprises delegates from 20 major countries. In recognition of this feat, Korea hosted the 5th G20 summit in Seoul in 2010. Due to a strong request from then-President Lee Myung-bak, Korea was the venue for the second Nuclear Security Summit (NSS) in 2012. The NSS is renowned as a gathering of the world's paramount leaders.

In October 2022, Seoul hosted the 26th Association of National Olympic Committees (ANOC) General Assembly, often referred to as the 'UN General Assembly of Sports'. With this event, Seoul claimed the distinction of having hosted the most ANOC general meetings, having previously been the venue for the 5th meeting in 1968 and the 15th in 2006. The ANOC Seoul General Assembly saw the participation of over 800 individuals and delved into contemporary issues. Attendees included National Olympic Committee (NOC) delegations from 205 countries, International Olympic Committee (IOC) chairs and members, heads of international sports federations, as well as representatives from the Court of Arbitration for Sport (CAS) and the World Anti-Doping Agency (WADA).

The MICE industry in Korea—which focuses on international conferences and exhibitions—has also been rejuvenated by international expositions, including the Daejeon World Expo held in 1993, a mere five years after the 1988 Seoul Olympics. This Expo spanned 93 days from August 7 to November 7 at the Daedeok Research Complex area.

Korea is gaining recognition as an ideal locale for prominent international conferences, due to its strategic geographical positioning and state-of-the-art urban infrastructure, most notably Incheon International Airport. Seoul is a global metropolis, boasting one of the world's most expansive airline networks, facilitating access for international travelers. The logistics systems via Incheon and Busan further enhance its appeal. Korea also wins praise for its premium hotels and globally recognized brand restaurants, efficient transportation grid, and secure societal environment. Its central position in the Asian landscape is undeniably advantageous. As hosts of numerous international conferences and exhibitions, convention centers including COEX in Seoul, BEXCO in Busan, and KINTEX in Ilsan have firmly established themselves on the global stage.

## E-SPORTS POWERHOUSE

While it may sound hyperbolic, there is a humorous saying circulating among foreigners:

"If you want to marry a Korean woman, you must first defeat her father in a StarCraft match."

The jest underscores the deep-rooted popularity of e-sports in Korea, spanning various demographics. Over the past two decades, Korea has consistently clinched titles in major e-sports

Chase Center in San Francisco, USA, the venue for the
League of Legends World Championship 2022 finals

championships, ranging from 'StarCraft' to 'Warcraft', 'League of Legends', and 'Overwatch'. In Korea, being a professional gamer is seen as a lucrative and prestigious career promising wealth, fame, and gratification. Dubbed the 'nation of e-sports', an astounding 500 million e-sports enthusiasts globally root for Korean players and their awe-inspiring skills.

In a remarkable turn of events in November 2022, two Korean teams clashed in the finals of the League of Legends World Championship, the pinnacle of e-sports contests. This championship identifies the top-performing team in 'LoL', the marquee game from international gaming juggernaut Riot Games. After a grueling face-off spanning roughly 4 hours and 30 minutes, the Korean professional team DRX staged an upset by defeating T1 (SK Telecom), fronted by Faker (Lee Sang-hyuk)—the three-time World Cup winner and celebrated 'King of LoL'—in a nail-biting 3-2 finish.

This electrifying match, punctuated by moments of raw emotion and an unexpected comeback, was streamed live worldwide. Data from e-sports charts reveal that the viewership for the 2022 LoL World Championship finals, hosted at the Chase Center in San Francisco, California, on November 6, 2022, peaked at an impressive 5.14 million.

# IS THE PC ROOM THE SECRET
# BEHIND KOREA'S E-SPORTS DOMINANCE?

The LoL World Championship is widely regarded as the pinnacle of major e-sports events. Amongst nations, Korea stands out with a record for the most victories in LoL tournaments. Out of 12 championships, Korean teams won the title 7 times and placed second on 5 occasions. Following Korea, China has 3 wins and 3 second-place finishes, and Europe boasts 1 win and 3 runner-up titles. On the individual team leaderboard, Korea's SK Telecom T1 is unparalleled, with 3 championships and 2 second-place finishes to their credit. Remarkably, every LoL championship-winning team since 2013 has featured Korean players, irrespective of the team's origin. Notably, all the mid laners (the players responsible for pivotal combat zones in LoL matches) were Korean.

Although Korea is lauded as an e-sports titan, it is worth noting that the country is not the birthplace of e-sports. The evolution of online games into competitive championships originated in the United States, which also introduced the concept of the 'professional gamer.' However, the world universally acknowledges Korea as the de facto 'home of e-sports'. This reputation stems from Korea's pioneering initiative: it was the first country to broadcast the StarCraft League. Though live broadcasts of e-sports are now commonplace, this trend traces its inception back to the StarCraft

The finals of the amateur e-sports competition, 'MK Challenge with Battleground', took place at the 'Facebook Gaming Arena' in 2018, a venue specifically designed for the game

© Maeil Business DB

League.

Korea's transformation into an e-sports juggernaut can be largely attributed to the infrastructure that led it to become an IT powerhouse. The country boasts over 10,000 PC rooms nationwide and this unique landscape, rare in other countries, played a pivotal role in propelling the online gaming industry. The Kim Dae-jung administration harnessed the IT sector as a catalyst for growth to overcome the challenges of the 1997 foreign exchange crisis. Embracing a vision of becoming a global IT leader, the administration actively championed the development of high-speed internet infrastructure. With the government's promotion of the internet network industry, the number of PC rooms throughout the nation surged.

These venues became popular haunts for teenagers passionate about online gaming, laying a robust foundation for the flourishing e-sports ecosystem. Given this infrastructure, both the young and old can effortlessly engage with games. It is rare to find a child who has not encountered gaming during their upbringing, signifying the vastness of the user base. This widespread accessibility ensures that Koreans can demonstrate their prowess in a variety of amateur competitions. Those showcasing potential are often recognized and steered towards a professional gaming trajectory.

Korea proudly stands as the host of the most abundant e-sports amateur competitions worldwide. Such competitions are even held at local PC rooms. A prime example is the President's Cup National Amateur e-Sports Competition, also known as KeG (Korean e-Sports Games), organized by the Korea e-Sports Association. KeG debuted in 2007 as the Minister's Cup, sponsored by the Ministry of Culture, Sports, and Tourism and was elevated to the status of the President's Cup by 2009. Unique in its distinction,

KeG is the only amateur e-sports competition worldwide to enjoy government sponsorship and has been instrumental in launching the careers of numerous professional gamers over the years.

Furthermore, Korean game developers have often launched games and held their own e-sports tournaments. Some of these events garnered such vast international interest that they evolved into global championships. Krafton, a significant investor in e-sports, unveiled its flagship game, Battleground, in 2017 and held the inaugral Battleground e-sports world competition a year later. The magnitude of this competition has since expanded, with events spanning the United States, Europe, Asia, and the Asia-Pacific region. The official competition website lists 90 professional teams from around the globe as participants and Krafton is proactively aiding the establishment of professional teams.

Korean game developer Smilegate introduced the video game series 'Crossfire', and held its first e-sports competition, 'CFS (Crossfire Stars)', in 2013. Players from around the globe vie for a collective prize pool exceeding $1 million in this event. Crossfire used this competition as a springboard to leap to the top of China's game rankings in 2014. Over a six-month span, approximately 100,000 gamers worldwide participate in the Crossfire game preliminary rounds. Notably, a competition was recently hosted on the African continent for the first time, and over 80% of Smilegate's sales are generated from overseas markets.

# KOREAN E-SPORT'S EXPLOSIVE GROWTH

Large corporations and premier gaming companies are increasingly diving into e-sports events, causing the Korean e-sports investment market to expand at an unprecedented rate. In a commitment to invest ₩50 trillion into the global gaming industry, which includes e-sports, Saudi Arabia channeled ₩920 billion into acquiring shares of NCSoft, a leading Korean game company, in 2022. This was facilitated through the Public Investment Fund (PIF), a sovereign wealth fund managing assets totaling an impressive ₩600 trillion. This investment maneuvered Saudi Arabia into the position of the second-largest shareholder of NCSoft with a 9.26% stake. Concurrently, Saudi Arabia also acquired shares in Nexon, which is listed on the Japanese stock market, securing a position as its second-largest shareholder with a 9.14% stake. The combined investments in these two companies by Saudi Arabia amount to an astonishing ₩3 trillion.

The e-sports industry is capitalizing on the rise of virtual currency to expand its reach. Cryptocurrency entities are making a mark as dominant sponsors in the e-sports domain, and are prominently displaying their virtual currency logos on e-sports team jerseys as well as orchestrating gaming events around non-fungible tokens (NFTs). Korean game developer Krafton is mulling over the incorporation of virtual currency and NFT into its flagship e-sports competition, 'Battleground'. In an related move, Bithumb, a Korean digital asset exchange, collaborated with e-sports specialist company 'Gen.G' in early 2022, ensuring that the Bithumb logo finds a place on the uniforms of Gen.G players.

Virtual currency is already making waves in the global e-sports market. In September 2021, Crypto.com, a virtual asset exchange based in Singapore, committed $15 million to display the Crypto.com logo on the uniforms of the LoL World Championship winners, Fnatic, for five years, and to introduce NFTs. Additionally, Coinbase, the largest cryptocurrency exchange in the United States, entered into a four-year partnership with the renowned e-sports team Liquid, towards the end of 2021.

# Taekwondo: From Korea's National Sport to a Global Phenomenon

In March 2023, Gwanghwamun Square in Seoul echoed with the spirited shouts of thousands of Taekwondo practitioners. Gathered from around the world, they descended upon the Square to attempt a Guinness World Record in honor of Taekwondo's designation as Korea's national sport in 2018. This endeavor was jointly organized by the Kukkiwon (also known as the World Taekwondo Headquarters), the Korea Taekwondo Association, and the Taekwondo Promotion Foundation. At the event, 12,533 individuals participated in the demonstration of Taegeuk Il Jang— the first of the eight Taekwondo forms. Of them, 12,263 sucessfully completed the demonstration, setting a new Guinness World Record. The previous record was 8,212.

Taekwondo has solidified its status as a global sport. Originating in Korea, Taekwondo is a traditional martial art that involves the use of hands and feet to attack and defend without weapons. It made its debut as a demonstration sport at the 1988 Summer Olympics and became an official Olympic sport in 2000. In 2018, Taekwondo was designated as Korea's national sport, further elevating its stature as a representation of the country. It continued its Olympic presence, and will be featured as an official sport at both the 2024 Paris and 2028 LA Olympics, marking its eighth and ninth consecutive appearance at the Olympic Games. Korea being the birthplace of the sport, many expected Korean athletes to dominate and win gold medals at international Taekwondo competitions.

But at the 2020 Tokyo Olympics, Korea did not any gold medals in the Taekwondo events. The eight gold medals up for grabs were distributed among seven countries: Russia claimed two gold medals, while the United States, Serbia, Uzbekistan, Italy, Croatia, and Thailand won one each. While it's indisputable that Korea is the birthplace of Taekwondo, the surging global interest and participation in the sport have made it increasingly challenging for Korean athletes to win medals at the Olympics or world championships. This trend is underscored by the fact that seven of the top 10 Taekwondo athletes in the world rankings by weight class are from countries outside Korea.

It took 50 years for Taekwondo to evolve into a global sport, starting with the opening of the first overseas Taekwondo 'dojang', or studio, in

Foreign students at the Taekwondo One Mind Festival
held at Gwanghwamun Square in Jongno-gu in 2023
practice the Taegeuk One Jang form

the United States in 1972. Kukkiwon has since inaugurated Taekwondo studios in 206 countries, surpassing the number of countries that maintain formal diplomatic relations with Korea (191 countries). Essentially, the influence of Taekwondo has expanded and there are 200 million individuals abroad who practice Taekwondo for both physical and spiritual discipline, with approximately 10 million holding Dan certificates issued by Kukkiwon. The enthusiasm for Taekwondo is so widespread that even in smaller nations like East Timor, Taekwondo-related festivals are held multiple times a year, fueled by the youth's active participation.

# TAEKWONDO: A MARTIAL ART CHERISHED GLOBALLY

Taekwondo's global appeal extends beyond the reach of the Korean Wave. It is beloved for its dual emphasis on physical strength and mental discipline. In January 2020, The New York Times spotlighted Frances Ramirez, an American single mother who reported a remarkable transformation in her two children, both diagnosed with attention deficit behavior disorder (ADHD), after they began Taekwondo training. This poignant tale cast a renewed global spotlight on the martial art. Benefitting from financial assistance provided by a Catholic charity, Ramirez was able to enroll her children in lessons. Expressing her gratitude, she remarked, "I felt so blessed to introduce Taekwondo to my children," noting the positive changes it brought about in their demeanor. In her view, the discipline instilled confidence and patience in them.

California has designated September 4th each year as 'Taekwondo Day'. This decision acknowledges Taekwondo's international stature as a sport that cultivates both physical and mental strength. The New York Times, in an article celebrating the martial art, said, "Taekwondo possesses a beauty that blends the grace of ballet, the precision of ice skating, the noble skill of boxing plus the concentration of chess."

Content centered on Taekwondo is also gaining traction. A

prime example is the webtoon "San Francisco Gallery" (2013), where artist Dolbae chronicles personal experiences. Dolbae, whose real name is Jang Hye-won, found solace in Taekwondo during a bout of deep melancholy. While wandering around her San Francisco neighborhood, she stumbled upon a martial arts center called Hwaranggwan, offering diverse martial arts lessons, including Taekwondo. Hoping it might alleviate her homesickness and elevate her spirits, she enrolled in classes. Along this journey, Dolbae's burgeoning passion for Taekwondo inspired her to create webtoons detailing the transformative effects of the martial art on her life. Consequently, Taekwondo played a pivotal role in her emergence as a full-time webtoon artist. Her webtoon garnered favorable reviews and a substantial viewership, leading to its eventual publication as a book.

Content related to Taekwondo is also experiencing tremendous popularity, especially among children. Taekwondo was featured in the Netflix animated series "Cocomelon," which has captivated children globally. As of August 2023, Cocomelon's official YouTube channel boasts 164 million subscribers. In the Taekwondo episode, the main character, JJ, along with his older sister, older brother, and friends, visits a Taekwondo dojang. They practice the martial art while singing joyful songs. This particular episode garnered 400 million views on YouTube alone.

In Korea, dojangs play a pivotal role in communities, especially for elementary school students. Lee Mi-young from Seongnam, Gyeonggi Province, shared that she enrolled her son in a dojang as soon as he began elementary school, acting on the advice of other mothers in her community. "At the dojang, kids interact with both younger and older students. This environment naturally teaches them about hierarchy, order, and other social rules that are challenging to learn in regular schools where they mainly interact with age-mates. Taekwondo has also helped my son in adjusting to school life by enhancing his focus, perseverance, and social skills," she explained.

© Cocomelon

Popular YouTube and Netflix content for children:
Cocomelon's episode about Taekwondo

Moreover, dojangs often function as an auxiliary childcare solution for working parents. When younger elementary students finish school between 12 p.m. and 1 p.m., a vehicle from the dojang collects them from their school gate, taking them to the premises. After their lesson, they are either dropped off at their home or transported to another after-school academy. Many Korean mothers are grateful to the dojangs for providing care for their children during working hours—a service that public schools cannot offer.

## TEACHING TAEKWONDO IN 206 COUNTRIES AROUND THE WORLD

The surging popularity of Taekwondo has led to a growing number of Koreans teaching the martial art in countries worldwide, with their influence being deeply felt in each nation. One such instructor, Jeong Seong-hee from Eumseong, North Chungcheong Province, currently teaches Taekwondo to the Thai Royal Guard. A Kukkiwon-certified 7th dan, Jeong also teaches at the United Nations Economic and Social Commission for Asia and the Pacific (UNESCAP) in Bangkok. Interestingly, UNESCAP has only two official sports clubs, Taekwondo and yoga.

Jeong trained in Taekwondo throughout his college and graduate studies, eventually opening a Taekwondo school in Cheongju,

North Chungcheong Province. His association with Thailand began when he engaged in cultural exchanges via the children's Taekwondo demonstration team from his school. In 2004, he received an invitation to become an instructor at the Royal Thai Police Academy, leading him to relocate to Thailand. Today, he is the General Manager of the World Taekwondo Academy in Thailand. Additionally, his roles in the country include being an adjunct professor at the Royal Thai Police Academy, an advisor to the Royal Guard, an advisory member for the Royal Thai Police, an executive vice-president of the Korean Teachers' Association in Thailand, and a member of the Southeastern Asia branch of the Peaceful Unification Advisory Council.

"There are countless posters and advertisements featuring Korean singers and Korea-related themes on the streets of Hong Kong. Hong Kong children hold a deep respect for Korean instructors when they come to learn Taekwondo, and that makes me truly proud," Park Sae-rom said during an interview with a foreign media outlet. Park is a Taekwondo instructor at YD Taekwondo, located in Tai Koo Shing, Hong Kong. In the interview, he expressed a renewed sense of pride in his Korean heritage. While in Korea, Taekwondo schools are commonplace and he never felt particularly unique, teaching abroad gave him a fresh perspective on the significance and global popularity of Taekwondo.

# The Power of the Korean Passport: Visa-free Entry to 192 Countries

As Korea solidifies its reputation as a global cultural powerhouse—producing numerous K-pop sensations as well as internationally acclaimed dramas and movies—more and more tourists are flocking to the country to immerse themselves in Korean culture. The Ministry of Culture, Sports and Tourism reported that the number of foreign tourists visiting Korea peaked at 17.5 million in 2019, just prior to the onset of the COVID-19 pandemic. This translates to one foreigner entering Korea every 1.8 seconds. In that same year, tourism generated a revenue of ₩25.1 trillion for Korea. Moreover, the economic contributions from foreign tourists to production and the job market were estimated at ₩46 trillion and 460,000 jobs respectively.

Since then, the influx of foreign tourists plunged to 960,000 in

2020 due to the COVID-19 pandemic, but the numbers are swiftly rebounding as COVID-19 recedes. In January 2023 alone, Korea welcomed 434,429 visitors, an increase of over fourfold compared to the previous year. Notably, 65% of these were returning visitors. The government has designated 2023 and 2024 as the 'Year of Visiting Korea to Experience K-Culture.' This marks the fifth time the government has designated a 'Year of Visiting Korea,' following similar initiatives in 1994, 2001, 2010, and 2018. The Ministry of Culture, Sports and Tourism projects that the number of foreign tourists will surpass 30 million by 2027, with the anticipated tourism revenue hitting $30 billion.

## KOREA'S ALLURE CAPTIVATES
## THE GLOBAL AUDIENCE

Foreign media outlets are increasingly captivated by Korea's allure, owing to its elevated status in the international community and the burgeoning popularity of Korean culture. British TV's 'Channel 5' garnered attention when it broadcast the three-part documentary 'Alexander Armstrong in South Korea' in November 2022 at 9 PM, during prime time. This documentary delved into the enchantments of Korea, exploring its rich food culture by posing questions like 'What is Mukbang?' and experiencing the traditional games featured in the globally-acclaimed Korean drama, 'Squid Game'.

Canadian travel-centric media outlet Travel praised Korea, stating, "There are abundant opportunities to immerse oneself in Korea's distinct culture. It is a land where history intertwines seamlessly with nature, offering a multifaceted travel destination that encapsulates everything a traveler seeks." The crux of this accolade underscored how Korean cities adeptly blend tradition with modernity, and historical reverence with future-forward innovation. In addition to its unique cultural facets and pristine natural landscapes, these attributes make Korea an irresistible draw for international visitors. Moreover, National Geographic Traveler, a renowned travel media authority, spotlighted Busan, choosing it as one of the '25 Breathtaking Places and Experiences for 2023' among countless Asian cities.

## THE SECOND-MOST POWERFUL PASSPORT IN THE WORLD, WITH VISA-FREE ACCESS TO 192 COUNTRIES

According to the Korea Tourism Organization's 'Korea Tourism Statistics', 28,714,000 Koreans traveled abroad in 2019, prior to the onset of the COVID-19 pandemic. This figure represents over half of Korea's total population in 2019, or 51,765,000. In other words, 55.5% of the Korean population ventured overseas that year. Consequently, it has become a common sight for Incheon International Airport to be bustling with Koreans departing for their international destinations, especially during holiday seasons. However, it's not only international travel that is popular; as of 2021, 93.3% of Koreans had also explored domestic destinations.

On a global scale, Koreans exhibit a pronounced affinity for travel. As per the World Tourism Index released by the Korea Culture and Tourism Institute in 2021, Koreans spent $32.7 billion on tourism in 2019. This positioned Korea 10th globally in tourism expenditure, following China, the United States, Germany, the United Kingdom, France, Russia, Canada, Australia, and the United Arab Emirates. Moreover, the average annual tourism expenditure per Korean ($632) surpasses that of individuals in Italy ($507) and the United States ($406). Notably, even amid the COVID-19 pandemic in 2021, when international borders were largely sealed and strict social distancing measures were in place, Korea ranked 6th in global tourism spending.

Passport power measures the number of countries a passport holder can enter without a visa, and Korea consistently ranks near the top on a global scale. The British consulting group, Henley & Partners, released the Henley Passport Index for the first quarter of 2023 using data from the International Air Transport Association

(IATA). According to this index, Korea's passport was 2nd among 199 countries worldwide, allowing Koreans visa-free entry to 192 countries.

Japan holds the top spot, granting its citizens visa-free access to 193 countries, while Singapore shares the second position with Korea, with both permitting entry to 192 countries. Germany and Spain are tied for 3rd place (190 countries), followed by a three-way tie for 4th place among Finland, Italy, and Luxembourg (189 countries). Austria, Denmark, the Netherlands, and Sweden jointly placed 5th, with visa-free access to 188 countries. Countries such as the United States, Belgium, New Zealand, Norway, Switzerland, and the Czech Republic, all of which allow visa-free travel to 186 countries, ranked 7th. In contrast, the North Korean passport, allowing travel to just 40 countries, ranked 102nd.

Korea's robust passport power is due to several factors. For example, Korean citizens are generally not prone to overstaying their visas abroad, and significantly boost the tourism sectors of countries they visit, often spending considerable amounts during their stays.

# Overseas Koreans Agency Supports 7.32M Korean Expats

As reported by the Ministry of Foreign Affairs in 2021, there are 7,325,143 Koreans residing in 193 countries, with the figure representing approximately 14% of the South Korean population. The United States hosts the largest number of Korean expatriates, with a count of 2,633,777—a 17.6% increase from 2015. The number of Koreans in China has been on the decline since 2015, making it the second-largest host country with 2,350,422 Koreans. Following China are Japan with 818,865 Koreans, Canada with 237,364, Uzbekistan with 175,865, Russia with 168,526, Australia with 158,103, Vietnam with 156,330, and Kazakhstan with 109,495.

By continent, Northeast Asia is home to 3,169,287 Koreans, North America houses 2,871,141, Europe has 677,156, South

Asia-Pacific accommodates 489,420, Central and South America host 90,289, the Middle East has 18,379 and Africa counts 9,471 Korean residents.

Korean expatriates have long been a vital link enabling domestic companies and talents to make headway internationally. Korean merchants and businesspeople of Korean origin have now firmly established themselves on the global stage, their influence now rivaling that of those of Chinese descent. The network of Korean business professionals abroad has immense potential and has solidified its position as a significant national asset for Korea. Notably, the network of Korean expatriates in the financial sector is particularly active on Wall Street in New York. During the foreign exchange crisis of 1997, remittances from Korean residents in Japan played a crucial role in helping the nation avert a bankruptcy crisis.

The World Korean Business Convention was formed to support Korean merchants and entrepreneurs who, despite starting with little, built their businesses globally. In 2022, this Convention celebrated its 20th anniversary, underscoring its pivotal role in fostering the network of Korean expatriate business professionals. The 21st World Korean Business Convention, held at the Anaheim Convention Center in California, USA, in October 2023 marked the first time the event was hosted outside of Korea. Choosing the United States as the venue was a nod to the 120th anniversary of Korean immigration to America and the 70th anniversary of the

Korea-U.S. alliance.

The endeavors of Korean entrepreneurs in distant parts of the world are noteworthy, and Kim Jeom-bae is an excellent example. Kim is the CEO of Al Kaus Overseas Trading in Oman and also serves as the Chairman of the African and Middle East Korean Merchants Association, as well as presiding over the 20th World Korean Business Convention. Often referred to as the 'godfather of Korean merchants in Africa and the Middle East,' Kim moved to Oman in 1976. He initially worked as an ocean fishing boat captain and base manager before forming Al Kaus Overseas Trading in 2000. When the company he had partnered with, responsible for operating two of his ships, went bankrupt, Kim acquired the vessels and today, Al Kaus Overseas Trading boasts three 1,000-ton and two 350-ton trawler net vessels. These vessels operate in the Somali waters of the Indian Ocean, with their base in Muscat, the Omani capital. In 2021, the company's sales surpassed $30 million.

For several decades, Kim has actively assisted Korean companies find their feet in Oman. He has effectively acted as a 'guide' for Korean firms and their personnel, easing their transition and settlement in the region. When GS Caltex sought entry into Oman, Kim even traveled to Yeosu to provide insights into the local way of life. Key Korean construction enterprises that ventured into Oman in the early 2000s, including Daewoo Engineering & Construction, Hyundai Engineering & Construction, and GS

Engineering & Construction, also benefited from Kim's assistance. He also champions ESG (Environmental, Social, and Governance) initiatives in Africa, which include constructing wells in water-deprived regions and sponsoring eye surgeries for those with vision impairments. Given that his company's revenues stem from the waters near Somalia, he feels a deep responsibility to give back to the local communities.

In June 2023, after 26 years of dedicated service, the Overseas Koreans Foundation was disbanded. It was subsequently re-opened as the Overseas Koreans Agency, which provides a 24-hour one-stop service point for overseas Koreans, covering everything from immigration processes to tax-related matters. This evolution paved the way for a more structured and holistic support policy for Koreans residing globally.

# 10 REASONS WHY KOREA IS AN ATTRACTIVE DESTINATION

① 24-Hour Mukbang for the Diverse Culinary Palette

• Indulge in an array of traditional and street foods at affordable prices, available at traditional markets spread across the country.

• Dive into the world of 'Chimaek,' savoring Korean-style chicken and steak, as well as 'Gogi-ssam (pork belly wrap)'.

• Relish the convenience of 24-hour restaurants in urban hubs, ensuring a meal is available anytime, be it day or night.

• A culinary haven with a wide choice of eateries, boasting one restaurant for every 67 inhabitants (770,000 restaurants recorded in 2020, as per Korea Rural Economic Institute and Statistics Korea).

• Be within an arm's reach of globally-renowned restaurant brands like Gordon Ramsay Burger and Gucci Osteria.

TJ Media's Virtual Reality (VR) Karaoke                    © TJ Media

• Recently, innovative fusion Korean restaurants that reimagine traditional ingredients have been tantalizing taste buds worldwide, particularly in Seoul.

## ② Experience the Unique Korean Culture in Iconic Drama Settings

• Jjimjilbang: An all-in-one destination where you can relish baths, massages, meals, and entertainment.

• Karaoke: The ultimate spot to privately immerse yourself in favorite K-pop songs and dances without inhibition.

• Folk Village: Dive deep into Korea's rich history, enjoying traditional games and living like Koreans from the past.

• Delivery Culture: Indulge in almost any delicacy, delivered right to your location, eliminating the need to visit a restaurant.

• Discover the magic of Korean home cooking, including: A versatile Korean-style electric rice cooker capable of preparing everything from rice and porridge to stews and soups; The kimchi refrigerator, specifically designed to store and ferment a year's worth of kimchi; and a wide assortment of meal kits.

## ③ The Immense Scale of Supermarkets: Korea, a Shopper's Paradise

• With over 50,000 convenience stores scattered throughout the country, you can effortlessly find what you need anytime, 24/7.

• Order online, and your items can be at your doorstep as soon as 30 minutes after placing the order, or at most, within two days.

• Effortlessly shop for daily

essentials at neighborhood supermarkets, which rival the size of expansive shopping malls.

• Dive into a unique shopping experience at traditional markets and roadside shops nestled in alleys.

④ **Mountains, Rivers, and Skyscrapers Everywhere! A Modern City in Harmony with Nature**

• Mountains and rivers are everywhere crisscrossing the nation, and one can still enjoy nature even amid the towering skyscrapers of Seoul.

• With three of the country's four boundaries bordered by the sea, beach resorts are always within easy reach.

• Apartments constitute 63.5% of all housing, creating a unique cityscape dotted with high-rise residences.

Meal kits occupy an entire shelf at Lotte Mart Zetaplex in Songpa-gu, Seoul

© Maeil Business DB

Suncheon Bay Nature Reserve, a UNESCO World Heritage Site

© Cultural Heritage Administration

## ⑤ Ever Thought of Visiting the Gangnam from "Gangnam Style"? Korea, the Birthplace of K-pop

• Following the global sensation that was Psy's "Gangnam Style", the Gangnam district in Seoul skyrocketed to fame, just as many other locales in Korea have been spotlighted in K-pop songs.

• Themed tours tracing the steps of K-pop stars, with stops such as 'The Tteokbokki enjoyed by BTS's Jimin', have gained popularity.

## ⑥ Stunning Vistas Await You! Korea's Gorgeous Natural Landscape

• The country boasts diverse natural sights, from the emerald seas of Jeju and the deep blue waters of Gangneung to the renowned night sea of Yeosu. Additionally, Suncheon is celebrated as the 'city of gardens', Tongyeong is admired for its scenic islands and sea, while Taean is sought after for its captivating sunsets.

Panoramic view of the Yeouido area as seen from Noryangjin, Seoul

• Korea's remarkable natural heritage, recognized as World Cultural Heritage sites, encompasses locations like Jeju Island's volcanic formations, lava tubes, and tidal flats in areas such as Seocheon, Gochang, Shinan, and Boseong~Suncheon.

⑦ Korea Offers Efficient and User-Friendly Urban Infrastructure Along with Free Wi-Fi

• A well-developed transportation infrastructure, including subways, buses, and the high-speed rail (KTX), ensures convenient travel. The entire nation is easily accessible, with Seoul to Busan taking approximately 2 hours and 30 minutes on the KTX.

• Most public places offer free Wi-Fi wireless Internet access.

• Stay connected with fast communication networks even in the subway or on remote islands.

• Experience efficient handling of various administrative and customer services.

• Public transportation remains available late into the night.

• Easily hail taxis, try the

A rider delivers convenience
store products to customers

© BGF Retail

misplacing or having your
belongings stolen. Even if you
inadvertently leave your cell
phone in a public area, it is
unlikely to be taken.

### ⑨ Warm Welcomes Await: Friendly Koreans Are Ready to Assist You

designated driver services, or
schedule home deliveries through
a variety of platforms.

### ⑧ Safety First: Korea's Low Crime Rate and Reliable Security

• Globally, Korea's crime index
ranks 116th (26.68), signifying it
as a country with a low crime rate
and that is very safe for travel,
even by international standards
(as reported by the U.S. research
institute, World Population
Review).
• There is minimal risk of

• Historically referred to as the
'Land of Courtesy in the East,'
Koreans are known for their
politeness and friendliness, even
towards strangers, ensuring that
visitors can easily seek assistance.
• In Korea, the culture prioritizes
the customer in the product and
service sectors. Thus, any issues
are typically addressed from the
customer's viewpoint.

### ⑩ Blending Time: Experience Korea's Past, Present, and Future in One Place

The "2024 Gucci Cruise Show" held at Gyeongbokgung Palace in Seoul in June 2023

• Korea preserves significant landmarks tied to its rich history, such as the Seodaemun Prison, which stands as a somber reminder of the pain endured during the Japanese colonial period.

• While rapid economic growth has given cities a predominantly modern aura, sites like the Gyeongbokgung Palace and other vintage structures offer glimpses into the lives of Koreans from decades or even centuries ago.

• An old adage goes, 'If you succeed in the Korean market, you will succeed globally.' In Korea, visitors can engage with cutting-edge technologies and services, ranging from service robots to AI-driven product recommendations.

PART 4

# KOREA,
# A COUNTRY THAT
# NEVER GOES DARK

"Indeed, I see many people here earning higher salaries than I do."

This is a remark made by former President Park Chung-hee in 1968 as he reviewed a list of salaries for employees at KIST (Korea Institute of Science and Technology). Founded in 1966, KIST was Korea's first comprehensive science and technology research institute and was established using the $10 million granted by the U.S. government as a gesture of gratitude for Korea's deployment of troops to Vietnam.

Dr. Choi Hyeong-seop, the first director of KIST, called for Korean scientists overseas to return to Korea. In an unprecedented move, he provided them with generous salaries to ensure they could dedicate themselves to research. For perspective, while national university professors earned a monthly salary of ₩30,000 at the time, KIST scientists were offered nearly ₩80,000, approximately three times that figure. This amount paled in comparison to international standards, but within was a groundbreaking approach in Korea. Dr. Ahn Young-Ok, an alumnus of Iowa State University who previously worked at the DuPont Research Institute, reflected, "The salary at KIST was about 30% of what I earned at DuPont."

Other researchers, who were not hired by KIST lodged complaints with the President's Office. They believed it was unfair for KIST to offer significantly higher salaries than professors elsewhere received. In response to the unrest, Park summoned Choi to discuss the remuneration of KIST researchers. For context, the president's own monthly salary at the time was ₩70,000. · When thus confronted, Choi said to Park, "If you deem this salary structure unfair, I am prepared to take a reduction in pay. But please refrain from slashing the salaries of the others." To this, Park simply responded, "Proceed as planned."

KIST's inception came at the price of deploying troops in the Vietnam War, and the institution's journey is intrinsically tied to the evolution of Korean science and technology. In its nascent stages, KIST researchers prioritized commercialization projects, largely because the nation's foremost objective was economic growth. Although it might appear somewhat peculiar from a contemporary perspective, one of the premier assignments for KIST's elite scientists was to devise technology capable of producing wigs that mimicked genuine hair using imported yarn. In 1969, KIST developed a yarn closely resembling authentic human hair, crafted from imported threads. Subsequently, as KIST grappled with increasing competition from international wig manufacturers for the same imported yarn, it embarked on a new endeavor in 1972: producing its own yarn. When the endeavor proved successful, the high-caliber yarn was lauded for its quality. This technology was then licensed to the industry for a significant fee of ₩200 million.

KIST's primary focus was on applied science with immediate commercial potential. Among its landmark accomplishments, KIST pioneered the development of Korea's first color television set in 1972; introduced the nation's inaugural minicomputer, Sejong No. 1, in 1975; produced fibers for optical communication in 1984; and showcased Korea's first humanoid robot, Sento, in 1999.

One nation took particular notice of KIST's impressive trajectory: Vietnam. The Vietnamese began to increasingly turn their attention towards Korea, largely influenced by the successes of soccer coach Park Hang-seo. Keen to evolve from a developing nation to a developed one, the Vietnamese government eyed Korea's meteoric rise as a potential blueprint. Recognizing KIST's pivotal role in Korea's growth, Vietnam embarked on plans to create a comprehensive research institute akin to KIST. To realize this vision, they sought assistance from Korea.

"We envisaged the creation of a research institute in Vietnam modeled after KIST in Korea. As we are in the middle of industrializing and modernizing, we require a significant amount of scientific and technological resources. With 'V-KIST', the Vietnamese counterpart of KIST, we aim to leverage technology to its utmost potential by drawing on KIST's expertise. Our focus is on researching technology that can be commercialized promptly and producing products that genuinely bolster the economy," former Vietnamese Minister of Science and Technology Nguyen Quan said during a 2021 appearance on a Vietnamese TV current affairs program.

In the show, he shared his anticipation for the inauguration of V-KIST, a collaborative endeavor between Korea and Vietnam. Initiated in early 2023, V-KIST is a Vietnamese government research institute Opened by KIST. Just as former Vietnam national soccer team coach Park instilled a belief in the Vietnamese players that "we can do it, too," transforming Vietnam into a dominant soccer force in Southeast Asia in a short period of time, V-KIST aims to elevate Vietnamese science and technology to unparalleled heights.

The V-KIST initiative was sparked during the Korea-Vietnam summit in 2012. During the meeting, then-Vietnamese Prime Minister Nguyen Tan Dung requested that then-President Lee Myung-bak facilitate a transfer of science and technology expertise. In response, the Korean government commissioned KIST to create a comprehensive research institute in Vietnam. The funding for this project took the shape of 'arm's length' official development assistance (ODA). The Korea International Cooperation Agency (KOICA), under the aegis of the Ministry of Foreign Affairs, partnered with Vietnam to cover the establishment costs, with each party contributing half of the required funds. The name V-KIST was proposed by the Vietnamese governement and notably, V-KIST is a unique instance where a comprehensive research institute symbolizing one nation incorporates the name of another nation within its own.

For Korea, the inception of V-KIST holds profound significance. In 1965, when the per capita income hovered below $100, the United States extended aid to Korea in return for the deployment of Korean troops to the Vietnam War. The Korean government debated the optimal use of these aid funds, with suggestions ranging from poverty eradication to industrial support. During this period, Park Chung-hee proclaimed, "Science and technology are Korea's future," and directed that a science and technology research institute be built. This decision allocated an additional $10 million from the national budget to the $10 million in aid received from the United States and as a result, KIST came into existence.

There are many tales highlighting Park's fondness for KIST. Beyond the aforementioned high salaries, he often visited KIST, engaging with its employees over drinks. Given the elevated salaries at KIST during that period, many influential figures aimed to secure positions for their children there. However, it is said that Park thwarted all such attempts, advising the first director, Dr. Choi Hyeong-seop, to "Ignore them." Reportedly, if someone was dressed in a KIST uniform, store owners would extend credit to them, even if they were strangers. This gesture stemmed from the widespread belief that KIST employees earned a substantial income. Interestingly, surveys conducted amongst young children consistently revealed that the most sought-after future profession was that of a 'scientist.'

Once the government committed to offering scientists an

environment where they could wholly focus on research, they began to showcase their full capabilities. KIST spearheaded industrialization, achieving milestones including developing Korea's first computer, pioneering semiconductor technology, and laying the foundation for automobile technology. KIST also played a crucial role in the conceptualization and establishment of the Pohang Iron and Steel Co. and the advancement of the electronics industry. KIST's contributions were instrumental in Korea's swift ascent in the realms of science and technology, earning the country the status of a 'miracle'. It is entirely apt to equate the history of KIST with the trajectory of Korean science and technology. With its profound influence on the evolution of Korean science and technology, KIST is now poised to play a pivotal role in the economic enhancement of other nations.

# From Aid Beneficiary to
# Science and Technology Benefactor

'Dream of the Future.' This is the title of the final chapter of the
'Report on the Establishment of the Korea Advanced Institute of
Science (now KAIST)' penned in 1970 by Frederick E. Terman, the
vice president of Stanford University, who is often heralded as the
father of Silicon Valley. Terman envisioned that by 2000, the Korea
Advanced Institute of Science and Technology would evolve into
"An educational institution of science and engineering of global
renown. A school that fosters leaders across diverse sectors, spanning
politics to economics. An institution pivotal in elevating the quality
of life for Koreans." True to Terman's foresight, KAIST, in tandem
with Seoul National University, has matured into a leading research-
driven university in Korea, and is widely recognized for its pivotal
role in the nation's economic ascent. The natural question that arises

is, why did Terman, the architect behind Silicon Valley, speak about the future trajectory of KAIST?

On April 8, 1970, then-President Park Chung-hee greenlit the establishment of an independent graduate school of science and technology, heeding the suggestion of John Hannah, the then-head of the United States Agency for International Development (USAID). In 1960, while Hannah was president of Michigan State University, he granted a special scholarship to the former Minister of Science and Technology, Jeong Geun-mo. After obtaining his doctorate from Michigan State University, Jeong served as a research professor at the Massachusetts Institute of Technology (MIT). During his tenure at MIT, he penned a paper in which he contended that "to curb the brain drain from developing countries, a top-tier specialized graduate school in science and engineering should be instituted within these countries." Moved by this argument, Hannah approached Park with the idea to establish the Korean Academy of Sciences. Recognizing the merit in the proposal, Park swiftly endorsed and advanced the initiative.

A working committee dedicated to the foundation of the National Academy of Sciences was initiated, and by August 1970, the Korean Academy of Sciences Act was birthed. This distinctive legislation embedded several pioneering measures, including ensuring research autonomy, pledging government contributions, and instituting exceptional provisions for the compulsory military service, which included exemptions. In essence, the act declared, "the government will support you fully, you just concentrate on research." To found the Korean Academy of Sciences, the government used a $6 million loan procured from USAID.

Subsequently, funded by the USAID loan, the Korean Academy of Sciences was built and opened in Hongneung, Seoul in 1973 and the first batch of students was welcomed in March of the same year. In September, a commemorative lecture was delivered by Dr. Walter Bratton, winner of the Nobel Prize in Physics in 1956. In the 2023 'QS World Universities' rankings, KAIST was 1st in Korea and 24th globally in the engineering category. Additionally, it placed 8th spot among Asian universities. Impressively, in the 'World Emerging University Rankings' for 2021, evaluated by the British university assessment body, THE, KAIST ranked 4th globally among institutions with a history of less than 50 years.

## TOP TIER SCIENCE AND TECHNOLOGY-TO-GDP RATIO

Once one of the world's poorest nations, Korea has experienced rapid growth, thanks in large part to bold investments in science and technology that KIST's formation heralded. Globally, Korea's astounding ascent is often referred to as the 'Miracle of the

Han River.' Although the term has waned in usage, during the 1990s Korea was frequently cited as one of the 'Four Dragons of Asia' alongside Singapore, Taiwan, and Hong Kong. These four dragons symbolized the nations that saw rapid growth in Japan's wake. Within a mere half century, Korea rebuilt itself from the devastations of the Korean War, emerging as one of the world's top 10 economic powers. Despite their relatively brief existence, Korean corporate giants like Samsung Electronics, Hyundai Motor Company, and SK Hynix now confidently rival global brands with centuries-long histories.

Korean global companies share a common trait: their growth is anchored in science and technology. Recognizing the significance of investing in science and technology, these companies allocate substantial funds to R&D annually. Korea's R&D investment as a percentage of its GDP is unparalleled globally. In 2021, Korea's total expenditure on research and development topped the ₩100 trillion mark for the first time, totaling ₩102.1352 trillion. The ratio of R&D spending to GDP was 4.96%, positioning Korea second globally behind Israel, renowned for its innovation prowess.

Each year, Korea and Israel vie for the top spot in terms of the R&D investment-to-GDP ratio. In 2000, Korea's ratio stood at a mere 2%, but it has witnessed a substantial surge over the past two decades. The lion's share of Korea's R&D investments is driven by the private sector, with private investments amounting to ₩78.403 trillion, which makes up 76.4% of the overall R&D investment. Dissecting R&D expenditures by phase, developmental research claims the largest slice (64.2%) with ₩65.5647 trillion, followed by applied research at ₩21.4704 trillion and basic research at ₩15.1002 trillion.

Korea boasts 586,000 professionals dedicated to science and technology research, placing it fourth globally behind China, the United States, and Japan. With 16.7 researchers per 1,000 economically active individuals and 9.1 researchers per 1,000 inhabitants, Korea ranks prominently in both metrics on a global scale.

# K-Power on Display at the Olympiad

During his tenure as U.S. President, Barack Obama frequently expressed his admiration for Korea's educational system and the extraordinary zeal that Korean parents have for their children's education. On multiple occasions—in formal speeches, interviews, and even during a summit with then-President Lee Myung-bak—he lauded the fervor Korean parents have for education and extolled the merits of Korea's educational framework, essentially championing Korean education.

It is inevitable that some have critiqued Obama's endorsement of the Korean education system, pointing out potential drawbacks, such as exorbitant private education costs—among the highest globally—and the intense academic pressure on students, many of whom study up to 12 hours daily. Even Lee was reportedly "embarrassed" when President Obama commended Korean education during their summit.

It is plausible to argue that the United States—the preeminent global power with unparalleled access to information—would not be oblivious to the negative aspects of the Korean education system. Nonetheless, Obama's emphasis was likely on the fact that education lies at the heart of Korea's meteoric rise from one of the world's most impoverished nations to a top-10 global economy within a mere fifty years.

His motivation could also stem from the observation that American elementary, middle, and high school students' mathematics and science scores not only trailed those of Korean students in the Program for International Student Assessment (PISA), but also ranked near the bottom among developed nations. He might have had an aspiration to emulate Korea's educational dedication, given the pressing need for educational reform in the United States. to uphold its stature as the world's dominant power. This naturally leads to the question: just how proficient are Korean students?

*"In South Korea, teachers are known as nation builders."*
_From Barack Obama's 2011 State of the Union Address

*"In places like Korea and Finland, where the education system is doing really well··· teaching is respected as a profession."*
_From Barack Obama's 2014 town hall meeting

# THE BEST ACADEMIC ACHIEVEMENTS AMONG OECD COUNTRIES OVER THE PAST 20 YEARS

PISA is a tool developed by the Organization for Economic Co-operation and Development (OECD) to evaluate the academic achievement of students 15 years old and older in each participating country. Although the assessment has been conducted every three years since 2000, the 2021 edition was postponed due to the COVID-19 pandemic, making the 2018 PISA the most recent data.

In 2018, 710,000 individuals from 79 countries participated, with 37 being OECD member countries and 42 non-members. From Korea, 6,876 middle and high school students across 188 schools took part in PISA, and they demonstrated impressive achievement across all areas. The average reading score for Korean students was 514 points, the math average was 526 points, and the science average was 519 points; all these scores topped the OECD average. Korea ranked between 2nd and 7th for reading, between 1st and 4th for math, and between 3rd and 5th for science. In comparison to the 2015 PISA results, while the average scores of OECD member countries decreased in all areas, Korea saw an increase in both math and science scores. Since PISA's inception in 2000, Korea has consistently held top rankings in reading, math, and science.

Korean parents have long held the belief that educating their children is both a 'virtue' and their 'duty,' irrespective of their financial circumstances. Historically, in Korean society, education was seen as the most effective ladder out of poverty. It was not uncommon for parents, even those in impoverished conditions, to sell cows—often a farmer's most valuable asset—to finance their children's college education. In an era where the majority lived in poverty, those who dedicated themselves to rigorous study could gain admission to prestigious universities and subsequently secure lucrative professions as doctors, judges, prosecutors, or positions at major corporations. The prevailing sentiment was that competing for top university spots and esteemed job placements would benefit not just the individual, but the nation as well. This fervent commitment to education was instrumental in Korea's transformation from an impoverished nation to a developing one, and subsequently, to its status as a developed country.

Statistical indicators related to education echo this narrative. In 2021, Korea's higher education completion rate stood at 51.7%, a figure that has consistently risen since 1997. This rate denotes the percentage of individuals aged 25 to 64 who have graduated from a tertiary institution. In comparison, the 2021 OECD average was 41.1%—over 10% lower than Korea. Among the younger demographic aged 25 to 34, Korea's higher education completion rate is an impressive 69.3%. Furthermore, Korea's expenditure per student stands at $13,341 for primary education and $17,078 for secondary education, figures which surpass the OECD averages. As for the proportion of public education spending relative to GDP, Korea allocates 3.4% to primary and secondary education, again exceeding the OECD average.

## EXCELLING IN THE SCIENCE OLYMPIAD

Not only do Korean students boast high average scores, but they also consistently shine in the International Olympiad competitions, which are reserved for top-performing students from around the world.

In the 2022 International Mathematics Olympiad, Korea placed second. Competing against 589 students from 104 countries, Korean participants won three gold and three silver medals—ensuring that every Korean participant went home with a medal. The results placed China in the top spot, followed by Korea, with the United States in third, Vietnam fourth, Romania fifth, Thailand sixth, Germany seventh, and a tie between Iran and Japan for eighth. Italy and Israel shared the tenth place. In the 2022 International Physics Olympiad, Korea ranked second overall, winning four gold medals and one silver. At the International Chemistry Olympiad, the Korean team placed fifth with two golds and two silvers.

## KOREAN STUDENT ENROLLMENT IN THE U.S. ON THE RISE POST-COVID

According to the Open Doors report—a comprehensive annual survey conducted by the Institute of International Education (IIE)—the number of Korean students studying in the United States declined due to the onset of the COVID-19 pandemic. However, there was a resurgence in 2022, when the count of Korean students in the United States, either pursuing undergraduate or

graduate courses, or participating in Optional Practical Training (OPT) and other training programs, was 40,755. This marked a 3.2% increase from the previous year and among the international student demographics, Koreans represented the third largest group at 4.3%, following China with 290,086 students (30.6%) and India with 199,182 students (21%).

Moreover, a notable number of Korean students are enrolled in top-tier American institutions. Data from the Harvard Worldwide website indicates that, in 2018, 317 Koreans were enrolled at Harvard University, making them one of the largest international groups after those from Canada, China, and India. As of the most recent data, excluding Korean Americans, 1,413 Koreans have earned degrees from Harvard University. Although Harvard University has not disclosed the specific breakdown of students by country recently, it is estimated that the representation of Korean students remains significant.

# KOREAN STUDENTS PERSUE
## OVERSEAS STUDIES AT MORE LOCATIONS

Historically, Korean students have shown a strong preference for studying in the United States over other nations. However, recent trends indicate a diversification in their choice of study destinations. According to the Ministry of Education, there has been a consistent decline in the number of Korean students pursuing education abroad since 2017, with the figure hitting 124,320 in 2022. A detailed breakdown by country reveals that the percentage of students studying in the United States and China has fallen below 50%, while there has been an uptick in the numbers heading to Japan, Canada, Germany, and France.

This decline in overseas studies is attributable to a combination of factors, with the COVID-19 pandemic and Korea's diminishing birth rates playing a part. Additionally, the trend that gained popularity in the early 2000s, where students would go abroad either to bypass Korean schooling or to commence their education overseas at a younger age, appears to be waning.

# KOREANS EXCEL IN INTERNATIONAL
# YOUTH SKILL OLYMPICS

In the 1960s, when the majority of Koreans were barely making ends meet, Bae Jin-hyo, the eldest among seven siblings, began working at a small shoe store in Busan at the age of 15. He worked there to earn a living and support his family. Later, he moved to Seoul in search of better opportunities and landed a job at a shoe-making store. Here, he honed his craft in shoemaking. He aimed to compete in the 16th International Youth Skill Olympics held in Madrid, Spain, on July 15, 1967. However, Korea initially chose not to participate in the shoemaking category, believing that the nation stood little chance in a field that demanded both industrial proficiency and design expertise.

But with the backing of the shoe store where he was employed, Bae managed to enter the competition and won the gold medal. When he landed at Gimpo Airport with his gold medal on July 27 of that year, he was greeted with a hero's reception, namely a grand car parade stretching to Seoul.

Subsequently, Bae earned the moniker "the young man who crafted shoes for the Spanish princess" and the store where he had worked soared in popularity. Earning medals at the International Youth Skill Olympics not only paved the way for individual successes but also set the stage for South Korea to establish itself as a leading nation in skills, largely through its manufacturing prowess.

The International Skills Olympics originated in Spain in 1947 and was inaugurated as an international competition in 1950, with the biennial contest welcoming youth aged 17 to 22. Recognizing the competition's significance early on, Korea viewed it as an avenue to bolster the nation's technological prowess. Backed by government policies that emphasized technical expertise, coupled with a societal mindset and the conviction that mastering a single skill can lead to success, Korea quickly distinguished itself in the International Youth Skills Olympics.

Korea made its debut in the competition in 1967, placing third at its next appearance. By 1977, Korea secured the top spot, taking the global community by surprise. From that point until the 1991 edition, Korea consistently claimed the same spot. Over the 24 contests spanning from 1977 to 2022, Korea placed first 19 times, a record for the International Youth Skills Olympics.

While China has held onto the top spot since 2017, Korea remains a close second. In the 2022 International Youth Skills Olympics Special Competition, Korea was the runner-up, winning 11 gold, 8 silver, and 9 bronze medals, showcasing its prowess in IT fields like cybersecurity and information technology. Furthermore, Korea continued its legacy of excellence by bagging gold in areas such as welding and molding, where it has traditionally excelled.

# Went to Catch Fish, Ended Up Building an Antarctic Science Base

Korea, a nation known for its active deep-sea fishing industry, dispatched its first research vessel, Anderby Land, to the Antarctic in 1978. The mission aimed to test the viability of catching krill, a marine resource plentiful in distant oceans. Successfully harvesting krill could position it as a lucrative export item for Korea during a period when the country was focused on economic development and boosting exports. To support this initiative, the Fisheries Agency (now known as the Ministry of Oceans and Fisheries) agreed to cover half of the expenses, and the North and South Fisheries, a deep-sea fishing company, spearheaded the Antarctic project. In the following two years, North and South Fisheries managed to catch 511 tons of krill.

Although the catch was modest, it was a significant first step in Antarctic deep-sea fishing. At that time, no one had ventured into Antarctic waters, and the route was largely unknown. The vessel 'Nambuk', belonging to North and South Korea Fisheries Co., Ltd., carried 94 crew members, five investigators, and six newspaper reporters. The research team studied the tools and methods for krill fishing and explored its ecology and distribution. The krill harvested in Antarctica was utilized as fishing bait, animal feed, and fertilizer. Engaging in krill fishing in Antarctic waters led Korea to join the Convention on the Conservation of Antarctic Marine Living Resources, a step necessitated by international obligations.

The journey to Antarctica for deep-sea fishing reflected the Korean spirit of vision and determination. But the venture did not end there. The Korea Marine Boys Federation proposed promoting Antarctic exploration to foster a sense of adventure and determination among the youth. With the economy rapidly developing, there was widespread Korean enthusiasm for such ventures. This development was underpinned by a collective ethos of "We can do it" and "Let's do it together."

In 1984, the Korea Marine Boys Federation inaugurated the 'Korean Antarctic Observation Expedition Team' and began preparations for the expedition. Subsequently, the Ministry of Foreign Affairs joined the effort, adding scientists from the Ocean Research Institute to the expedition team. In November 1985, the Korean Antarctic Exploration Team became the sixth in the world to climb Vinson Massif, which has an altitude of 4,892 meters. They also visited Antarctic bases in Chile and China. With the 1988 Seoul Olympics on the horizon, the Korean group's Antarctic exploration became a topic of national conversation. It raised awareness in the international community that the country, known for the Miracle on the Han River, was now embarking on significant ventures ahead of hosting the Olympics.

Korea's foray into Antarctica proceeded smoothly. The government took steps to join the Antarctic Treaty, becoming the 33rd member in 1986. Following this step, Korea decided to establish an Antarctic base in 1987, recognizing the need for long-term scientific research and resource development.

## CONSTRUCTING KING SEJONG STATION IN ANTARCTICA

Just three months after deciding to build an Antarctic base, a team of scientists and engineers surveyed the prospective site for the base. In October 1987, a team of Korean engineers embarked for Antarctica, equipped with the materials and equipment necessary for building the base.

A construction ship, loaded with materials, arrived at King

George Island, Antarctica, on February 15 of the same year and groundbreaking ceremony was held on December 16. Remarkably, within just one year from the decision to build the base to breaking ground, all the preparatory steps proceeded smoothly. Construction was feasible only during the Antarctic summer, so around 180 workers labored intensively from 7 a.m. to 10 p.m. during this season, occasionally extending their work until 2 a.m.

King Sejong Station in Antarctica was completed on February 17, 1988, a scant two months after the groundbreaking. With this achievement, Korea became one of the nations with a permanent base in Antarctica, capable of supporting year-round habitation. Despite being about 40 years behind some developed countries, the construction of a base dedicated to basic science and research in the 1980s was a notable leap in Korea's research and development history, especially as the nation was then primarily focused on industrial research.

The establishment and operation of King Sejong Station, coupled with the resulting research outcomes, enabled Korea to become the 23rd Antarctic Treaty Consultative Party (ATCP) in 1989, giving the country a say in Antarctic governance. In 1995, Seoul hosted the 19th Antarctic Treaty Consultative Meeting, cementing Korea's standing within the international community.

King Sejong Station in Antarctica is currently focused on various research topics including Antarctic pollution, tectonic

Panoramic View of King Sejong Station at Sunset

activity, future resources such as gas hydrates, undersea earthquakes, glacier collapse, and biodiversity, alongside atmospheric and space observations. In the mid-2000s, the necessity for an additional base in Antarctica beyond King Sejong Station, became apparent. This was due to the limitations in the scope of Antarctic research stemming from the absence of an inland base. A survey team was deployed to establish this second base between 2007 and 2010. Eventually, the coast of Terra Nova Bay along the Ross Sea coast in Antarctica was chosen as the site for this new construction.

Following the decision on the construction site, a public contest was held to name the second base. The name ultimately chosen was the Antarctic Jang Bogo Station, honoring the historic Korean figure Jang Bogo, who pioneered the Maritime Silk Road in the 9th century that facilitated international logistics and cultural exchange. The name reflects a determination to continue his spirit of pioneering and challenge. The construction of this second base was completed on February 12, 2014, taking one year and nine months from its inception. With this achievement, Korea became the 10th country to operate two or more permanent bases in Antarctica, 29 years after a 17-member Antarctic observation expedition team first explored King George Island in 1985.

## FROM ANTARCTICA TO THE NORTH POLE

Korea's polar exploration efforts didn't stop with Antarctica. Since 1969, the Korean government has shown interest in the Arctic Ocean, particularly for pollock fishing in the Bering Sea. Interest in Arctic scientific exploration grew following the construction of King Sejong Station in Antarctica in 1988. However, Korea's move toward the North Pole began in earnest quite serendipitously.

In 1999, China initiated its first exploration of the Arctic using the icebreaking research vessel 'Seollong'. In a gesture of international cooperation, China invited Korean scientists, along with those from Russia, Japan, and Taiwan, to join the expedition.

Researchers from the Korea Polar Research Institute had their first opportunity to explore the icy waters of the Arctic aboard the Seollong vessel. Although it was a passive form of research that was reliant on a Chinese vessel, they were able to gather crucial initial data, paving the way for Korea's future ventures into the Arctic.

At the Korea-Norway summit, alternately held in Oslo and Seoul in December 2001 and January 2002, the two countries agreed to cooperate in Arctic scientific research. In March 2002, the Korea Institute of Ocean Science and Technology (KIOST) leased a building to serve as the Arctic Dasan Science Station from a Norwegian company operating the Arctic research base, Ny-Ålesund. Officially opened on April 29, 2002, the Arctic Dasan Science Station became Korea's first Arctic science base and the 12th such facility in the world.

The base was named 'Dasan' following an open contest. Dr. Kang Seong-ho, who suggested the name, explained his choice in his book, stating, "Jang Yeong-sil might be the first scientist that comes to mind when thinking of notable Korean scientists, but his name can be challenging for foreigners to pronounce." He added, "I chose Dasan because it's easier for foreigners to say and remember." Dasan was the pen name of Jeong Yak-yong, a Silhak scholar during the late Joseon Dynasty. Jeong was a polymath with expertise in politics, law, economics, agriculture, engineering, geography, and medicine. He was also an engineer who contributed to the construction guidelines for Suwon Hwaseong Fortress under King Jeongjo.

Suwon Hwaseong Fortress, constructed under his guidance, is recognized as a UNESCO World Heritage Site. With the inauguration of the Arctic Dasan Science Station, Korea has established a solid foundation for comprehensive polar research, with scientific bases in both the Arctic and Antarctic. The Arctic Dasan Science Station conducts research in various fields, including the sea ice in the Arctic Ocean, atmospheric and space environment observation, and the monitoring and exploration of marine and terrestrial ecosystems, as well as polar biological resources.

Korea succeeded in building two bases, one in Antarctica and another at the North Pole, but the missing piece was an icebreaker capable of breaking surface ice to open routes through the ice-covered seas. Initially, Korea relied on icebreakers from other countries, which often made it challenging to conduct research where and when Korean researchers desired. To address this issue, Korea leveraged its outstanding shipbuilding technology to begin constructing an icebreaker that would match its stature as an Antarctic Treaty Consultative Party (ATCP). In May 2008, Korea's first icebreaker, the 'Araon,' was launched. With the construction of Araon, Korea became the seventh country in the world to domestically build an icebreaker.

Araon Supplying Winter Essentials to the Sejong Science Base

## KOREA'S GOAL FOR A 6TH
## ANTARCTIC INLAND BASE BY 2030

Araon, a medium-sized icebreaking research vessel, weighs about 7,500 tons and can accommodate 85 people. Capable of breaking through 1-meter-thick ice at a speed of 3 knots (approximately 5 km/h), Araon is well-equipped for polar exploration. It houses 51 types of research equipment, enabling simultaneous studies on the atmospheric environment, ozone layer, and marine biological resources, while monitoring changes in the polar regions.

Additionally, its heliport facilities ensure safe navigation routes. Being a relatively recent addition to the fleet, Araon boasts advanced capabilities, making it a versatile icebreaker for global missions. It primarily supports research in the Arctic from August to September and in the Antarctic from November to March.

Korea's ambitions extend further, with plans to build the world's sixth Antarctic inland base by 2030, along with constructing a 15,000-ton next-generation icebreaking research vessel. This vessel aims to spearhead international collaborative research in the high-latitude Arctic Ocean. Although Jang Bogo Station is located in Antarctica, its coastal position makes it difficult to consider it a true inland base.

As of now, there are only five countries that have built bases in Antarctica: the United States, Russia, Japan, France and Italy (jointly), and China. When this new base is completed, it will be Korea's third in Antarctica, following the King Sejong Science Station and the Jang Bogo Science Station.

Korea also plans to invest ₩277.4 billion in constructing a 15,000-ton next-generation icebreaking research vessel, which is expected to be completed by 2026. This cutting-edge vessel will be capable of breaking through 1.5-meter-thick ice at a speed of 3 knots. Surpassing the Araon's capabilities, which can only break through 1-meter-thick ice, the new vessel will enable Korea to expand its exploration into the high-latitude Arctic Ocean.

# Korea Poised to Become a Space Powerhouse

August 1992 marked a significant milestone when a rocket was launched from the Guiana Space Center in French Guiana, carrying the low-orbit satellite KITSAT-1—affectionately nicknamed "Our Star-1"—developed by the KAIST Satellite Research Center. This 50 kg micro-satellite, equipped with broadcasting, communication, and ground observation equipment, was a major achievement. Just three years after initiating its research and development in 1989, Korea successfully launched KITSAT-1, becoming the 25th country in the world to operate its own satellite.

It was affectionately nicknamed "Our Star," but it wasn't entirely our own creation: The satellite was not built solely with Korean technology. At the time, lacking satellite expertise, Korea relied on support from international researchers. The Korean government sent five KAIST graduates to the University of Surrey in the United Kingdom, renowned for its satellite development experience, to gain necessary knowledge. Consequently, some questioned, "Is Our Star-1 truly a byproduct of our technology?" There were even sarcastic remarks suggesting it should be called "Their Star" instead of "Our Star."

Now, 30 years later, Korea has advanced to the point of independently building a lunar orbiter. December 28, 2022, is a monumental date in the history of Korea's space industry, because it is the day when Danuri, Korea's first lunar orbiter built with indigenous technology, successfully entered an orbit 100 km above the moon. Influenced by the moon's gravity—just one-sixth of Earth's—Danuri will orbit the moon for about a year beginning in early 2023, undertaking various exploratory missions. The Danuri satellite, which is still circling the moon, was developed solely by Korean researchers, including the orbiter's main body and five payloads (one was developed in collaboration with the National Aeronautics and Space Administration).

With the successful launch of the Danuri satellite, Korea became the seventh country in the world to explore the moon, joining the ranks of the United States, Russia, China, Japan, the European Union, and India. Koreans take great pride in this achievement, ascending from being the 25th country to possess a satellite with the successful launch of Our Star-1, to becoming the seventh nation

A view of the Earth taken by Danuri, Korea's first lunar probe

© Korea Aerospace Research Institute

to explore the moon, all within just thirty years. This milestone indicates that Korea is now comparable to nations classified as 'space powers.' Although Korea's technological capabilities still lag behind the leading space powers, this achievement lays significant groundwork for Korea to continue striving and keeping pace in the arena of space exploration.

Danuri is equipped with the 'Shadow Cam' developed by NASA, designed to photograph the 'permanently shaded areas' in lunar polar impact craters which are hidden from sunlight. These shaded regions are critical to the success of NASA's 'Artemis Project', an ambitious lunar exploration initiative aiming to send humans to the moon again, 50 years after Apollo 17's landing in 1972. These areas are considered potential landing sites for a manned lunar and Korea's lunar exploration vehicle, Danuri, thus plays a pivotal role in supporting the Artemis project.

## FROM 'THEIR STAR NO. 1' TO 'MOON EXPLORATION'

It was in October 1957 that the former Soviet Union launched the Sputnik 1 satellite, to usher in the space age. This event spurred a sense of urgency in the United States, which subsequently launched its own satellite, Explorer 1, into space in January 1958. Compared to these space-faring powerhouses, Korea's journey in space exploration started modestly. From the 1960s to the 1980s, Korea's focus was primarily on immediate survival and economic development, leaving little room for space aspirations.

But Korea's indomitable spirit soon changed this trajectory. Despite initial setbacks and the dismissive labeling of KITSAT-1 as 'Their Star', Korea steadily increased its technological input in subsequent projects, including KITSAT-2 and KITSAT-3. These efforts bore fruit, and soon Korean technology was robust enough to develop and operate various types of satellites, including science and technology satellites, multipurpose satellites, next-generation small and medium-sized satellites, and the Chollian series.

Today, approximately 20 Korean-made satellites have been launched, with nine currently operational. The degree of technological independence tops 90%, a remarkable rise in just three decades. This growth is a testament to Korea's emerging status as a formidable player in satellite production and operation, matching the capabilities of long-established space powers.

There still is a hurdle that Korea must overcome to establish itself as a space powerhouse: the development of a launch vehicle. Although Korea's first space launch vehicle, Naro-1, was successfully introduced in 2013, marking Korea's entry into the 'Space Club' of nations capable of independently manufacturing and launching both space launch vehicles and satellites, the first stage of the rocket, crucial for breaching the atmosphere, was of Russian origin. According to the 2020 Technology Level Assessment report by the Korea Institute of Science and Technology Evaluation and Planning (KISTEP), there is an 18-year technological gap between Korea and the United States in the field of space launch vehicle development and operation.

Developing launch vehicles is a monumental task, requiring not only a decade or more of consistent research but also a budget potentially in the trillions of won. Countries like the United States and Russia are particularly hesitant to transfer critical technology related to first-stage rockets. This hesitancy stems from the dual-use nature of such technology: while a satellite-mounted launch vehicle is intended for peaceful purposes, the same technology can be adapted to create intercontinental ballistic missiles—weapons of mass destruction.

What is less commonly known is that since 1990, Korea has been earnestly working towards the independent development of launch vehicles. In July 1990, under the guidance of the Korea Aerospace Research Institute, Korea developed the first-stage solid rocket, named Science Rocket, and the second-stage solid rocket, called Medium Science Rocket. Both rockets' test flights were successful, but they were limited by low flight altitudes and their inability to carry satellites.

Starting in 1997, Korea embarked on the challenging development of a liquid sounding rocket, KSR-III (Korean Sounding Rocket-III), a project made difficult by the complex nature of liquid rocket technology. Such technology, essential for space development, is favored for its scalability and controllability. KSR-III, developed and launched entirely using Korean technology, achieved a flight duration of 231 seconds and reached an altitude of 42.7 km. Korea's aspiration to launch a small satellite by 2005 using domestically developed technology reached a pivotal juncture in 2002 with the signing of a technology agreement with Russia, marking commencement of the Naro Space Center project.

The Korean government's strategy aimed to expedite the acquisition of core launch vehicle technology by collaborating with Russia, ultimately progressing towards self-reliant space technology. However, the arrangement placed Russia in control of producing the first-stage launch vehicle, while Korea was responsible for the second stage. Russia's policy of restricting access to the first stage's technology under the pretext of 'technology protection' meant that when the Naro-1 launch finally succeeded in 2013, it was met with mixed reactions and deemed only a "half-success" by some critics.

## ONE STEP CLOSER TO DEVELOPING AN ADVANCED LAUNCH VEHICLE

However, Korean researchers did not relent. Despite the challenges, they accumulated numerous essential skills related to launch vehicle operation during their collaboration with Russia for the Naro project. A launch vehicle comprises both first and second stages, but successful launches require a comprehensive, integrated system. The collaboration with Russian experts was crucial, enabling the Korean team to glean diverse knowledge about launch vehicle technologies. It is humorously noted that Korean scientists used vodka as a gift for their Russian counterparts, facilitating the exchange of valuable insights over drinks.

Generally, projectiles are categorized as 'extreme technology.' While the principles and construction methods of projectiles are well-established, actual implementation is a separate, complex issue. One longstanding challenge, 'combustion instability,' where a launch vehicle's fuel doesn't burn correctly, has been known since the 1930s, yet its precise cause remains elusive and long-term investment and experience are critical for mastering launch vehicle technology. Thanks to the Russian collaboration, Korean researchers have steadily built up their technological expertise.

At 5 p.m. on October 21, 2021, eight years after the successful launch of Naro, Korea dispatched another launch vehicle into space from Oenarodo, Goheung, North Jeolla Province—the same location where Naro previously took flight. This was Nuri, a three-stage launch vehicle developed entirely by Korea. Even though Nuri did not achieve its intended orbit, it was hard to label it an outright failure. Given that both the crucial first stage and the second stage operated as intended, the predominant sentiment was one of optimism towards the forthcoming era of 'New Space' in space development.

International media noted, "Though Korea might have missed

the mark slightly during its maiden test launch, the nation has unmistakably established itself as a contender in launching magnetic satellites." Historical data reveals that, across a century of human rocketry, the maiden voyage of a rocket has a 73% probability of failure. Most of these failures are due to explosion or orbital deviation of the first or second stage rocket. In Nuri's case, both the first and second stages of its tri-stage design functioned flawlessly.

In its subsequent launch on June 21, 2022, Nuri successfully soared into space. This signaled Korea's arrival as a nation capable of not only developing space launch vehicles but also transporting them beyond the Earth's atmosphere and operating satellites deployed therein. After three decades of relentless research and development in space technology, Korea proudly stands as the seventh nation globally to devise its own launch vehicle and send it into space on its own terms.


## THE SIGNIFICANCE OF THE SUCCESSFUL THIRD LAUNCH OF NURI

Then, on May 25, 2023, Nuri was successfully launched for the third time. This launch was particularly momentous because it carried an actual satellite, unlike the previous two which utilized a satellite simulator for practice. The third launch was more than just a trial; it demonstrated to the world the fact that Korea is capable of launching actual satellites.

Nuri's successful launch after three tries has profound implications. Until this achievement, Korea had been dependent on launch vehicles from other countries to send satellites into space. This reliance meant not only having to pay millions of dollars per launch but also having to align with the scheduling constraints of those countries. Furthermore, the inability to launch satellites at its will limited Korea's participation in 'New Space'—the burgeoning private enterprise-centered space industry.

This launch marked a pivotal change; Korea now has the capability to send its domestically developed satellites into space using its own launch vehicles. This provides a valuable alternative for many countries wanting to possess a satellite but having to depend on foreign launch vehicles due to a lack of their own. Nuri is slated for continuous launches in the future, with plans to offer commercial satellite launch services as Korea builds a reputation for reliability in this domain.

In terms of technology, one of the primary features of the Nuri is its 'liquid fuel' propulsion. Rockets can be powered by either solid or liquid fuel, depending on their intended purpose. For the 'peaceful purpose' of deploying a 1.5-ton practical satellite into Earth's orbit—in other words, launching an artificial satellite into space—liquid fuel is generally preferred. This preference stems from the fuel's capability for precise control; it can be sprayed as needed. However, managing liquid fuel requires sophisticated technology to effectively cool parts, control gas pressure, and manage jetting. Liquid fuel engines offer higher 'specific impulse' (a measure of fuel efficiency) compared to solid fuel engines, allowing more payload to be sent into space with less fuel.

## EMERGENCE OF PRIVATE LAUNCH VEHICLE COMPANIES

On March 20, 2023, a significant milestone advanced Korea's space development technology: Innospace, a private space launch vehicle company, successfully conducted its first test launch. The test vehicle, 'Hanbit TLV,' independently developed by Innospace, was launched from the Brazilian Air Force's Alcântara Space Center at 2:52 pm local time on March 19.

This launch was a triumph. The Hanbit TLV is a hybrid rocket designed as a first-stage prototype, aimed at verifying the flight performance of the engine for a second-stage launch vehicle, the 'Hanbit Nano,' which is slated for a test launch later in 2023.

After initiating its commercial service with 'Hanbit Nano,' Innospace aims to commence commercial operations with a launch vehicle capable of carrying a 150 kg payload in 2023, followed by a vehicle built for a 500 kg payload in 2026.

Space is a burgeoning sector that Korea is keen to capitalize on, as it represents a future growth engine of immense potential. The global race to cultivate the space industry, considered a veritable golden goose, is intensifying. Euroconsult, a consultancy specializing in space markets, reported that the global space industry was valued at $370 billion in 2021. This figure surpasses the memory semiconductor market, worth ₩225 trillion, and is nearing the non-memory semiconductor market's valuation of ₩550 trillion. The space market is expected to grow rapidly, potentially doubling by 2030 to reach an estimated $642 billion.

Launch vehicles, in particular, are deemed a critical cornerstone of the space sector as they are the sole means of transporting materials and humans beyond Earth. Fortune Business Insights, an international market research company, projects that the global space launch service market will expand by 12.6%, from $12.6 billion in 2021 to $14.2 billion in 2022 and the market could swell to $31.9 billion by 2029. Furthermore, SpaceX, the current frontrunner in the launch vehicle market, is valued at up to $150 billion, topping Lockheed Martin's market capitalization of $118.9 billion.

The successful launch of Nuri and the rise of private launch vehicle enterprises such as Innospace have carved a path for Korea to gear up for the New Space era. It is true that Korea has not yet mastered the technology to launch heavy satellites or spacecraft over 3 tons into space, as SpaceX does, nor has it started to develop reusable launch vehicles to reduce costs. When compared with the six space superpowers—the United States, China, Russia, Japan, India, and the European Union—Korea still has considerable ground to cover technologically. Nevertheless, Korea has made significant strides in the production of small to medium-sized satellites, which are currently in high demand, marking its entry into the space industry race.

Around 300 domestic companies contributed to the development of Nuri, including major players like Hanwha Aerospace, Hanwha Systems, and Korea Aerospace Industries (KAI). The private sector has been instrumental in this journey, with Hanwha Aerospace developing the core 75-ton liquid engine for Nuri; S&H engineering the turbo pump; Innocom fabricating the tanks; KAI overseeing the integration of the entire system; and Hyundai Heavy Industries constructing the launch platform. While space development was once primarily a government-led initiative, it has increasingly transitioned to private industry involvement.

Furthermore, the 2021 agreement between Korea and the United States to terminate missile guidelines—following their revision in 2020—has provided an impetus for expanding the breadth of launch vehicle development in Korea. With the conclusion of these guidelines, Korea is no longer subject to limitations on the range, payload weight, and type of fuel for its space launch vehicles. The lifting of fuel constraints, in particular, has established a foundation for the private sector to vigorously pursue the solid launch vehicle market, which presents lower barriers to entry in terms of technological complexity and production costs than its liquid-fueled counterparts.

To foster long-term and sustained space development, the government is also moving towards the creation of the Korea Aerospace Administration, the country's equivalent of NASA. This entity will be dedicated to invigorating the aerospace industry, which is increasingly private-sector-driven, and aims to ensure that space development transcends merely stirring national pride or showcasing technological prowess. The goal is to transform space exploration into a catalyst for the rejuvenation and economic advancement of Korea's space industry.

"My fascination with space has been unwavering since 1969. Virgin Galactic aspires to pioneer commercial space travel for the world."

During the 11th World Knowledge Forum in 2010, I had the opportunity to engage with Sir Richard Branson, Chairman of the Virgin Group. Recognized as a paragon of innovation, he spoke about entrepreneurship with fervor and declared his determination to venture into 'space'. True to his word, Virgin Galactic made history by becoming the first private company to successfully

Nuri, the launch vehicle developed independently by Korea, ahead of its launch

conduct a commercial space flight in 2021.

There was a time when space development and space travel were relegated to the realm of science fiction. It was not only cost-prohibitive but the technology was underdeveloped and there was little to be gained for humanity. I never doubted his determination, but must admit that even I saw it as somewhat of a foolhardy venture. However, times have changed. With rapid technological advancement and the emergence of private space companies, space is now being viewed as a lucrative market.

# Powering Korea Via Nuclear Plants

The world is turning its attention once more to Korea's nuclear power technology. Following the Fukushima nuclear disaster in March 2011, there was a surge of interest in renewable energy sources like solar and wind, and a global trend toward phasing out nuclear energy emerged. However, the narrative has shifted recently. In the wake of the conflict in Ukraine, nations that were once leaning toward nuclear decommissioning are now acknowledging the imperative of energy security. Moreover, there is consensus that nuclear power plants, which offer a steady supply of electricity without carbon emissions, are essential for achieving carbon neutrality goals.

With the world's top nuclear power technology and cost-effectiveness in the large nuclear power plant market, Korea made strategic early investments to take the lead in the small and medium-sized nuclear power plant market. In 2012, Korea underscored its technological superiority by being the first in the world to receive the 'Smart Reactor' certification for an integrated nuclear reactor.

*"If the U.S. government does not support private companies in the development of small modular nuclear power plants (SMRs) through cost-sharing, other countries such as Korea will seize jobs and profits by selling nuclear reactors to U.S. power companies."*

_Christopher M. Mowry, CEO of B&W, USA, in written testimony to the US Senate Appropriations Committee on July 14, 2011

*"Korea is striving to become a leader in nuclear technology. The country is at the forefront of SMR projects, especially in the field of SMART reactors."*

_U.S. Senator Lamar Alexander in his keynote speech at the SMR Conference on May 22, 2012

For over a decade, U.S. senators have recognized Korea's small nuclear reactor technology as a competitive threat to the U.S. industry and have been emphasizing the need for the government to support American companies. This clearly demonstrates Korea's prominence in the small nuclear power plant market, which is gaining attention as a next-generation nuclear power solution, to the point that it has been on the American political radar for the past ten years.

French President Emmanuel Macron, who was previously been an advocate for nuclear phase-out in alignment with Germany, has now reversed his stance and announced the 'Nuclear Power Renaissance Plan,' which involves constructing 14 new nuclear power plants by 2050 and postponing the decommissioning of existing reactors. This shift represents a pragmatic approach to ensure a stable electricity supply while aiming to achieve zero carbon emissions by 2050.

Japan has also been adamant about not building new or expanding nuclear power plants since the Fukushima nuclear disaster. However, it recently changed its policy towards the construction of new next-generation nuclear power plants. The United Kingdom has also announced its intention to increase the proportion of nuclear power generation in its total power sources from the current 16% to 25% by 2050. To achieve this goal, the U.K. is planning to build eight new nuclear power plants by 2030. In the United States, there is an allocation of $6 billion to support the continued operation of existing nuclear power plants, in addition to a plan to provide $1.36 billion for the development of NuScale's newly emerging small modular nuclear power plant.

After the inauguration of the Yoon Seok-yeol government in 2022, South Korea abolished the previous government's nuclear phase-out policy and shifted its focus to 'relaunching the nuclear power industry.' The Yoon administration plans to restore the nuclear power industry ecosystem and increase the proportion of nuclear power generation to more than 30% by 2030. In response to the growing demand, Korea is also actively engaged in exporting nuclear power plants.

# THE FIRST GROUP OF KOREANS TO LEARN
# NUCLEAR POWER PLANT ENGINEERING

Korea's history of nuclear power plant development dates back to the 1950s. At a time when Korea was recovering from the devastation of the Korean War, the Korean government sent 237 first-generation nuclear engineers to the United States and Europe to learn nuclear technology. Each individual's education cost the government $6,000, a significant investment for Korea, one of the poorest countries with a per capita income of only $60 at the time. Nevertheless, the government pushed forward with this ambitious initiative, recognizing that for a resource-poor country that could not produce even a drop of oil, self-sufficiency in electricity was the top priority for survival and prosperity.

Before the Korean War, Korea was dependent on hydroelectric power plants, but most of them were located in North Korea. The Korean peninsula had a power facility capacity of 1.72 million kW (kilowatts), but only 198,740 kW, or 11.5%, could be generated in South Korea. Electricity was essential for national growth, and relying on electricity purchases from other countries could present a significant hurdle. This motivated the Korean government to turn to nuclear power. In March 1956, the government formed the 'Atomic Energy Department' within the Ministry of Education (currently the Ministry of Science and ICT) and selected nuclear energy scholarship students to send to the United States and other countries. Their mission was straightforward: they were tasked with gaining the knowledge to make Korea self-sufficient in nuclear technology.

In 1958, Korea signed a contract with GA (General Atomic), an American military and nuclear power company, to build a research reactor. Ground was broken in 1959 to construct the TRIGA Mark-II Training and Research Reactor out of the ashes of war, and it commenced full-scale operation in March 1962. The Triga Mark-2 operated until 1995 and played a major role in helping Korean engineers gain knowledge related to nuclear energy. Korea established the Atomic Energy Commission in 1956 to build nuclear power plants and began investigating candidate areas for domestic nuclear power plant construction with the assistance of the International Atomic Energy Agency (IAEA) in 1963. In 1969, Gori, South Gyeongsang Province, was selected as the site for the first nuclear power plant, and a construction contract was signed with Westinghouse.

Ground was broken for Gori Unit 1 in 1971, and construction was completed in 1978. As with many industries in Korea at the time, the construction of Gori Unit 1 relied heavily on foreign technologies. The cost of building the power plant was ₩156 billion. Following the construction of Gori Unit 1, Korea began to actively foster nuclear talent and successfully designed 'Hanaro,' a 30MW (megawatt) nuclear reactor, in the 1980s independently. This marked a significant step towards Korea achieving independence in nuclear power plant technology. The first Korean standard nuclear power plants, 'Hanul No. 3 and No. 4,' were completed in succession in 1998 and 1999.

## THE WORLD'S 4TH NUCLEAR POWER PLANT EXPORTER

Encouraged by the localization of nuclear power plant design technology and equipment, as well as by confidence gained from the experience of nuclear power plant construction and operation, investments in research and development (R&D), and human resource development, the Korean nuclear industry ventured into overseas markets and succeeded in exporting the APR1400, a Korean-designed nuclear power plant, to the United Arab Emirates (UAE) in December 2009.

With this achievement, Korea became the world's fourth-largest exporter of nuclear power plants, following the United States, France, and Russia. Korean nuclear technology has been acclaimed abroad. In 2018, Bloomberg conducted a comparison of the competitiveness of nuclear power plant construction among five countries: Korea, the United States, France, Russia, and the

United Kingdom. At that time, the construction cost per kW was the lowest in Korea at $3,717. China's price was $4,364, Russia's ranged from $5,271 to $6,250, France's was $7,809, and the United States' price was $11,638—nearly three times that of Korea. The cost for Korea to build one nuclear power plant was ₩5.6 trillion. Compared to Russia (₩7.8 trillion) and France (₩10 trillion), Korea had an overwhelming competitive advantage in terms of cost.

Korea excelled not only in price competitiveness but also in technology. The Korean-made nuclear power plant, the APR1400, received design certification from the U.S. Nuclear Regulatory Commission (NRC), an honor that nuclear powerhouses France and Japan have yet to achieve. This certification is essentially a license granted by the United States to Korea, allowing the construction of a Korean-style nuclear power plant in the country. Korea is the only country other than the United States to have been granted this certification. Additionally, the EU-APR1400 design developed by KHNP (Korea Hydro & Nuclear Power) also obtained EUR certification, enabling the construction of Korean-developed nuclear power plants in Europe.

In January 2023, UAE President Mohamed bin Zayed Al Nahyan met with President Yoon Seok-yeol during Yoon's state visit to the the country. He expressed his trust in Korea by stating, "I decided to invest $30 billion in Korea because of my trust in Korea, a country that keeps its promises under any circumstances." He praised

Korean companies for fulfilling their contracts despite unexpected challenges, such as COVID-19. The Barakah Nuclear Power Plant Units 1 and 2, which have started commercial operation, now provide 60% of Abu Dhabi's electricity and contribute to 15% of the UAE's total electricity production. It is noteworthy that the projects faced almost no delays in the transition from contract to commercial operations, which is considered unprecedented among nuclear power exporting countries.

Currently, only a handful of countries have nuclear power plant construction capabilities, including Korea, the United States, France, the United Kingdom, China, Russia, and Japan. However, the United States, France, and the United Kingdom have not built nuclear power plants within their borders for a long time, leading some to say that their nuclear power plant ecosystems have collapsed. While they were faltering, Korea, led by Doosan Energy, was solidifying its nuclear ecosystem value chain. Although Korea's nuclear power plant ecosystem faced challenges for a while due to the nuclear phase-out policy, the nuclear power industry is preparing for a second leap forward in response to the growing demand for nuclear power to achieve carbon neutrality. This preparation is supported by the strong commitment of the Yoon Seok-yeol government to nuclear power.

Korea is also expected to stand out in the emerging market for small and medium-sized nuclear power plants. In 2012, Korea became the first country in the world to obtain standard design approval for a SMART nuclear power plant, an integrated nuclear reactor. This achievement laid the foundation for Korea to be a step ahead of other countries. SMART nuclear power plants have a small power generation capacity—only one-tenth the size of large nuclear power plants—and their construction costs are low, at around ₩1 trillion. They also feature a desalination function that converts seawater into freshwater, making them an excellent power source capable of supplying electricity to desert areas.

## SETTING A WORLD RECORD
## IN NUCLEAR FUSION

Although its commercial application is some distance away, Korea's mastery in nuclear fusion technology is unparalleled and this technology is expected to be a significant contributor to power generation by the 2050s.

Nuclear fusion power generation, which uses the fusion of hydrogen atoms to create helium, differs fundamentally from traditional nuclear power generation, which depends on nuclear fission. Nuclear fusion is akin to creating an 'artificial sun' on Earth, replicating the sun's energy production process to generate heat. Nuclear fusion's potential for generating substantial energy from minimal fuel—far exceeding that of traditional nuclear power—carries high expectations. Nevertheless, the intricacies of simulating such extreme conditions have made the technology's implementation challenging. In a collective effort to surmount these challenges, six nations—Korea, the United States, Russia, Japan, China, India, and the European Union have jointly funded the construction of 'ITER,' an experimental nuclear fusion reactor in France, to further persue nuclear fusion's commercial viability.

Creating an Earth-bound equivalent of the sun's environment entails producing temperatures upwards of 100 million degrees Celsius. By heating a blend of deuterium and tritium in a toroidal (doughnut-shaped) reactor chamber, scientists aim to induce a fusion reaction at these exceedingly high temperatures to form a plasma state. However, maintaining stability of this plasma, which is as unpredictable and unbridled as a 'wild horse' at such extreme temperatures, is a significant technical obstacle. Korean researchers are leading the way in this venture, developing unmatched technological expertise to stabilize plasma at 100 million degrees Celsius.

Korea has been setting the world record for the longest ultra-high temperature plasma maintenance time annually since 2018. In 2021, KSTAR, a superconducting nuclear fusion research device, achieved stable plasma maintenance for 30 seconds, operating as an artificial sun, and there are plans to extend this duration to 300 seconds by

Inside of KSTAR, a Korean Superconducting Nuclear Fusion
Research Device

2026. Academic experts anticipate that maintaining ultra-high temperature plasma for 300 seconds could pave the way for the commercialization of nuclear fusion power generation. While some skeptics deem nuclear fusion power generation impractical, Korean researchers are proving them wrong by continually breaking new ground.

# Waiting for a Nobel Prize

"I can't win it. You can leave."

There was a period when a Korean scientist was frequently named as a potential Nobel Prize laureate in Science. In anticipation of the Nobel announcement, reporters camped outside both his laboratory and residence, prepared to broadcast the potentially historic moment. However, the scientist dismissed the possibility, stating, "I really can't win it. They won't give me the Nobel Prize." His skepticism proved accurate when reporters departed in a wave of disappointment after the announcement of the winners, mirroring the sentiments of the scientists, journalists, and the expectant public.

In Korea, the saying goes that "Scientists become sinners every October," referring to the period when Nobel Prizes in scientific fields are awarded. A humorous yet telling episode occurred during the National Assembly audit when a legislator queried the Minister of Science and ICT about the country's Nobel Prize prospects, questioning the return on substantial annual R&D investments and the persistent absence of a Nobel laureate in science.

Korea's neighbors have garnered several Nobel Prizes in the sciences. Japan has produced 25 Nobel laureates in science, who were either born in the country or hold Japanese nationality. In China, a Chinese scientist won the Nobel Prize in Physiology or Medicine in 2015. Among the three Northeast Asian countries— Korea, Japan, and China—only Korea has yet to win a Nobel Prize in Science. This fact stings Korean pride, especially given the country's dramatic economic rise, known as the 'Miracle on the Han River,' was driven by daring investments in science and technology and the presence of global corporations like Samsung Electronics and Hyundai Motor Company.

The Korean obsession with the Nobel Prize reached a peak when, in 2014, a Korean scientist appeared on the 'expected winners by field' list published by the academic information firm Clarivate during the Nobel Prize season. The anticipation was palpable, bolstered by statistics showing that "14% of those highlighted by Clarivate eventually won a Nobel Prize in Science." However, a win for Korea has yet to materialize. Despite being featured in Clarivate's predictions almost annually since then, no Korean scientist has taken home the prize. Their research is undoubtedly world-class, but the Nobel Prize in Science honors those whose work represents groundbreaking discoveries or has significantly impacted humanity, which high-caliber research does not necessarily achieve.

As the pattern of falling short for the Nobel Science Prize repeats itself annually, journalists no longer set up camp outside scientists' homes or pre-emptively prepare for Nobel announcements. The media and public excitement about Clarivate's predictions has also waned.

Korea's rapid economic expansion has been driven by a 'fast-following' strategy, prioritizing applied and commercial technologies over basic scientific research. The Nobel Prize in Science is awarded for pioneering work in pure science, which seeks to unravel the mysteries of nature and life and discover the principles governing natural phenomena. This realm of study is often dubbed 'the science of advanced countries' and contrasts with applied science's focus on utility and economic viability. For Korea, a country long fixated on survival and rapid growth, investing heavily in basic science has proven challenging.

# FROM A WIG EXPORTER
# TO A DARK MATTER RESEARCHER

In response to critiques of its performance in basic science, the Korean government founded the Institute for Basic Science (IBS) in 2012, thereby committing to foundational scientific inquiry. The IBS has astounded the science and technology community with its exceptional support for research fellows. The government funds 100% of research expenses and provides comprehensive administrative support, enabling researchers to dedicate themselves entirely to their work. Group directors enjoy autonomy and have complete authority to manage their teams—a system many scientists would deem perfect, offering support without micromanagement.

Funding for IBS researchers can be as high as ₩10 billion, depending on the project. Performance evaluations prioritize 'quality' over 'quantity,' relying on peer assessments from top-notch scholars. The compensation for IBS researchers is on par with prestigious global institutions, such as Germany's Max Planck Institute and Japan's RIKEN. This level of support is unprecedented and reflects Korea's intention to bridge the gap with leading nations in basic science.

IBS is delving into fundamental research areas, including dark matter, plant senescence, neuroscience, and climate change, as well as exploring new natural phenomena such as RNA, carbon nanotubes, and laser technology. Prominent academic journals, such as *Nature* and *Science*, have highlighted the launch of IBS in feature articles, signaling international recognition of Korea's increased focus on basic science—a field historically neglected within the nation.

IBS was named a 'Rising Star in Basic Science' by Nature Index in 2016, which gauges the caliber of basic science based on publications in prominent academic journals. Out of 100 candidates identified as rising institutions, Nature Index highlighted 25 that have notably driven national growth or markedly improved their international standings. Among these, Nature Index likened IBS to Japan's RIKEN and Germany's Max Planck Institute for its remarkable role in advancing basic science. The commendation noted that within four years, IBS's rating surged by over 4,000%.

According to Clarivate Analytics, IBS had a Highly Cited Papers (HCP) ratio of 5.29% in 2016, five years post-establishment. This figure outshines that of the Max Planck Institute's 2.77% and RIKEN's 2.18%, indicating that IBS's research is of superior quality and impact.

*Nature*'s special issue in May 2020, titled "Korea's Change of Direction," recognized the country's swift progress in basic science—and came 27 years after *Nature*'s 1993 special issue on Korean science and technology. The 2020 issue reflected on Korea's strategic shift to 'first mover' status by prioritizing investment in foundational research and pioneering R&D.

In its review, *Nature* posited that "IBS is the crowning achievement of Korea's public investment in basic research," commending it as parallel to the renowned Max Planck Institute and RIKEN. The review also highlighted that over the past three years, the proportion of researchers relocating to Korea from overseas exceeded the global average. This trend is seen as evidence of Korea's successful strides in diminishing scientific insularity.

## WOO JANG-CHUN, THE SCIENTIST WHO REVISED
## DARWIN'S THEORY OF EVOLUTION

"Up until now, I have worked hard for the sake of Japan, my mother's country, and not to fall behind the Japanese. But from now on, I will do my best for Korea, my father's country. I promise I'll bury my bones in this country."

Dr. Woo Jang-chun, whom most people believe developed 'seedless watermelon,' was born in 1898 to a Korean father and a Japanese mother. Raised in Japan, he faced discrimination due to his Korean heritage. Despite these challenges, he was diligent in his studies and earned admission to the Tokyo University of Economics in 1916, graduating in 1919. He subsequently worked at the Agricultural Experiment Station under the Japanese Ministry of Agriculture and Forestry, focusing on breeding science until 1937. During this period, he authored more than 20 research papers.

Woo gained international recognition with his cross-breeding thesis, published in 1935. The idea came to him upon observing rape flowers flourishing in fields of cabbage and radish, which led him to propose the theory of 'synthesis of species.' He substantiated his theory through rigorous experimentation.

To appreciate Woo's contributions, one must understand the scientific context of his time. According to Darwin's theory of evolution, all organisms can interbreed within their own species, with species evolving through natural selection. The prevailing belief was that crossbreeding between different species was rare, hindered by 'interspecies barriers' and 'breeding barriers' that made crossbreeding more difficult with greater evolutionary distance. Even when crossbreeding did occur, it was generally thought to result in infertility or genetic complications. This understanding explained why hybrids like ligers and tigons, produced from lions and tigers, are typically sterile. Such was the widely accepted scientific knowledge.

But in contrast to this knowledge, Woo observed rape blossoms in fields of radish and cabbage and hypothesized that crossbreeding could occur between different species within the same genus. He proposed that new species created in this way could be fertile and propagate. Using this principle, he believed humans could cultivate new plant species by interbreeding different plants to our advantage. Through his research, Woo validated his theories, challenging and revising the long-standing scientific consensus. What may seem self-evident today was, at the time, revolutionary. Educational textbooks were rewritten to incorporate his findings, and many of the fruits and vegetables in our current diets owe their existence to his work. Consequently, his work is heralded in academia as marking the dawn of modern plant breeding and considered to be of Nobel Prize-level significance.

Most people attribute the creation of the seedless watermelon to Woo but it was actually Dr. Hitoshi Kihara of Japan who developed it. When Woo arrived in Korea in 1950, his aim was to enlighten Koreans on the significance of plant breeding, and during this educational process, he introduced the seedless watermelon, leading to a widespread misconception that he was its creator. However, it was Woo's theory of species synthesis that laid the groundwork for creating seedless watermelons.

Woo's reputation is evidenced by the efforts made following Korea's liberation: the Korean government formed the 'Woo Jang-chun Return Promotion Committee' and initiated a campaign to persuade him to return to Korea. An agricultural science research institute was established in anticipation of his arrival so that he could commence work without delay. Upon his arrival on March 8, 1950, he declared, "I will live for the sake of Korea." Indeed, he dedicated the rest of his life to breeding research in Korea until his death in 1959. Among his notable contributions, Woo advocated for tangerine cultivation on Jeju Island and achieved significant advancements in improving potato strains in Gangwon Province, as well as developing delicious and disease-resistant varieties of cabbage and radish.

PART 5

# KOREAN
# COMPANIES
# THAT MADE THE
# IMPOSSIBLE,
# POSSIBLE

The concept of the Internet of Things (IoT) existed even 30 years ago. In the 1990s, before the widespread adoption of personal mobile communications such as mobile phones, pagers—also known as beepers—were a global sensation for instant communication. Although considered obsolete today, for those in their forties and beyond, pagers were once a coveted gadget, akin to the modern smartphone.

When someone left a number on your pager, the typical response was to find a payphone, dial the number, and say, "Can I talk to the person who paged me?" to connect with the caller. Pagers also offered a voice messaging feature; you could dial a pager's number and leave a voice message that the recipient would alerted to by a 'beep' sound, allowing about a minute for the recording. After the message was sent, the pager would alert the owner, who could then play back the message via a telephone.

At the height of their popularity in 1994, Samsung C&T introduced 'X-bing,' the world's first remote control pager. Its operation was straightforward: by attaching an auxiliary device to household appliances, such as an electric rice cooker, the appliances could be activated remotely using a phone call with the user's specific number and password. This innovation meant that one could turn on the rice cooker from work before heading home. It was also capable of starting the car and controlling lights, heating, and air conditioning systems. What is now routine with IoT technology and smartphones was, at the time, a remarkable demonstration of the foresight of researchers who envisioned such possibilities in the early 1990s.

# Small Korean Companies That Conquered Global Niche Markets Worldwide

Korea's economic and industrial structure is centered on large corporations, often overshadowing small and medium-sized enterprises (SMEs). While these conglomerates garner hundreds of applications for each position, SMEs struggle to attract candidates. Nonetheless, despite these challenging circumstances, numerous local SMEs are carving out dominant positions in the global market with their unique technological prowess.

## A SMALL YET MIGHTY LOCAL COMPANY CONQUERS THE WORLD WITH STRAWS

Straws are ubiquitous, found in convenience stores, supermarkets,

and cafes alike. Yet, it is a Korean company that holds the distinction of being the world's largest straw producer, having also pioneered the Z-shaped straw to prevent liquid backflow. This innovation has led to impressive annual sales nearing ₩200 billion, all of which was achieved by selling straws that cost only ₩5 each.

This company, Seoil, boasts a commanding presence, holding over 30% of the global straw market share. Despite its classification as an SME, Seoil operates local factories in six countries, including Korea, Indonesia, the United States, China, and Türkiye. It has further expanded its global footprint with sales subsidiaries in the United Kingdom and Japan.

Seoil is a prominent supplier of straws to many companies, including the world's largest food corporations, Nestle and Pepsi. It was the first to develop the U-shaped straw, commonly seen in convenience stores, as well as the Z-shaped straw designed to prevent the backflow of drinks. Aligning with the surge in demand for environmentally friendly products, Seoil has recently developed and commercialized U-shaped paper straws, a first in the industry. Remarkably, these paper straws retain their shape even when wet. With a workforce of approximately 1,500 both domestically and internationally, Seoil has been producing and selling straws since 1979 without ever incurring a loss, rightfully earning the title of a 'recession-proof company.'

## HJC: THE ORIGINATOR OF THE KOREAN WAVE IN MOTORCYCLE HELMETS

Unbeknownst to many, a formidable Korean company has been leading the global motorcycle helmet market, giving rise to what some refer to as the 'Korean Wave' in this sector. This company, HJC (originally known as Hongjin Crown), began as a small motorcycle helmet manufacturer. Since its founding in 1971, HJC rapidly secured the number one spot in Korea's domestic market. Its foray into international markets was equally successful, achieving top positions when it entered the U.S. market in 1992 and the European market in 2001. With over two decades of industry leadership, HJC has maintained an unbroken record as the global leader in market share.

HJC began as a manufacturer of motorcycle interior materials before acquiring Seoul Helmet in 1974 and shifting its focus to producing motorcycle helmets. At that time, the Korean motorcycle helmet market was heavily reliant on imports from Japan and other countries. By locally producing the manufacturing equipment for helmet production, HJC significantly enhanced its price competitiveness. When it entered the United States market, the company dedicated itself to rigorous research in order to meet the stringent certification standards in the country. HJC achieved the top spot in the U.S. motorcycle helmet market in 1992, roughly a decade after entering it, and has remained at the forefront ever since. Upholding the belief that "a company that does not engage in research cannot survive," HJC reinvests 10% of its annual sales into R&D. In 2022, HJC reported sales of ₩184.2 billion and an operating profit of ₩12.4 billion.

# DOMINATING THE GLOBAL HAT MARKET WITH ₩500 BILLION IN SALES

Among the plethora of small yet powerful Korean companies, some stand out as world leaders in the hat industry. Given the vast array of hat types and the dynamic market, the top contenders can vary based on market segmentation. However, it is indisputable that these robust Korean enterprises have carved out a dominant position in the global arena.

Yupoong, established in 1974, is a prime example, specializing in ODM and OEM services. With facilities in Vietnam and Bangladesh, Yupoong produces a staggering 120 million hats annually. The company's 2022 sales figures hit ₩514.9 billion, positioning it at the pinnacle of the global market. Its operating profit margin of 23.6% in 2022 places Yupoong among the most profitable firms in its league.

Young An Hat, another noteworthy Korean hat manufacturer, evolved from its humble beginnings as a street vendor in Cheonggyecheon in 1959. By the 1970s, it had become an exclusive supplier of fan service hats for the Los Angeles Dodgers and today, the company exports 12 million sports hats annually to the United States. Despite being a Korean enterprise, Young An Hat has no retail presence in Korea and does not engage in OEM delivery. Producing approximately 100 million hats per year, the company once boasted a market share of up to 40% of the global hat market.


## KOREAN BUTANE GAS HEATS
## INTERNATIONAL MARKETS


Three decades ago, Japan was at the forefront of the butane gas industry as its pioneer. The landscape dramatically changed following Korea's back-to-back hosting of the 1986 Asian Games and the 1988 Seoul Olympics. Visitors to these events took note of Koreans using portable 'Blue Star' gas stoves to cook food anytime, anywhere. This demonstration of convenience captivated international guests, who sought the same butane gas in their countries upon returning home.

The 1995 Kobe Earthquake played a pivotal role in changing market dynamics. It severely impacted Japan's energy infrastructure, causing a surge in butane gas demand. With Japan's domestic production unable to fulfill the sudden spike in demand, it began to import supplies from Korea. This shift presented Korean butane gas firms with significant export opportunities, ultimately propelling Korea to a leading position in the global butane gas market.

Taeyang, the most renowned manufacturer of portable butane gas products, commands a 60% share of the global market. When combined with the shares of other Korean manufacturers like

Dae Ryuk Can and OJC, Korea's total market share rises to 90%. Notably, Dae Ryuk Can was awarded the $70 million Export Tower in 2022 for its explosion-proof butane gas product, 'Max Butane', recognizing the company's significant contribution to increasing exports.


## AT THE FOREFRONT OF THE ARTIFICIAL LEATHER AND WIND TOWER MARKETS


In the realm of artificial materials, DK&D stands out as a Korean company leading the global market with a 30% share in the production of 'non-woven fabric' used in synthetic leather. This turn towards synthetic materials gained momentum in the 2000s as animal protection groups rallied against the use of natural leather, sparking consumer interest in alternatives that mimic the real thing. Established in 2000, DK&D has pioneered the development of a synthetic leather that is not only lighter than natural leather but also replicates its texture. This innovative material has found applications in Nike sneakers, car seats of leading automotive companies, and cases for Apple's iPad.

Huvis is another Korean success story, becoming the world leader in the PPS fiber market in 2018, outperforming giants like Toray. Founded in the year 2000 as a joint venture between SK Chemicals and Samyang Corporation, Huvis was the first in Korea to develop PPS fiber in 2009. This 'super fiber' is known for its heat resistance and chemical stability, making it indispensable in the automotive and home appliance sectors. Its production demands such advanced technology that only a few companies globally, including Japan's Toray, have the capability to manufacture it.

In the cosmetics industry, a Korean company's products are used by nearly a quarter of the world's 7 billion people. If you're using products from global cosmetic giants such as L'Oréal, Nu Skin, Johnson & Johnson, or popular Korean brands such as The Face Shop, you're likely a consumer of products made by Cosmax. This mid-sized Korean enterprise specializes in the research, development, and production of cosmetics and health supplement foods via Original Design Manufacturing (ODM). Cosmax partners with over 600 companies globally, providing them with customized products that are then marketed to consumers. Although it operates as a B2B entity and remains relatively obscure to the average consumer, Cosmax's sales are approaching the ₩2 trillion mark.

As global interest in eco-friendly power generation grows, CS Wind, a Korean mid-sized company, is leading the wind tower market with 16% of the global market share. Wind power generates electricity by rotating large blades, increasing demand for wind towers that act as supporting pillars. Despite having only about 100 employees, CS Wind now leads the market thanks to its technological excellence. The durability of wind towers is critical, as they must withstand strong winds; it is said that none of CS Wind's towers have ever failed to date. In 2021, CS Wind acquired a 100% stake in a U.S. plant from Vestas, the Danish wind power company operating the world's largest wind power tower, for $150 million. The following year, Bloomberg reported that the U.S. Inflation Reduction Act (IRA) would benefit Korean renewable energy companies, naming CS Wind as one of the prospective beneficiaries.

Shinhwa Intertek, recognized by the Ministry of Trade, Industry, and Energy as a "small but strong company" in materials, parts, and equipment, has established itself as a reputable manufacturer. The company produces 'optical films' used to minimize light loss in displays such as LCD monitors. Shinhwa Intertek supplies its films to major corporations, including Samsung Electronics and various global IT firms. In 2021, the company pioneered the development of a film suitable for use in next generation displays, commanding a 40% share in the optical film market.

Many slot machines in Las Vegas, USA, are manufactured and supplied by Kortek, a Korean mid-sized company that specializes in industrial monitors. Visitors to Las Vegas have likely seen a wide array of casino slot machines, not only in hotels but also at the airport. Kortek stands as the leading company in the field of monitors for casino slot machines, commanding a global market share of over 50%. Branching out into other areas, Kortek has also penetrated the electronic whiteboard market and now produces various specialized monitors for medical and aviation use, as well as for kiosks.

Faber-Castell is a storied German manufacturer of writing instruments with a 260-year history, while Bic is the largest manufacturer of writing instruments in France. These prestigious companies share a common supplier: a Korean company named UNI. Founded in 1958, UNI initially dealt in pigments and dyes imported from Japan. In 1988, it began to produce pigments domestically and by 1997, had entered the writing ink market, quickly becoming competitive with German and Japanese manufacturers. Despite its modest size, with about 50 employees, UNI leads the global market share in the fancy ballpoint pen ink sector due to its advanced technology. The company also innovated a 'gel' type of neutral ink, which addresses the limitations in both water-based and oil-based inks. UNI currently generates more than 80% of its sales from international markets, including China, India, and Southeast Asia.

# The Authority of Korean-Made Semiconductors

In 1983, the Mitsubishi Research Institute in Japan issued a report that affronted Korea's national pride. Titled "Five Reasons Why Samsung Cannot Succeed in the Semiconductor Industry," the report detailed the alleged insurmountable barriers facing Samsung in its nascent semiconductor endeavor. This was particularly provocative given that only a few months earlier, in February 1983, Lee Byung-chul, the then-chairman and founder of the Samsung Group, had proclaimed his intent to enter the semiconductor business with a declaration made in Tokyo, titled 'Why We Should Enter the Semiconductor Business'.

The Mitsubishi Research Institute's report claimed that Samsung Electronics would struggle due to a small domestic market, weak ancillary industries, inadequate social overhead capital, the company's lack of scale, and inferior technology. At the time, the semiconductor industry was considered the exclusive realm of developed countries, necessitating substantial capital and sophisticated technology. Despite Samsung's rapid growth, the prevailing opinion was that breaking into the semiconductor sector was an unrealistic aspiration for the company. The market was then dominated by the United States and Japan, collectively referred to as the G2. Intel, reflecting the industry's dismissive attitude, purportedly labeled Lee a 'megalomaniac.'

Even within Korea, there was skepticism regarding the semiconductor industry. In 1982, the Korea Development Institute (KDI) published a report stating, "The semiconductor industry is only viable in countries with a population of over 100 million, a per capita income of $10,000, and domestic consumption accounting for more than 50% of GDP. It is impossible for Korea, as we lack the technology, manpower, and financial resources." If the Mitsubishi Research Institute and KDI were to reflect on what they wrote at the time, they would likely be embarrassed.

Four decades after that report, Korean semiconductors are at the forefront of the global market, illustrating just how incorrect the U.S. and Japanese predictions were. The American and Japanese companies that once dominated the global semiconductor scene in the 1980s and 1990s have dwindled, and Korean companies like Samsung Electronics and SK Hynix now hold an unrivaled leading position with a significant market share in the DRAM sector.


## THE ONCE UNATTAINABLE DREAM OF BECOMING A SEMICONDUCTOR POWERHOUSE IS NOW REALITY

Samsung began as Samsung Electronics Industries in 1969, initially manufacturing and selling white home appliances and audio equipment. The company produced its first black-and-white TV and, with technological and financial backing from Sanyo Denki, exported it to Panama. In 1974, Samsung Electronics expanded its horizons by acquiring Korea Semiconductor.

It is rumored that even the executives of Samsung Electronics were initially opposed to the acquisition of Korea Semiconductor. At the time, Samsung was still trailing behind Japan in the television industry, and venturing into the high-tech semiconductor sector was deemed overly ambitious. Nonetheless, then Vice Chairman Lee Kun-hee personally financed the acquisition of a 50% stake in Korea Semiconductor, and purchased the remaining shares three years later. In 1978, Korea Semiconductor was renamed Samsung Semiconductor and subsequently became part of Samsung Electronics in 1979.

In December 1983, just ten months after Samsung Electronics

entered the semiconductor market, it accomplished a remarkable milestone by developing Korea's first 64K (kilobit) DRAM, becoming the third in the world to do so. At the time of Korea Semiconductor's acquisition, Korea lagged nearly three decades behind American and Japanese companies. This gap was dramatically closed to only 3 to 4 years following the development of the 64K DRAM. Samsung Electronics then continued to gain momentum, rapidly enhancing its semiconductor technology.

Initially aiming to rival Japanese firms, Samsung Electronics, pivoted towards a new management philosophy focused on creating "the world's best products" in the 1990s. This shift enabled Samsung to not only catch up to but also overtake its Japanese competitors in technological excellence. In 2007, a survey by the American consulting firm Andersen Analytics of 1,000 American college students found that 57.8% believed Samsung Electronics was a Japanese company and only 9.8% correctly identified it as Korean. This misconception underscored the extent to which Samsung's products matched or even surpassed the Japanese products that were once renowned for their 'technological prowess'.

Samsung Electronics has also become the 'people's company'. As of 2023, the number of investors holding shares in Samsung Electronics exceeded 6 million. With around 14 million investors in the domestic stock market, this statistic reveals that every second Korean stock investor owns shares in Samsung Electronics, a significant lead over LG Energy Solution and SK Hynix, which have 800,000 and 950,000 investors respectively. In the KOSPI market, Samsung Electronics alone commands a 16% share of market capitalization, significantly outpacing LG Energy Solution and SK Hynix, which stand at 5.8% and 2.7% respectively.

As a globally recognized corporation, Samsung Electronics represents Korea on the world stage. The company was valued at $87.7 billion, approximately ₩115 trillion, in the 2022 'Best Global Brands' ranking by Interbrand, placing it fifth worldwide.

Moreover, Samsung Electronics surpassed Google in YouGov's 2022 ranking of best global brands, grabbing the top spot for the first time. Additionally, Samsung has been named first in Forbes' 'World's Best Workplaces' for three years running, from 2020 through 2023.

## THE RESILIENCE OF SK HYNIX

SK Hynix is a leader in the global memory market, sharing the position with Samsung Electronics. The company's origins trace back to its establishment as Kukdo Construction in 1949. It was rebranded as Hyundai Electronics Industry in 1983 and marked its entry into the semiconductor business by manufacturing Korea's first 16KB SRAM in 1984. The company made headlines again in

1995 by developing the world's first 256MB SDRAM, showcasing its innovative capabilities.

Hyundai Electronics thrived in the semiconductor industry, until it merged with LG Semiconductor in 1999, emerging as a consolidated semiconductor enterprise. But the semiconductor industry started declining in 2000. Faced with financial difficulties, Hyundai Group divested various divisions, leaving only Hyundai Electronics Memory, which later became Hynix Semiconductor.

Hynix was put under a creditor-led workout program in 2001. Although it weathered this storm, the 2008 global financial crisis precipitated another industry downturn, sparking an intense competition among memory semiconductor manufacturers—a 'chicken game' that led to the exit of several German and Japanese firms. Hynix was also taken over by SK Group in 2011.

At the time, SK Group's main businesses were in petrochemicals and telecommunications, and it was on the lookout for a new growth engine. Meanwhile, Hynix needed an owner with robust financial backing. Following the acquisition, SK Group provided full support to SK Hynix, which returned to profitability in the second quarter of 2012. Since then, the company has reported record sales and operating profits annually and has pioneered many firsts in the industry, including the launch of high-capacity mobile DRAM in 2013.

# KOREAN SEMICONDUCTORS COMMAND
# A 70% GLOBAL MARKET SHARE

As of the fourth quarter of 2022, Samsung Electronics and SK Hynix's shares in the global DRAM market stood at 45.1% and 27.7% respectively, culminating in a commanding global market share of 72.8% for the two giants. It is fair to say that more than 70% of electronic devices worldwide likely incorporate semiconductors from either Samsung Electronics or SK Hynix.

These two trailblazers in the memory sector are also aggressively investing to bolster their presence in the non-memory segment. The semiconductor landscape is bifurcated into memory and non-memory chips, with the former category responsible for data storage and the latter for data processing. Non-memory semiconductors, which act as the 'brains' of electronic devices, require more sophisticated technology to develop. As per the 2022 figures, memory chips account for 30% of the semiconductor market, with non-memory chips making up the remaining 70%.

Non-memory semiconductors are produced in greater variety but in smaller quantities than memory semiconductors. As processors of information, their development necessitates advanced technical expertise. In the non-memory semiconductor market, the top four industry leaders are Intel and Qualcomm from the United States, TSMC from Taiwan, and Broadcom, with Samsung Electronics in

**Share of Semiconductor Exports in Korean Exports**

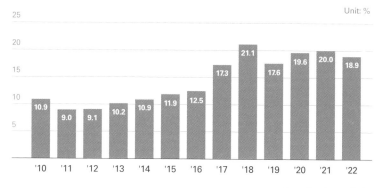

Unit: %

Source: Korea Customs Service,
Ministry of Trade, Industry, and Energy

fifth place.

Samsung Electronics plans to invest ₩300 trillion by 2040 to build the world's largest system semiconductor complex in Korea. This ambitious project aims to cluster 150 related enterprises, including material, component, and equipment suppliers, as well as fabless companies, around five state-of-the-art semiconductor production facilities. SK Hynix has also set the stage for expansion by acquiring Key Foundry, a non-memory semiconductor business, in 2022.

## SAMSUNG AND APPLE VYE
## FOR SMARTPHONE MARKET SHARE

Samsung is vying with Apple for the top spot in the global smartphone market share in addition to competing in semiconductors. Market research firm Canalys reports that in 2022, Samsung led with a 22% share of the global smartphone market, followed by Apple at 19%. The struggle for dominance in the smartphone market is so fierce that the two giants vie for supremacy with each passing quarter. Samsung's market share tends to dip when Apple launches a new product. Conversely, Samsung's releases often propel it ahead, creating a see-saw dynamic between the two companies.

In the first quarter of 2023, Samsung maintained the lead with a 22% market share, while Apple followed closely with a 21% share, a narrow 1% point difference. Apple had a surge to 25% in the fourth quarter of 2022 coinciding with a new product launch, overtaking Samsung's 20%. However, this lead was short-lived, as Samsung regained the upper hand after the initial sales spike for Apple's new product subsided. Samsung has emerged as a contender in the smartphone arena, pursuing Apple since the iPhone revolutionized the market. When Apple started the iPhone phenomenon, Samsung responded with the introduction of the Galaxy series. It was an uphill battle for Samsung, which held only a 9% market share in 2010 compared to Apple's 16.1%.

However, Samsung rapidly caught up with Apple by successively incorporating new technologies into its smartphones. In 2010, Samsung unveiled a large-screen smartphone featuring an AMOLED display. The following year, the company introduced the 'Note' series with its complementary 'S Pen', melding analog touch with mobile technology. In 2014, Samsung launched a waterproof smartphone, and in 2016, it released a model equipped with the world's first dual pixel sensor, enabling DSLR-quality photography on a smartphone. Then, in 2019, Samsung unveiled the foldable 'Z Series' smartphones. With these innovations leading the charge, Samsung began to surpass Apple in the global smartphone market share by 2011.

# Korean Cars: Come So Far, Got so Far to Go

How far would Hyundai Motor Group's cars reach if lined up end to end? Since its founding in 1962 until January 2023, Hyundai has sold a total of 147,749,384 vehicles globally.

To estimate the total length, one could multiply the number of sold vehicles by the length of each model. The currently available Avante model is 4.7 meters long, the Sonata is 4.9 meters, and the Santa Fe is 4.8 meters. The best-selling Hyundai model is the Avante, with 14.73 million units sold. Naturally, larger vehicles like buses and trucks would significantly exceed these lengths. Using the Avante's length for this mental exercise, the combined length of all Hyundai vehicles sold amounts to approximately 694.42 million meters, or around 690,000 kilometers. To put that in perspective, given that the distance from Earth to the Moon is 380,000 kilometers, lining up every Hyundai car ever sold would span a round trip to the Moon and back.

Mount Everest, the tallest mountain on Earth, is 8,849 meters high. With the average height of a vehicle being between 1.4 and 1.6 meters, let's use 1.5 meters for calculation purposes. This yields a total stacked height of 221.62 million meters for all sold Hyundais, equivalent to stacking cars 25,000 times higher than Mount Everest.

While this record is impressive, Hyundai's sales figures are modest compared to those of other global automakers like Toyota and Volkswagen Group. However, the landscape is shifting and as electric vehicles take center stage in the car market, Hyundai is at the forefront of this pivotal change.


## "SORRY, ELON MUSK, HYUNDAI IS QUIETLY DOMINATING THE EV RACE"

That was the rather provocative headline of a Bloomberg article published on June 26, 2022 that highlighted Hyundai's elevated status in the electric vehicle (EV) era. From January to May of 2022, Hyundai sold 21,467 units of its electric vehicle models, the Ioniq 5 and EV6, in the U.S. market. These models have been so well received that they are said to be "crafted with soul ground into them". Hyundai's sales figures placed it second only to Tesla,

© Hyundai Motor Group

Ioniq 5, Hyundai's electric vehicle

stunning the automotive industry with its rapid ascent. In an interview with Bloomberg, Joseph Yoon, a vice president at the research firm Edmunds, remarked, "Hyundai and Kia are sweeping the electric vehicle market."

Of course, Tesla still ranks first with a commanding lead in the global electric vehicle market, having sold 200,000 units in the U.S. market between January and May 2022. The Bloomberg article might seem a bit exaggerated when you consider that Tesla's sales were ten times those of Hyundai's electric vehicles, which hold the second-largest market share. Nonetheless, Bloomberg awarded Hyundai high marks for placing second place in electric vehicle sales, overtaking established automakers like GM and Ford.

While it took Tesla 10 years to reach annual sales of 20,000 electric vehicles, it was a remarkable accomplishment for Hyundai to hit that number within just one year of launching its dedicated electric vehicle line.

Just five days before the Bloomberg article's publication, Tesla CEO Elon Musk acknowledged Hyundai's performance. He tweeted a photo indicating that in the first quarter of 2022, Hyundai and Kia captured a 9% share of the U.S. electric vehicle market—more than doubling the shares of Volkswagen at 4.6% and Ford at 4.5%. Musk's accompanying remark, "Hyundai is doing pretty well," suggests he recognizes the competition from the Korean automaker.

# From a Clunker to a Luxury Car

This story begins with Hyundai's Pony model, which was first exported to Saudi Arabia in 1976. Desert sand infiltrated the car's air conditioning systems, causing them to fail. When the air conditioning ceased functioning, the temperatures inside the vehicles rose dramatically, leading to melting seats and deformed steering wheels.

In 1986, Hyundai targeted the North American market—the world's largest for automobiles—by exporting the Excel model and promoting it with the claim, "Don't just buy on credit. You can own two Excels for the price of one." The starting price for the Excel was $4,995, which was less than half of the North American average car price of $12,500 at that time.

Capitalizing on this aggressive pricing strategy, Hyundai

managed to sell 168,882 units of the Excel in the U.S. market in that year alone. The success caught the attention of the U.S. business magazine Fortune, which named Excel as one of America's top 10 products of the year. The following year, sales of the Excel model soared to 263,610 units, overtaking Toyota as the leading seller of imported compact cars in the U.S. Buoyed by these numbers, in 1988, Hyundai confidently released the mid-size Sonata and the sporty Scoupe models.

However, the success was short-lived. Hyundai's technical expertise at the time was not on par with its Japanese and American competitors. Frequent malfunctions were compounded by slow repair services due to an underdeveloped Hyundai warranty service center network in the U.S. In a country where owning a car is essential, the damage to Hyundai's reputation was swift and severe due to these delays. Consequently, a narrative took hold that Hyundai cars were 'cheap and of poor quality.' Despite significant sales, Hyundai's image in the U.S. became synonymous with subpar reliability.

At the time, Hyundai was often the butt of jokes on popular American talk shows and dramas. One joke, titled "one of the 10 pranks you can do in space," suggested "placing a Hyundai logo on the inside of a spacecraft" as a prank. This implied that the sight of the Hyundai logo might cause an astronaut to fear they would not make it back to Earth. Ultimately, in 1989, sales of the Excel plummeted to 180,000 units, and once they fell, they struggled to recover.

Hyundai cars were once derided as "cheap" or as "models where you buy two for the price of one." However, in 1999, the situation began to shift, allowing Hyundai to be recognized as a 'cost-effective car.' It was during this period that Chairman Chung Mong-koo took charge of the U.S. market by prioritizing 'quality management' based on his confidence in Hyundai's technological capabilities. Hyundai regained American consumer interest with its groundbreaking offer of a '10-year, 100,000-mile warranty'— an offer unprecedented in the automotive industry at that time. No car company had ever guaranteed its vehicles for that long before, as offering such a lengthy warranty without confidence in product quality could be financially disastrous.

Hyundai succeeded in garnering recognition for the quality of its vehicles through its marketing of a 10-year warranty, a strategy no other car companies had attempted before and the perception of the market has evolved accordingly. Hyundai differentiated itself by offering cars that were not just low-priced but also high-quality and cost-effective. In 2004, U.S. Business Week acknowledged Hyundai's commitment to quality management in an article titled "Hyundai: Kissing Clunkers Goodbye," signifying Hyundai's transformation in the North American market from a 'cheap car' label to a 'cost-effective car' reputation.

Hyundai's Excel, which gained popularity thanks to an advertisement claiming "you could buy two cars for the price of one," is a notable chapter in the company's history

In 2008, USA Today published an article with the headline, "Surprise! Hyundai proves it's a master of luxury with Genesis." Launching the Genesis model that year, Hyundai ventured into the premium market. A mere year later, in 2009, the Genesis astonished the industry by being named 'North American Car of the Year.' In January 2010, the economic magazine Fortune appraised Hyundai's ascent to fourth place in the automotive industry, above Ford, commenting, "Hyundai's speed of development is such that it deserves a speeding ticket."

Riding on Genesis's reputation, Hyundai rose to 5th place in sales volume in the North American market in 2021, overtaking Japan's Honda, known as the 'Honda of Technology.' It has been 35 years since Hyundai entered the North American market, and in 2022, the company's global sales hit 6,840,500 units. This impressive figure positioned Hyundai third globally after Toyota and Volkswagen Group, marking the first time it reached such a height since claiming 5th place in 2010. This rapid increase in sales volume was accompanied by a rise in prices. In the past, Korean products were often sold at higher prices domestically and for less overseas, but this is no longer the case. In 2022, the sales prices of Hyundai and Kia vehicles in the United States were approximately 10 to 50% higher than in Korea.

## "I SURVIVED THANKS TO GENESIS"

In February 2021, golf champion Tiger Woods was involved in a serious car accident in California, USA. Woods was in LA for the Genesis Invitational Golf Tournament and was driving a GV80 provided by Genesis, the tournament's sponsor, at the time of the mishap. The U.S. police report revealed that Woods's vehicle hit a median, struck a tree, and rolled over multiple times before coming to a halt. Despite the severe damage to the front of the vehicle, the deployment of airbags and the intact cabin structure were credited with saving Woods's life; he would have faced a potentially fatal outcome otherwise. This incident inadvertently served as a significant endorsement for Hyundai's safety reputation in the U.S. market. Before the crash, many Americans still associated Hyundai cars with their 1980s quality levels. However, widespread media coverage of Woods's accident highlighted the safety features of the GV80, substantially enhancing the prestige of both Genesis and Hyundai. The GV80 model reaffirmed its safety credentials by achieving the top rating in the rigorous crash tests conducted by the Insurance Institute for Highway Safety in the United States.

Reflecting Genesis's elevated standing, the brand's sales figures and pricing in the North American market have seen remarkable growth. The average sales price of a Genesis rose from $46,328 in September 2020 to $62,033 in March 2023.

Similarly, U.S. sales figures soared from 21,233 units in 2019 to 56,410 units in 2022, contrasting with the sales decline of established luxury brands such as Audi and Lexus.

---

# BECOMING A LEADER
# IN THE ERA OF ELECTRIC VEHICLES

The automobile industry bestows numerous awards, with the 'North American Car of the Year,' 'European Car of the Year,' and 'World Car of the Year' viewed as the most prestigious. In 2022, Hyundai clinched two of these top three automotive awards, thanks to its Ioniq 5 and EV6 models, the company's pioneer electric vehicles.

The electric vehicle market has seen explosive growth since the onset of the COVID-19 pandemic, with electrification becoming a critical focus for global automakers. Aside from Tesla, most automakers had only been experimenting with electric vehicles on a 'test' basis by retrofitting hybrid or conventional internal combustion engines with batteries, rather than developing bespoke electric vehicles. But with more governmental support for electric vehicles and the rising interest in ESG (Environmental, Social, and

Governance) principles, electrification has become an unstoppable trend. Automakers that traditionally focused on internal combustion engines, like Ford, GM, and Hyundai, have been compelled to quickly shift towards electric vehicles. In the realm of electrification, Hyundai is now seen not as a follower but as a leader, and the statistics stand as a testament to this transformation.

There is an accolade known as the 'Top 10 Engine Awards,' selected by Wards Auto, an automobile media outlet. This award is recognized as prestigious enough to be referred to as the 'Oscar' of automotive powertrain technology, and in the electrification sector, Hyundai has been demonstrating remarkable performance making other automakers pale in comparison.

Among the 280 car brands honored as 'Top 10 Engines of the Year' by 2022, BMW and Ford have each received the award 39 and 38 times respectively. When compared to Nissan's 22 awards and Honda's 21, it is evident that the United States, Germany, and Japan have almost monopolized the title for the world's best engine. However, looking at the last decade alone, the landscape is changing. Since Genesis first made its mark on Wards Auto in 2009, Hyundai has consistently been included on the list of award-winning vehicles, particularly shining in electrified models, such as electric, hydrogen, and hybrid vehicles.

Starting in 2014, hydrogen vehicles, hybrids, and electric vehicles began to be recognized among the top 10 engines. Hyundai has won the eco-friendly powertrain category seven times, beginning with the Tucson hydrogen fuel cell vehicle in 2015 and most recently with the IONIQ 5 in 2022. Since the introduction of this category, 26 eco-friendly car brands have won accolades, with Hyundai representing 26.9% of these recognitions. Whereas Hyundai was once a 'follower' in the conventional internal combustion engine vehicle market, it has now firmly positioned itself as a 'leader' in the environmental automobile field.

Hyundai has set an ambitious goal to sell 3 million electric vehicles in the global market by 2030. To capture the giant North American electric vehicle market, the company is constructing a factory dedicated to electric vehicles in Georgia, USA, which is expected to begin production in the first half of 2025. Hyundai Motor Group Metaplant America (HMGMA) is projected to produce 300,000 Hyundai, Genesis and Kia electric vehicles a year.

## KOREA'S AVENGERS TAKE CHARGE OF THE FUTURE NEW INDUSTRY OF HYDROGEN

An unusual scene unfolded at the H2 Mobility + Energy Show in September 2021 at KINTEX in Goyang, Gyeonggi Province. As unmanned drones took flight at Hyundai Motor's booth, SK Group Chairman Chey Tae-won was seen capturing the moment on his smartphone. Hyosung Group Vice Chairman Cho Hyun-sang, stationed beside him, did the same. Other leading business figures— Hyundai Motor Group Chairman Chung Eui-sun, POSCO Group Chairman Choi Jeong-woo, and Lotte Group Chairman Shin Dong-bin—were also present, observing closely. These conglomerate heads gathered for the launch ceremony of the 'Korea H2 Business Summit.' They were collectively dubbed the 'Hydrogen Avengers,' likening them to the cinematic 'Avengers' whose heroes come together.

Hydrogen is regarded as a plentiful and clean energy source. Fuel cell vehicles that run on hydrogen generate electricity through the chemical reaction of hydrogen with oxygen to create water. The use of hydrogen extends beyond vehicles; with hydrogen buses and hydrogen-powered cars already on the market, the potential exists to build ships powered by hydrogen fuel as well. The construction of a liquefied hydrogen plant would enable the mass supply of hydrogen, allowing power plants to utilize it as a fuel source. The widespread use of hydrogen for energy could lead to a significant reduction in carbon emissions produced by human activity.

Korean companies have traditionally been labeled as 'fast followers,' but they now have the potential to be "first movers" in the hydrogen vehicle sector, akin to their progression in the electric vehicle sector. Hyundai has been proactively pursuing research and development in the hydrogen economy, positioning itself at the forefront of this field. The company embarked on developing hydrogen electric vehicles powered by hydrogen-based batteries in 1998 and created a hydrogen electric version of the Santa Fe model by 2000. In 2005, Hyundai achieved a milestone by localizing the hydrogen fuel cell system, thereby cementing its leadership in the technology. In 2013, Hyundai marked a significant industry achievement by mass-producing the world's first hydrogen vehicle, the Tucson FCEV. With strategic investments in hydrogen technology, Hyundai secured its technological prowess before the widespread advent of electric vehicles. Hyundai has led the global market since 2018, outpacing Japan's Toyota in sales of its hydrogen car, the 'Nexo'. Beyond the Nexo, Hyundai also developed the Xcient hydrogen truck, the world's first mass-produced large hydrogen truck, and has exported a total of 47 units to countries, including Switzerland, starting in 2020.

# One Out of Two Electric Vehicles Worldwide Uses a Korea-Made Battery

Electric vehicles powered by Korean batteries are becoming a common sight on the roads of many countries, including Korea, the United States, and Europe. Korean companies account for 53.4% of the batteries used in electric vehicles globally, excluding China.

In 2022, around 3 million electric vehicles were sold worldwide outside China. Of these, at least 1.5 million units are powered by batteries manufactured by LG Energy Solution, Samsung SDI, and SK On. This fact underscores the prominence of Korean-made batteries, which is far greater than generally perceived. U.S. President Joe Biden, representing the world's most powerful country, has personally engaged with Korean battery manufacturers to ensure a stable supply for the United States.

# BIDEN PERSONALLY STEPS IN STATING THE U.S. CANNOT DO WITHOUT KOREAN BATTERIES

In 2019, LG Energy Solution filed a lawsuit with the U.S. International Trade Commission (ITC), accusing SK On of 'violating trade secrets in battery manufacturing.' In February 2021, the ITC ruled in favor of LG Energy Solution. The verdict means SK On is not only barred from building a battery factory in the United States for the next ten years but is also prohibited from supplying batteries. Consequently, the construction of SK On's battery factory in Georgia was at risk of an immediate halt.

However, it was the U.S. government, not SK On, that was most dismayed by the ruling. This was because the American market was in dire need of Korean-made batteries. Korean companies were the only ones capable of producing and reliably supplying large quantities of secondary batteries, which are essential to electric vehicles.

During his election campaign, Joe Biden had pledged to convert half of the new cars sold in the United States to electric vehicles by 2030. The ITC ruling threatened to make this goal unattainable, potentially undermining the Biden administration's promise and America's competitiveness in the electric vehicle market. With U.S. automakers at risk of failing to produce electric vehicles on schedule, the Biden administration was compelled to get involved in the dispute between the Korean battery manufacturers. As the tension between the companies escalated, foreign media began to report that the U.S. government was stepping in to mediate.

Although it is unclear whether the intervention of the U.S. government played a role, the high-stakes trade secret dispute between LG Energy Solution and SK On, dubbed the 'litigation of the century' in the wake of the smartphone patent war between Apple and Samsung, was settled amicably on April 12, 2021. The resolution was welcomed by the U.S. government, with White House Press Secretary Jen Psaki commenting at the time that the U.S. needed a strong, diverse, and robust U.S.-based electric vehicle battery supply chain to meet the growing global demand.

It was uncommon for the White House to issue a statement on litigation between foreign companies in the United States. Taking an extraordinary step, Biden explicitly referred to the settlement as a win for American workers and the automotive industry. Reflecting on the agreement between LG Energy Solutions and SK On, The Washington Post reported, "The settlement marks a victory for President Biden, who is committed to creating jobs and establishing a robust electric vehicle supply chain in the United States."

# SECONDARY BATTERIES
# CANNOT BE MADE BY JUST ANYONE

The production of secondary batteries for electric vehicles is a feat that only a few companies around the world can claim, with the list including Korea's LG Energy Solution, SK On, and Samsung SDI, as well as Japan's Panasonic. While China's CATL and BYD also manufacture batteries, their technology falls short of satisfying the stringent requirements of global automakers such as Ford, GM, BMW, and Audi, due in part to their growth within the relatively insular Chinese market.

Moreover, the escalating trade tensions between the United States and China have rendered collaboration between Chinese and American firms nearly untenable. Panasonic has found it challenging to satisfy Tesla's demand, and its cautious approach to investment has hindered the expansion of production capacity. In this context, Korea emerged as the reliable partner for the United States. However, a legal dispute erupted between two of Korea's battery giants, LG Energy Solution and SK On, complicating matters. The U.S. government stepped in to mediate, leading to a resolution where SK On agreed to pay LG Energy Solution close to ₩2 trillion in damages. This agreement permitted both parties to continue their battery production operations in the United States.

When China is excluded—as it represents the largest market

for electric vehicles with a preference for local brands—Korean companies command a majority share of the global market. As per SNE Research's 2022 data, LG Energy Solution holds the top position outside China with a 29.7% market share. CATL is in second place with 22.3%, followed by Panasonic with 17.1%, SK On with 12.7%, and Samsung SDI with 11.0%.

## GLOBAL DEPENDENCE ON K-BATTERIES IS RISING

The 2019 Nobel Prize in Chemistry was awarded to three scientists for their contributions to the development of lithium-ion batteries. Among the laureates was Akira Yoshino, a professor at Meijo University in Japan, honored for inventing the world's first commercial lithium-ion battery in 1985. At that time, Yoshino was employed by Japanese secondary battery materials company Asahi Kasei. Owing to his pioneering work, Japan gained a dominant foothold in the secondary battery market during the 1990s, with companies like Panasonic, Sony, and Sanyo Electric commanding over 90% of the global market share.

In Korea, LG Chem, formerly known as Lucky-Goldstar, began researching secondary batteries in 1992. By 1996, the research unit was incorporated into LG Chem, marking the start of serious development efforts in this area. LG Chem achieved a milestone in 1998 by becoming the first Korean company to set up a mass production system for lithium-ion batteries. In 2000, began developing the world's first sizable lithium-ion battery suitable for use in electric vehicles. Meanwhile, Samsung SDI entered the lithium-ion battery market in 1994 and, despite being a newcomer, quickly made its mark by launching high-capacity products in the small battery segment.

According to secondary battery market research conducted by the Industrial Technology Information Institute (ITI), in 2006, Japanese companies held a 52% market share in secondary batteries, followed by Korean firms with 24%, and China with 18%. By 2008, Japan's share had declined to 47%, Korea's had increased slightly to 25%, and China's share rose to 24%. This shift indicates a rapid catch-up by Korean companies, particularly LG Chem and Samsung SDI, considering that Japanese firms accounted for 90% of the market share in the early 2000s.

As Korean battery manufacturers continue to lead the global market, a value chain centered around domestic small and medium-sized enterprises (SMEs) is being strengthened. Material companies, such as EcoPro BM, L&F, and POSCO Chemical, which provide anode and cathode materials, are becoming significant players in the secondary battery market. European battery manufacturers are increasingly sourcing materials and components from Korea. Despite

**Global Battery Market Share by Country (ex-China) in 2022**

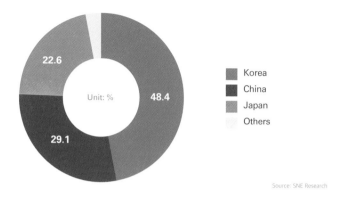

Unit: %

22.6
48.4
29.1

- Korea
- China
- Japan
- Others

Source: SNE Research

Korea's lack of abundant raw materials required for secondary battery production, such as lithium, cobalt, and aluminum, the country's secondary battery value chain is becoming more robust with the growth of companies specializing in the recycling of materials, finished products, and, more recently, waste batteries.

The secondary battery industry is characterized by its complex technology and a multitude of factors influencing the final product. Companies frequently encounter numerous trials and errors, and the timeframe for recovering their investments is unpredictable. LG Energy Solution, for instance, spent 20 years from the commencement of its research before seeing a profit in the electric vehicle battery sector. Samsung SDI also took 16 years to start seeing returns. Thanks to long-term and continuous investment,

Korean secondary battery companies have been able to secure a leading position in the global market. The distinct corporate culture in Korea, which supports patient investment based on the CEO's vision, has positively contributed to this success as well.

The vast experience, technological advancement, and sustained investment required in this field create significant barriers to new entrants. To lessen reliance on Korean battery technology, Europe established the 'European Battery Association,' where member countries collaborate through this association to procure raw materials and cultivate their own battery manufacturing capabilities. Initiatives such as these have led to the creation of numerous companies, including Northvolt and ACC; however, these new ventures are still in the early stages of development.

European battery manufacturers are projected to hold a mere 4% market share, with a production capacity of 102GWh (gigawatt hours) by 2025. This figure pales in comparison to LG Energy Solution's anticipated production capacity of 520GWh for the same year. Northvolt, which is seen as the frontrunner among European companies, commenced battery production in December 2021. But it still grapples with low production yields and the need to upgrade its facilities, often resorting to Korean equipment. This situation suggests a prolonged period before any significant reduction in the global electric vehicle industry's reliance on Korean battery manufacturers is realized.

# Korea's Defense Industry: Largest Arms Export Since the Nation's Founding

The 'Lightning Project' was a pivotal weapons development initiative launched by the Agency for Defense Development in 1971, under President Park Chung-hee's regime. Following the Korean War in 1950, Korea relied heavily on the U.S. military for defense. But the urgency for a self-reliant defense heightened following the 'Kim Shin-jo Incident' in 1968, where North Korean spies infiltrated the Presidential Blue House, and the subsequent abduction of the U.S. Navy ship 'Pueblo' by North Korea.

As detailed in the 'Defense Policy Research' paper titled *40 Years of Development and Achievements of the Korean Defense Industry* , in January 1970, Park ordered the creation of a defense industry development department. This led to the foundation of the Korea Institute for Defense Development in August of the same year.

Progress in defense research and weapon production was swift. By November 1971, the basic policy for weapon development had been established, and the 'Lightning Project' was inaugurated without delay. The development of the first weapon prototypes, including rocket launchers, carbines, and mortars, was completed by December of the same year, with satisfactory performance reviews. Full-scale weapon production was underway by January 1972, and by April, the second round of prototype evaluations had been finalized. The speed and efficiency of Korea's defense industry evolution indeed mirrored the 'lightning' pace implied by the project's name.

Bolstered by the "we can do it" ethos fostered by the Lightning Project in the defense sector, Korea has developed a variety of weapons, enhancing its national defense capabilities. In 2022, Korea marked a significant milestone, reaching an extraordinary $17 billion in defense exports. Before 2020, Korea's defense exports averaged about $3 billion annually. This figure rose sharply to $7.25 billion in 2021 and then set a new record in 2022, bolstered by substantial exports to Poland. Korea's annual defense imports stand at around $5 billion, with the sector achieving a trade surplus beginning in 2021—a first since the 1970s when Korea first ventured into the defense industry.

# POLAND'S AFFINITY FOR
# KOREAN MILITARY HARDWARE

The spike in Korea's defense export figures in 2022 is largely attributable to Polish contracts. In that year, Poland imported Korean arms valued at $12.4 billion in total, including Hanwha Aerospace's 648 K9 self-propelled howitzers for $2.4 billion, 288 K239 multiple launch rocket systems priced at $6 billion, Hyundai Rotem's 980 K2 tanks for $3.36 billion, and 48 of KAI's FA-50 light combat aircraft, among other items.

Poland's substantial procurement of Korean military hardware was spurred by urgent security concerns following Russia's invasion of Ukraine in February 2022. Sharing a border with Russia, Poland recognized the need to significantly bolster its defense capabilities swiftly to deter any potential Russian military threat. As Poland provided Ukraine with weapons, including self-propelled guns and armored vehicles, its own arsenal dwindled. Confronted with the urgent task of replenishing its armaments, Poland looked to Korean defense manufacturers, known for their ability to deliver a stable supply of cost-effective weaponry quickly. In contrast, American defense manufacturers were not only pricier but also had longer production lead times, a reality shared by other European defense producers from countries like France and Germany.

The Voice of America (VOA), the U.S. government-operated

broadcasting service, offered an analysis of the Korean defense companies' significant arms deals with Poland, stating, "Korea's strategy of targeting niche markets proved effective." Drawing on insights from various military experts, VOA reported, "Korea has actively engaged in the defense industry market since the 2000s and is now presenting itself as a provider of economical alternatives to expensive American equipment for countries facing acquisition challenges, rather than competing head-on with market leaders such as the United States." VOA also remarked on the competitive pricing and commendable quality of Korean weaponry.

## HYUNDAI ROTEM EXPORTS K2 TANK FOR THE FIRST TIME

Hyundai Rotem distinguished itself in the 2022 weapons export market to Poland, moving beyond its public perception as merely a 'railway company' producing trains and subway cars. In August 2022, Hyundai Rotem signed an export contract with Poland for the K2 tank, valued at ₩4.4992 trillion. As Korea's sole tank manufacturer, Hyundai Rotem has been committed to developing Korean tanks since 1976, when it was named a premier defense company specializing in tank production. The company released its first Korean tank, the K1, in 1984 and by 2014 had started mass-

producing the advanced K2 tank.

The K2's 120mm smoothbore gun has enough firepower to destroy most of the tanks operated by North Korea. Designed with an automatic loading system, the K2 tank needs a mere three crew members for optimal operation, as opposed to the four needed by previous models and boasts top speeds of 70 km/h on roads and 50 km/h across rough terrain. Equipped with sophisticated technology, the tank features an Identification Friend or Foe (IFF) system, automatic target tracking, and the ability to submerge to depths of up to 4.1 meters.

Serving as the backbone of the Korean military, the K2 tank matches global performance standards. Hyundai Rotem's autonomous development capabilities not only assure mastery over core technology but also flexibility in meeting consumer requirements, facilitating the production of customized tanks.

Hyundai Rotem's production capacity was also boosted by the

orders from Poland. In March 2023, Hyundai Rotem delivered five K2s to Poland, three months ahead of the original shipping schedule. The company was able to expedite the K2 order by maximizing work efficiency through reallocating personnel to high-demand teams and implementing special overtime work. Poland, needing weapons as soon as possible, chose Korea for its fast and stable production capacity. Hyundai Rotem validated Poland's decision by delivering the order early.

## HANWHA DOMINATES THE GLOBAL SELF-PROPELLED ARTILLERY MARKET

The Hanwha Group played a pivotal role in exporting weapons to Poland, with a history deeply intertwined with the Korean defense industry. Hanwha Aerospace, a defense subsidiary of Hanwha Group, was initially founded as Samsung Precision Industries in 1977. It was renamed Samsung Techwin in 2000 and became Hanwha Techwin in June 2015 after Hanwha acquired it from Samsung. The company underwent another name change to Hanwha Aerospace in 2017 and merged with Hanwha Defense, consolidating its focus on the defense sector.

Hanwha Aerospace's K9 self-propelled howitzer, first deployed by the Korean military in 1999, is a 155mm, 52-caliber weapon with an 8-meter barrel length. South Korea ranks second after Germany in developing this type of artillery. With a range of 40 km, the K9's automatic fire control system enables the gun to fire within 30 seconds of a fire command. It boasts a rapid-fire capacity of 6 to 8 rounds per minute for up to three minutes and a sustained fire rate of 2 to 3 rounds per minute over an hour.

The K9 self-propelled howitzer is acclaimed for having the best performance in the world, commanding a global market share of over 50% and ranking first in the global self-propelled howitzer market share. Hanwha Aerospace secured a contract worth ₩3.2 trillion with the Polish government in 2022 to supply the self-propelled howitzer K9 and 155mm ammunition. Should the K9 be delivered to Poland without any issues, its share in the global self-propelled howitzer export market is expected to soar to 70% by 2023 and effectively dominate the global self-propelled artillery market.

Korea Aerospace Industries (KAI) is Korea's foremost aviation company, formed by the merger of the aviation divisions of Samsung Aerospace, Hyundai Space and Aircraft Co., and the aviation business division of Daewoo Heavy Industries during the financial crisis in 1999. KAI took on the role of developing and producing various aircraft shortly after its founding, including the KT-1 basic trainer, the T-50 advanced trainer, the FA-50 light attack aircraft, and the KUH-1 Surion utility helicopter. In addition to aircraft, the company is also involved in developing a range of satellites, such as

FA-50 developed

multi-purpose practical satellites, next-generation medium-sized satellites, and geostationary composite satellites. The successful test flight of the next-generation Korean fighter, the 'KF-21 Boramae,' positions Korea to potentially become the eighth nation to develop and produce its own fighter jets using indigenous technology.

KAI is set to export 48 FA-50 light attack aircraft to Poland, marking the largest deal since the company first exported the domestically-produced T-50 supersonic advanced trainer in 2011. This export is also significant as KAI's first foray into the European market. The FA-50 is designed for specialized tactics and combat missions and is highly interoperable with the F-16. It is also considered well-suited for training missions aligned with fifth-generation fighters such as the F-35.

# The First Korean President to be Invited to the NATO Summit

President Yoon Seok-yeol attended the North Atlantic Treaty Organization (NATO) summit held in Spain in 2022, the first time in the NATO's 73-year history that Korea was invited to the summit.

NATO was established in 1949 as a collective security system centered around the United States and Europe. Korea's invitation to the summit holds significant international political and diplomatic weight, signifying that U.S. and European security cooperation organizations are extending their reach to Korea amidst the unstable international climate triggered by Russia's invasion of Ukraine and growing tensions between the United States and China. Korea's participation at the NATO summit underscores its burgeoning influence in the global arena and NATO members' interest in the capabilities of the Korean defense industry.

However, Korea's invitation to NATO was not merely a nod to its enhanced global standing. In light of the war in Ukraine, European nations are increasingly intent on bolstering their defense capabilities. Yoon's invitation was a recognition of Korea's potential to significantly bolster NATO's armaments. In essence, these nations view Korea as a prospective security and defense ally for NATO.

That makes sense, given that the Korean defense industry, which was developed in response to the confrontation with North Korea, boasts considerable competitiveness. Korea ranked 6th in the 'Most Powerful Countries of 2022' list published by the American weekly magazine *US News & World Report* (USNWR) in January 2023, climbing two spots from its 8th place in 2021. The 'most powerful countries' ranking is based on six indicators: leadership, economic influence, political influence, international alliances, military strength, and exports. Korea scored a total of 64.7 points across these categories, including leadership (22.5 points), economic influence (79.8 points), political influence (48.6 points), international alliances (66.4 points), military strength (79.1 points), and exports (84 points). The United States topped the list with 100 points, followed by China with 96.3 points, Russia with 92.7 points, Germany with 81.6 points, and the United Kingdom with 79.5 points. Following Korea, France, Japan, the United Arab Emirates, and Israel were ranked from 7th to 10th, respectively.

Focusing solely on military power, Korea is classified as a powerful country. Global Firepower (GFP), an American agency that evaluates military strength, has compared and ranked the military capabilities of countries annually since 2006. As of 2023, Korea is placed sixth, after the United States, Russia, China, India, and the United Kingdom. Pakistan, Japan, France, and Italy follow Korea in the top ten rankings. Korea was ranked 11th in 2016 and 2017 but climbed to 7th in 2018 and has held onto 6th place since 2019.

GFP ranks over 40 items including weapons, troops, and defense spending, excluding nuclear weapons. While some critique GFP rankings for not considering nuclear capabilities and for oversimplifying the comparison of military power indicators, they are nonetheless regarded as a useful gauge of a country's military strength. By these measures, Korea's defense capabilities are acknowledged as having reached a notable level.

According to the *2022 Global Defense Market Yearbook* published by the Agency for Defense Development, Korea's defense expenditure in 2021 was $50 billion, placing it 10th worldwide, after the United States, China, India, Russia, and the United Kingdom. In terms of arms sales by the world's top 100 defense companies, four Korean firms ranked in the top ten in this category, with total exports in military supplies valued at $6.5 billion.

Korea also holds a significant position in the 'defense science and technology' sector that is critical for the future of national defense capabilities. Based on the "National Defense Science and Technology Level Survey by Country" released by the Agency for Defense Technology Promotion in 2022, Korea is 9th in defense science and technology, following the United States, Russia, France, Germany, the United Kingdom, China, Israel, and Japan. Government statistics for 2022 report the Korean Army's strength as 365,000, with an additional 70,000 Navy personnel, including the Marine Corps, and 65,000 Air Force members, totaling around 500,000 troops. The military's equipment includes approximately 2,200 tanks, 3,100 armored vehicles, 5,600 artillery pieces, 410 fighter jets, 700 helicopters, and a reserve force of 3.1 million.

## BOLSTERED BY DEFENSE DONATIONS, KOREA IS NOW FOSTERING A DEFENSE INDUSTRIAL BASE

After the 'Kim Shin-jo Incident' in 1968, where North Korean commandos infiltrated and stormed the Blue House, the Korean government initiated a defense donation campaign in 1973 to raise the necessary funds for weapons development. The government recognized the urgent need for a robust armament to counter North Korean aggressions, but state finances were insufficient to cover the costs at the time.

It may seem unbelievable to today's generation, but at that time, citizens contributed to national defense funding through various channels, including schools, municipal offices, and local government institutions. Corporations gathered defense donations and conveyed them to the government on behalf of their employees or corporate entities. Records from the National Archives reveal that ₩60.9 billion was accumulated via this initiative from 1973 until the campaign concluded in September 1988. These defense funds enabled the procurement of F-4D fighters and 500 MD helicopters, as well as the development of indigenous armored vehicles.

Today, the Korean defense industry has positioned itself as a dynamic pillar for national economic growth. The Yoon Seok-yeol administration has publicized plans to construct a defense industrial complex in Changwon, aspiring to elevate the defense sector to a leading global industry. On March 15, 2023, Yoon declared, "Changwon has been chosen as the prospective location for the national industrial complex, which aims to nurture pivotal industries such as defense and nuclear energy as well as bolstering exports.

The national industrial complex for defense and nuclear power in Changwon is poised to be developed with an estimated investment of ₩1.4 trillion to cover an area of around 3.39 million square meters by the year 2030. South Gyeongsang Province, where Changwon is situated, has an established defense industry value chain. This is evident from the production facilities for the K2 tank and K9 self-propelled howitzer—stalwart exports in the national defense industry— as well as for the FA-50 light combat aircraft. Moreover, Changwon hosts 17 companies designated as national defense manufacturers, including prominent names like Hyundai Rotem and Hanwha Aerospace. The city is also a hub for key players in the nuclear sector such as Doosan Energy and various collaborating firms.

# A Country That Owns the A380
# Super-large Passenger Aircraft

## MINUS ₩10 TRILLION VS. PLUS ₩238.3 BILLION

In 2020, while COVID-19 pandemic wreaked havoc globally and caused widespread financial losses for airlines, Korean Air was a notable exception. Korea's national flag carrier, the airline recorded a surplus when major U.S. airlines, including Delta Air Lines, American Airlines, and United Airlines, reported operating losses ranging from $6 billion to as much as $12 billion. Japanese carrier All Nippon Airways also saw an operating loss of $3 billion. In contrast, Korean Air not only avoided losses but also recorded a profit. Cho Won-tae, Chairman of Korean Air, was recognized as 'Person of the Year' by Orient Aviation, a prestigious aviation industry publication in the Asia-Pacific.

The onset of the COVID-19 pandemic in early 2020 dealt a severe blow to the global aviation sector, causing a steep decline in demand. Starting in March, passenger flights of domestic airlines were largely grounded due to route suspensions and reductions in service. The prospect of international travel became a distant thought for many, and airlines were among the first to feel the impact. Merely keeping aircraft on the tarmac entailed considerable expense. With flights canceled, the financial shortfall for airlines increased and their deficits grew exponentially. As a result, larger airlines with more aircraft experienced heavier losses.

Korean Air, ranking as the world's 10th largest airline by fleet size, was initially devastated alongside its competitors. However, the company quickly pivoted to leverage Korea's export-driven economic structure by capitalizing on the rise in air cargo demand— even as passenger demand plummeted. Recognizing the surge in the need for cargo transport, Korean Air fully utilized its fleet of 23 large cargo planes. Furthermore, to handle the increase in export cargo, the airline converted passenger aircraft by removing seats to create additional cargo space.

During this period, Korean Air's workforce also made sacrifices to cope with the downturn. Approximately 10,000 employees, constituting around 70% of the total workforce, rotated in taking a month-long leave. Executives also voluntarily accepted pay cuts of up to 50%.

Through its astute strategy of reconfiguring passenger aircraft for cargo use, Korean Air posted an operating profit of ₩238.3 billion in 2020—despite the complete halt in international passenger flights. While the global airline industry grappled with the challenges posed by the pandemic, Korean Air seized the opportunity to expand its market presence by beginning the process of acquiring Asiana Airlines and scaling up its cargo operations. With proactive measures such as increasing paid-in capital, Korean Air was able to lower its debt ratio to about 200%.

In June 2021, Korean Air was honored as the 2021 Airline of the Year by the esteemed global aviation publication *Air Transport World*. The Airline of the Year accolade is so highly regarded it's often referred to as the 'Oscars' of the aviation sector and confirmed Korean Air's status as one of the world's top airlines, both in prestige and performance.

Other international competitors such as America's Delta Air Lines, American Airlines, and the Air France/KLM Group that failed to adapt swiftly faced operational funding deficits, necessitating tens of millions of dollars in government aid to stay afloat.

# ONE OF EIGHT A380 OPERATORS

Korean Air has been a pioneer in Korean civil aviation since its takeover of the state-operated Korean Air Corporation in March 1969, which was then plagued by chronic deficits and has since flourished into an influential global carrier. Starting with a modest fleet of seven propeller aircraft and one jetliner, Korean Air has, over half a century, grown into one of the largest international carriers, boasting a fleet of 166 aircraft. From a mere ₩3.6 billion in sales in its inaugural year, the airline's revenue has soared beyond the ₩10 trillion mark. Initially, the airline served only three Japanese destinations; it now flies to 107 cities in 42 countries.

During the challenging 1970s, Korean Air made audacious investments to carve out its place in the global market. As foreign airlines began acquiring large jet fleets, Korean Air followed suit, choosing to purchase jets over propeller-driven aircraft. In a two-year span, Korean Air acquired eight new YS-11 jets and introduced the Boeing 747 in 1972, committing to a vast financial outlay amid modest passenger demand. Despite some viewing this as a rash gamble, Korean Air took the strategic step, anticipating growth in future travel demand.

In 2003, Korean Air ambitiously acquired the A380, a superjumbo passenger aircraft once deemed so costly that few airlines dared to purchase it. By the close of 2022, there were only eight carriers globally that boasted the A380 in their fleet, among them Britain's British Airways, Emirates from the UAE, Australia's Qantas, Qatar Airways, Singapore Airlines, and both Korean Air and Asiana Airlines. Even with Germany's Lufthansa and Etihad Airways of the UAE, which have announced intentions to purchase the A380, the total comes to just ten airlines.

The A380 measures 73 meters in length and 79 meters in wingspan, capable of accommodating up to 853 passengers with a fuel capacity of 320,000 liters. This colossal aircraft carries a price tag between $300 million and $400 million. Upon its introduction to the market in the early 2000s by Airbus, the A380 was so popular that it earned the moniker "the hotel in the sky." However, the steep costs associated with the A380, including a monthly storage fee nearing a million dollars—exclusive of maintenance and inspection costs—limited the number of buyers. Ownership of the A380 has subsequently become a benchmark for classifying airlines as either 'large' or 'medium-sized.'

Korean Air, recognizing an opportunity, promptly endorsed the purchase of the A380 in 2003 and received its first aircraft in 2011, becoming the sixth carrier worldwide to operate the model. By introducing the A380, Korean Air not only bolstered its position in the premium sector but also distinguished itself as the first Northeast Asian airline to deploy the superjumbo, enhancing its market competitiveness.

Korean Air was ranked 9th in *Skytrax*'s "World's 100 Best Airlines 2022," scoring high marks in the quality standards maintained by this British airline and airport rating organization. *Skytrax* issues this distinguished list annually, drawing on extensive evaluations of in-flight entertainment, food quality, seat comfort, staff service, and price satisfaction. Korean Air's progress is commendable, rising from 34th in 2019 to 22nd in 2020, and then to 13th in 2021, before breaking into the top ten.


## THE WORLD'S BEST AIRPORT: INCHEON INTERNATIONAL AIRPORT


In April 2022, Luisito Comunica, a popular Mexican YouTuber with 40 million subscribers, shared his encounter with a spot well-known to Koreans in one of his videos: Incheon Airport. His footage from a layover at Incheon International Airport captured his audience's attention when it was shared on his channel, sparking widespread interest.

During his visit, Luisito was particularly taken with 'Airstar,' the robotic airport guide at Incheon. Airstar operates autonomously, engaging with people through spoken interactions, and providing information on demand via its touchscreen interface. Upon entering a flight number, Airstar offers guidance to the check-in counter and directions for navigating the airport. After his experience, Luisito expressed his admiration for Incheon, stating, "I thought the best airport was Qatar Airport, but Incheon International Airport is more impressive." His video sparked global interest in the airport, highlighting how significant an airport's role is in shaping the first impression of a country. Whether for leisure or business, the experience at the airport can significantly influence one's perception of their stay. Incheon International Airport serves as a vital showcase of South Korea's prowess, impressing travelers in the brief period of their transit or arrival.

Firstly, Incheon Airport offers fast internet, as expected from a country known for its IT prowess. Wi-Fi is accessible throughout the facility, allowing travelers to enjoy unlimited internet access. Service counters for telecommunications companies are conveniently located across the airport for those who need connectivity services at competitive prices. Additionally, there's a notable cultural aspect visible at the airport: personal belongings are typically respected, so much so that you can leave your heavy suitcase outside a restroom or a store and expect it to remain untouched. This speaks volumes about the safe environment at the airport.

Incheon International Airport is also recognized for having some of the quickest arrival and departure processing times in Northeast Asia. The efficiency is impressive to foreigners and has been documented by media outlets such as Business Insider, whose

Facebook page in 2016 featured a video showcasing the airport's transit experience. The video highlighted the airport's clean and modern aesthetics, the availability of comfortable seating with charging facilities for smartphones and laptops, clean restrooms, and a tidy shopping area.

Korea's first international airport was Yeouido Airport. During the Japanese colonial era, it served as an air force base and training site, and became Korea's first international airport in 1953. This was followed by the opening of Gimpo International Airport in 1958, at a time when Korea was still developing and international travel by air was a luxury few could imagine. As the country's economy grew and the number of air travelers increased, the need for a new airport to succeed Gimpo Airport became apparent, particularly as noise complaints rose due to its proximity to the city center. A feasibility study for a new airport commenced in 1969, and two decades later, in 1990, Yeongjong Island in Incheon was selected as the location for the new airport.

Incheon International Airport opened in March 2001 after the completion of its first phase of construction, which spanned from 1992 to 2000 at a cost of ₩5.6323 trillion. The process used about 450,000 sheets of design drawings which, if stacked, would equal the height of a 15-story building. The land for the airport, created by reclaiming tidal flats, was 18 times larger than the area of Yeouido, with the passenger terminal alone being equivalent to the size of 60 soccer fields.

The second phase, costing ₩3 trillion, extended from 2002 to 2008. This phase included the construction of a runway suitable for the takeoff and landing of very large aircraft such as the A380 and expanded the concourse and cargo terminal.

Incheon International Airport has earned numerous accolades. It was recognized as the 'Best Airport' among 1,800 airports in the Airports Council International (ACI) 'Roll of Excellence' in 2011. It has consistently placed first in the 'World Airport Service Quality (ASQ)' rankings for 12 years starting in 2005, just five years after it opened. Additionally, in a flight service satisfaction survey among airline pilots globally, the airport ranked first for six consecutive years beginning in 2012. In 2022, Incheon International Airport was awarded the Level 5 certification plaque, the highest level of the International Civil Aviation Organization's Customer Experience Accreditation Program—a world-first achievement.

# Korean Construction Companies Building Landmarks in the Middle East and Asia

The Petronas Twin Towers, a renowned Malaysian landmark, began construction in 1992 and was completed in 1998. Standing at a height of 451.9 meters, the skyscraper consists of two identical towers and was the tallest building in the world until the completion of Taipei 101 in Taiwan in 2003.

## CONSTRUCTING THE PETRONAS TWIN TOWERS: KOREA VS. JAPAN

"On Sundays, we forfeited our days off and worked tirelessly to outdo Japan. It was then I realized that patriotism intensifies when one is abroad."

The construction kick-off in 1992 sparked of a fierce contest of national pride between Korea and Japan. The Malaysian government awarded the contract for Tower 1 to Japan's Hazama Construction and for Tower 2 to Korea's Samsung C&T. The 1990s witnessed a potent rivalry between the two nations, which was equal to or more intense than today's competitive climate. Hazama Construction, already established as a leader in the industry, had a significant advantage, while Samsung C&T was at a disadvantage due to its lack of high-rise building experience. Hampered by initial setbacks, Samsung C&T started construction 35 days behind Hazama Construction. This delay set the tone for the remainder of the project, with Samsung C&T consistently trailing by a margin of four to eight floors.

Samsung C&T was resolute in its ambition to outpace its competitor. Employees sacrificed their holidays and dedicated their efforts to constructing Tower 2, even working through Sundays. One notable story tells of how, when approval for concrete pouring stalled due to the absence of a Malaysian supervisor, Samsung employees scoured city bars to locate one, ultimately securing the necessary permission.

Employing innovative construction techniques, Samsung rapidly closed the gap with the Japanese team and finished Tower 2 ahead of their rivals. The upset victory came as a shock to the world and a proud surprise to Koreans. The Japanese team's pride was

© Samsung C&T

Petronas Twin Towers in Malaysia, constructed
by Samsung in competition with Japan

particularly stung when their tower was found to be tilting by about
25mm. The competition extended to the installation of the 'spire'—
critical for claiming the title of the world's tallest building.

Expertise in welding was crucial for this stage. The Japanese company flew in skilled welders from Japan. Samsung C&T responded by doubling down, with workers forfeiting any time off. In the climactic last days, teams ate on-site and, in the final 72 hours, worked relentlessly overnight to finish the spire. On March 6, 1996, Samsung C&T triumphed by reaching the highest point a full ten days before Hazama.

The Petronas Twin Towers marked a turning point. Since their construction, Korean construction companies have demonstrated their prowess worldwide, securing contracts for significant landmarks globally. Currently, the tallest structure in the world is the Burj Khalifa in the UAE, soaring to a height of 828 meters. The rebar used in the building stretches over 25,000 km, which could span the distance from Korea to the United States if laid end-to-end. Its total floor area is 56 times that of Jamsil Stadium, and Samsung C&T also constructed this architectural marvel. The company embarked on the Burj Khalifa project in partnership with Belgium's Besix and the UAE's Arabtec, but Samsung C&T alone was responsible for constructing everything above 500 meters. The construction techniques that Samsung C&T employed for the Burj Khalifa have since become global standards for high-rise building.

# HOW WAS THIS BUILDING MADE POSSIBLE? HYUNDAI AND SSANGYONG ENGINEERING & CONSTRUCTION

However, Samsung C&T is not the only representative of Korean construction excellence. Hyundai Engineering & Construction secured the contract for Saudi Arabia's Jubail Industrial Port in 1976, which was heralded as the century's largest project, and went on to construct the National Museum in Doha, Qatar. There, Hyundai E&C exhibited its technical expertise, distinct from Samsung C&T's approach. The Qatar National Museum, which features a 'desert rose' design by respected architect Jean Nouvel, is acclaimed as 'the greatest masterpiece of the century' due to its unique architecture.

Created by assembling 316 disc-shaped "rose petals," the design of the Qatar National Museum was one that most construction companies would not even consider attempting. The discs were crafted by integrating 76,000 concrete panels into circular plates, with each disc taking an astonishing four months to construct. Partners withdrew from the project, citing technical challenges. Nevertheless, Hyundai Engineering & Construction overcame these hurdles and completed the National Museum—a feat widely regarded as a monumental challenge in construction.

Ssangyong Engineering & Construction has also ventured into

foreign markets. The company faced hurdles during the construction of Singapore's Marina Bay Sands Hotel, as the design required the building to lean at a precarious 52-degree angle. In the 2007 tender, 14 companies recognized for their technological expertise worldwide submitted bids. However, only four, including firms from Japan, France, and Hong Kong, alongside Ssangyong Engineering & Construction, were shortlisted as the final contenders. But all four companies struggled to devise a feasible construction method and doubted the possibility of reducing the construction timeline. Ultimately, Ssangyong Engineering & Construction successfully

© Ssangyong E&C

Another testament to Korean construction capability is the Marina Bay Sands Hotel in Singapore, constructed by Ssangyong E&C

erected this complex structure within the stipulated timeframe, and today, the Marina Bay Sands Hotel is an iconic Singaporean landmark.

In 2021, Ssangyong E&C completed 'Atlantis the Royal,' an opulent hotel in the UAE featuring 94 lavish swimming pools and a distinctive exterior reminiscent of stacked Lego blocks. Pop icon Beyoncé graced the pre-opening event, with the suite her family occupied commanding a rate of approximately $100,000 per night. The building's innovative design presented significant construction challenges. Reports suggest that executives from the Belgian company Besix, which collaborated on the construction, were taken aback by the project's complexity, remarking that it was an even more demanding job than the Burj Khalifa.

## KOREAN COMPANIES BUILD
## THE WORLD'S LONGEST 48KM BRIDGE

The world's longest bridge, the Sheikh Jaber Al-Ahmad Al-Sabah Causeway in Kuwait, spans an impressive 48.57km. Constructed by Hyundai Engineering & Construction (Hyundai E&C) and Combined Group Contracting Company (CS E&C) at a cost of ₩3.56 trillion, the project was a display of the prowess of Korean engineering. These two companies undertook the

Sheikh Jaber Al-Ahmad Al-Sabah Causeway in Türkiye,
built by Hyundai and CS construction companies

© Hyundai E&C

design and build aspects of the project concurrently. The combined technological expertise of the firms enabled the completion of the bridge within a mere 66 months.

The title of the world's longest suspension bridge was claimed by the Çanakkale Bridge in Türkiye, a joint effort by DL E&C and SK Eco Plant. Completed in 2022, this bridge extends 2,023 meters over its main span, surpassing the Akashi Kaikyo Bridge in Japan, which has a main span of 1,991 meters. Counting the approach spans at both ends, the Çanakkale Bridge measures a total of 4,608 meters. This bridge was constructed to mark the centennial of the Republic of Türkiye in 2023, and serves as a critical connection between the continents of Europe and Asia.

## THE WORLD'S LARGEST NEW CITY PROJECT, NEOM

New opportunities are opening up for Korean construction companies well-versed in building numerous skyscrapers and bridges worldwide. They are now turning their attention to Neom, which Saudi Arabia is ambitiously developing with a goal to complete the first phase by 2025 and the final phase by 2030. Neom, the designated name for a new city to be constructed over an area of 26,500 km$^2$ between the Saudi peninsula and Egypt, is set to be the largest construction project in human history, boasting a staggering total construction cost of ₩650 trillion.

Neom, which combines Greek and Arabic to mean 'new future', mirrors Saudi Arabia's aim to shift away an oil-centered economy. The city is planned to be self-sufficient and will feature "The Line," a linear urban stretch spanning 170 km; "Trozena," a vast eco-friendly mountain complex; and "Oksagon," an octagonal, sea-floating, high-tech industrial complex.

Building a new city from scratch requires building comprehensive infrastructure, including roads, transport systems, tunnels, and water and sewage facilities. Korean domestic construction firms are poised to secure contracts for Neom due to their proven global competitiveness. This venture presents significant opportunities for Korean companies, which have consistently taken on new challenges and built solid reputations in the construction sector.

Samsung C&T and Hyundai E&C have formed a joint venture to bid for and have received orders for part of Neom City's construction, which they are currently executing. The project of tunneling beneath The Line within Neom represents a substantial venture, valued at $1 billion.

# Korean Bio Industry
# Joins the Ranks of Big Pharma

The "2023 Bio International Convention (Bio USA)," held in Boston, USA, in June 2023, turned heads as the first major event since the COVID-19 pandemic. The event saw a threefold increase in the number of registered companies, including Big Pharma, to over 9,100 from 85 countries. The number of Korean companies participating in the event surged to 544, more than doubling from the previous year. This boost is a testament to the impressive growth of Korean pharmaceutical companies in developing and exporting rapid COVID-19 test kits, manufacturing vaccines, and treatments as CMOs (contract manufacturing organizations), as well as advancing innovative technologies such as messenger ribonucleic acid (mRNA), amid the pandemic.

Samsung Biologics, in particular, celebrated the completion

of its fourth plant in June 2023, which is now the world's largest production facility with a capacity of 604,000 liters, or approximately 30% of the total global CMO production. total. Concurrently, Samsung Biologics signed a letter of intent for a consignment production contract with Pfizer Ireland Pharmaceuticals valued at ₩535 billion. This contract represents 17.8% of its 2022 annual sales, which was ₩3.013 trillion, surpassing the previous record held by a contract with AstraZeneca worth $350.97 million. Under this new agreement, Samsung Biologics is set to produce biosimilars— generic versions of Pfizer's biopharmaceutical products—for tumors, inflammation, and immune disorders at its fourth facility.

## KOREA DOMINATES
## $75 BILLION BIOSIMILAR MARKET

Korea's consignment manufacturing capabilities are poised to get even more attention following the significant growth of the biosimilar market. Market research firm IQVIA Forecast Link projected that the biosimilar market would grow to an estimated $75 billion within the next decade. This surge is primarily due to the expiration of the patent for Humira, the top-selling drug worldwide, alongside subsequent patent expirations of major original drugs such as the autoimmune treatment Stelara, macular degeneration

Samsung Biologics employees inspect the production site
through a live virtual system

therapy Eylea, and osteoporosis medication Prolia.

From 2015 to 2020, the global biosimilar market expanded at an average annual growth rate of roughly 78%, amounting to a $17.9 billion market by 2020. It is forecasted to continue growing at an average rate of about 15% annually until 2030.

During the COVID-19 pandemic, Korean pharmaceutical and biotech companies were instrumental in the consignment production of vaccines and treatments that were exported globally. SK Bioscience gained prominence as a key vaccine manufacturer by securing consignment production contracts with AstraZeneca and Novavax early on in the pandemic. Samsung BioLogics is on track to surpass ₩1 trillion in sales for the first time in 2020 by processing large volumes of products, including COVID-19 vaccines and treatments from international firms including GlaxoSmithKline (GSK) and Eli Lilly. The company's sales are expected to hit ₩3.013 trillion in 2022, with further growth anticipated.

Additionally, Samsung Biologics plans a ₩7.5 trillion investment by 2032 to establish a 'second bio campus' in Songdo. The plan includes the construction of four new factories (numbered 5 to 8) and the expansion of large-scale antibody drug production facilities. An open innovation center is also in the works to nurture next-generation pharmaceutical technologies.

Celltrion is recognized as a biosimilar powerhouse alongside Samsung Bioepis. The combined production capacity of Celltrion's first and second factories in Songdo totals to 190,000 liters. With the expected commencement of commercial production at the third factory in June 2024 and the addition of a fourth factory currently under construction in Songdo, the Korean biopharmaceutical company is poised to have a total production capacity of 450,000 liters. Celltrion aims to increase its total production capacity to 600,000 liters by 2030, including production from overseas plants that are yet to be constructed.

In May 2023, SK Bioscience secured a contract from Merck & Co. (known as MSD outside the USA and Canada), a major U.S. pharmaceutical company, for the contract development and manufacturing (CDMO) of an Ebola virus vaccine. To date, the company has primarily focused on COVID-19 vaccines, securing volume contracts with multinational pharmaceutical companies like AstraZeneca and Novavax. But with this collaboration with MSD, SK Bioscience plans to broaden its CDMO business scope to include general vaccines in the future. SK Bioscience has previously announced an investment of ₩2.4 trillion over the next five years to position itself as a global leader in the vaccine and biotech industry. The company specifically plans to allocate ₩1.2 trillion for research and development efforts.

## KOREAN-MADE VACCINES AND DIAGNOSTIC KITS

During the COVID-19 pandemic, the diagnostic kits developed by Korean companies gained global recognition for their swift development, the government's quick emergency use authorization, and exceptional export performance. These domestic diagnostic kits experienced rapid growth amid the global spread of the COVID-19 pandemic. According to the Korea Customs Service, exports of diagnostic kits (including diagnostic reagents) saw a steep rise from just $253.26 million in 2019 to $2.17087 billion in 2020. The growth continued as exports hit $2,047.32 million in 2021 and a record $3,349.08 million in 2022, marking the highest performance to date. The COVID-19 antigen rapid diagnostic kit, developed by Celltrion in collaboration with Humasis—a specialist in in vitro diagnostics—is valued at approximately ₩730 billion and has been procured by over 25,000 sources, including U.S. military facilities, despite the implementation of the Buy American Act in September 2021.

Korean-developed vaccines are also on the rise. GC Green Cross, known for developing hepatitis B and chickenpox vaccines, has become the largest supplier of seasonal flu vaccines to the Pan American Health Organization (PAHO). The company has displayed remarkable capability by supplying around 50 million doses of flu vaccines from 2020 to 2022, even amid the pandemic. With robust exports, GC Green Cross's accumulated flu vaccine production recently surpassed 300 million doses. Considering that one dose is sufficient for one adult, this means that vaccines from GC Green Cross have immunized 300 million individuals worldwide against the flu.

# Not an Oil-Producing Country, but the World's Largest Exporter of Petroleum Products

"Oil was discovered near Yeongil Bay last December. We need to conduct further investigations to determine whether the reserves are substantial enough to be economically viable," President Park Chung-hee said during an annual press conference on January 15, 1976, revealing the discovery of oil in Pohang. This announcement was met with cheers from many who watched on television, as noted in the National Archives. Even Park appeared visibly moved, his eyes turning red during the conference. At the time, the government was covertly conducting oil drilling operations under presidential directives, recognizing the critical need for oil in economic development. The exact nature of the oil found in Pohang remains a subject of speculation. Some suggest that the oil could be from drilling machinery, while others contend it was genuine crude oil.

Despite its resource constraints, Korea has unearthed small quantities of oil and gas. In July 1998, Korea joined the ranks of oil-producing nations, placing 95th, with the successful extraction from a gas field off the coast of Ulsan. However, the gas produced was only sufficient for the daily consumption of 340,000 households. The production could fuel 20,000 cars per day, indicating its insufficiency to meet the country's overall demand. The gas and oil from the East Sea fields were piped underwater to Ulsan and predominantly used by industrial firms. The 'Donghae-1 Gas Field' ceased operations in 2017. Meanwhile, the 'Donghae-2 Gas Field,' which began production in 2016, concluded its supply on December 31, 2021.

Korea relies on imports for most of its energy needs, but it also possesses unparalleled capabilities in processing imported energy and selling refined products. In 2022, Korea imported crude oil valued at $95.5 billion—a staggering sum equivalent to approximately ₩125 trillion. It also exported oil-related products derived from processing the imported crude oil, with the total value of these exports hitting $63 billion, indicating that 60% of imported crude oil was re-exported after processing. The value of these petroleum product exports comprises 9.2% of Korea's total exports, ranking as the second-largest export item after semiconductors when considered as a single category. The combined export value of the four major oil refining companies—SK Energy, GS Caltex,

S-Oil, and Hyundai Oilbank—amounts to $57 billion, representing 90% of the total exports in oil products.

# WORLD'S 5TH LARGEST
# EXPORTER OF REFINED CRUDE OIL

In *Maecheonyarok*, a record by late Joseon Dynasty scholar
Hwang Hyeon, there is an account of Korea's first use of oil.
"It is said that oil originates from the West, in countries such as the
United Kingdom or the United States. Some believe it is harvested
from the sea, others that it is produced from coal, and there are those
who think it is made by boiling stones to obtain water. There are lots of
theories, but it is evident that it is a natural resource. Petroleum was first
utilized in Korea in the year 1880. Just about 180mL, which is roughly
equivalent to half a bottle of soju, can light a room for ten days."

Oil was introduced to Korea in 1880, and was primarily used
for lighting fires. The documentation describes how one hop,
approximately 180mL, could sustain a light for ten days. It is also
recorded that in the same year, the monk Lee Dong-in imported oil,
along with lamps and matches, from Japan.

Japan built Korea's first diesel plant after establishing 'Chosun
Petroleum Co., Ltd.' After liberation, the Korean government
set up the Ulsan Oil Refinery, but its completion was thwarted
by the outbreak of the Korean War in 1950. Subsequently, under
the five-year economic development plan, the Korea National Oil
Corporation (now SK Energy) began operating the Ulsan Refinery
in 1964, which began producing naphtha, a critical raw material for

the petrochemical industry. In 1967, Korea's first private oil refinery, Honam Oil Refining (now GS Caltex), was established via a joint venture between the Lucky Group and Caltex of the United States. Honam Oil Refinery achieved a milestone in 1981 by becoming the first Korean company to export petroleum products. In 1983, it became the first domestic refinery to win the $200M Export Tower Award.

S-Oil was originally established in 1976 as the Iran-Korea Petroleum Company, a joint venture between the Ssangyong Group and the Iranian National Oil Company. The company began joint management in 1991 after Iran withdrew and Aramco, the world's largest oil company, purchased a stake. Hyundai Oilbank was formed as a joint venture between Kukdong Petroleum Industry and Royal Dutch Shell and was later taken over by Hyundai when Royal Dutch Shell exited Korea in 1977.

According to statistical data published by global oil company BP, Korean oil refineries had a refining capacity of 3.572 million barrels per day in 2021. In terms of size, Korea ranks fifth globally, following the United States, China, Russia, and India. By company, SK Energy is the world's second-largest, while GS Caltex and S-Oil are the fourth and fifth largest respectively in crude oil refining capacity. The ratio of exports to domestic consumption among Korean refineries is approximately 1:1, illustrating that the export ratio is exceptionally high compared to that of other countries.

Panoramic view of the GS Caltex Yeosu plant

© GS Caltex

## CHEMICAL COMPANIES ON THE RISE

In September 1955, the Korean government began constructing the Chungju Fertilizer Factory with funding from the U.S. Department of State's Agency for International Development (AID). The factory, which was completed in April 1961, became a beacon of technological advancement akin to a modern IT company situated in Pangyo, in the context of the economics of that era. American engineers, assigned to facilitate technology transfer, lived nearby, creating an American community reminiscent of today's

Itaewon. It is said that former UN Secretary-General Ban Ki-moon, who hails from Chungju, honed his English skills by visiting this enclave as a student.

Fertilizers were critically needed in Korea during the 1960s to boost food production and escape poverty. Achieving self-sufficiency by 1975, the fertilizer sector later shifted to exports. However, by 1983, the Chungju Fertilizer Factory was shut down due to plummeting global fertilizer prices and diminishing demand. Despite its closure, the factory marked the start of Korea's ascent in the chemical industry.

The Chungju Fertilizer Factory, which leveraged advanced technology, established a foundation for Korea's proficiency in chemical plant management and engineering. This knowledge was propagated as engineers from Chungju contributed to the establishment of other key chemical plants, including Yeongnam Chemical, Jinhae Chemical, and Namhae Chemical, and shared their large-scale operational expertise. The subsequent creation of the Ulsan and Yeosu Petrochemical Complexes in the 1960s and 1970s respectively, propelled Korea into the forefront of the global chemical industry.

In the ethylene market, often referred to as the industry's 'ricebowl' alongside semiconductors, Korean companies such as LG Chem and Lotte Chemical command a significant share. With a 6.2% stake in the global market, Korea stands as the fourth-largest producer after the United States, China, and Saudi Arabia, manufacturing approximately 12.7 million tons annually and exports totaling around $55 million.

## KOREA'S TEXTILE REVOLUTION: DR. LEE SEUNG-GI AND THE DEVELOPMENT OF VINALON

The contribution of Dr. Lee Seung-gi, in developing the world's second major synthetic fiber is a fact known to few. Lee, born in Damyang, South Jeolla Province in 1905, attended Joongang High School in Seoul before relocating to Japan to pursue a degree at Kyoto University. There, he earned his doctorate in engineering in 1939, with a thesis that detailed research on vinalon, referred to as 'the first synthesis' in Japan. DuPont's development of nylon, the first synthetic fiber, occurred just a year prior, in 1938.

During World War II, Lee was incarcerated in a Japanese prison for his assertion that "Japan will definitely fall." After the war, he was released and returned to Korea, only to defect to North Korea in July 1950. There, he furthered the development of vinalon, which closely resembles natural fibers, and sparked a textile revolution.

Kim Il-sung praised vinalon as 'Juche fiber', promoting its widespread use as a cotton substitute in North Korea. Lee was also a recipient of the Lenin Prize in 1961, an award often compared to the Nobel Prize in communist countries. Historical accounts note that a bedridden Lee received wild ginseng from Kim Il-sung and a grand birthday celebration from Kim Jong-il on his 90th birthday.

# HALLYU
## How Korea Captivated the World

**초판 1쇄** 2024년 1월 4일

**지은이** 장대환
**펴낸이** 최경선
**편집장** 유승현   **편집2팀장** 정혜재

**책임편집** 이예슬
**마케팅** 김성현 한동우 구민지
**경영지원** 김민화 오나리
**디자인** 김보현 한사랑   **삽화** 양만금

**펴낸곳** 매경출판㈜
**등록** 2003년 4월 24일(No. 2-3759)
**주소** (04557) 서울시 중구 충무로 2(필동1가) 매일경제 별관 2층 매경출판㈜
**홈페이지** www.mkpublish.com   **스마트스토어** smartstore.naver.com/mkpublish
**페이스북** @maekyungpublishing   **인스타그램** @mkpublishing
**전화** 02)2000-2612(기획편집) 02)2000-2646(마케팅) 02)2000-2606(구입 문의)
**팩스** 02)2000-2609   **이메일** publish@mkpublish.co.kr
**인쇄·제본** ㈜M-print 031)8071-0961
**ISBN** 979-11-6484-647-4 (03300)